IMAGES
of America

CARTHAGE
1940–1990

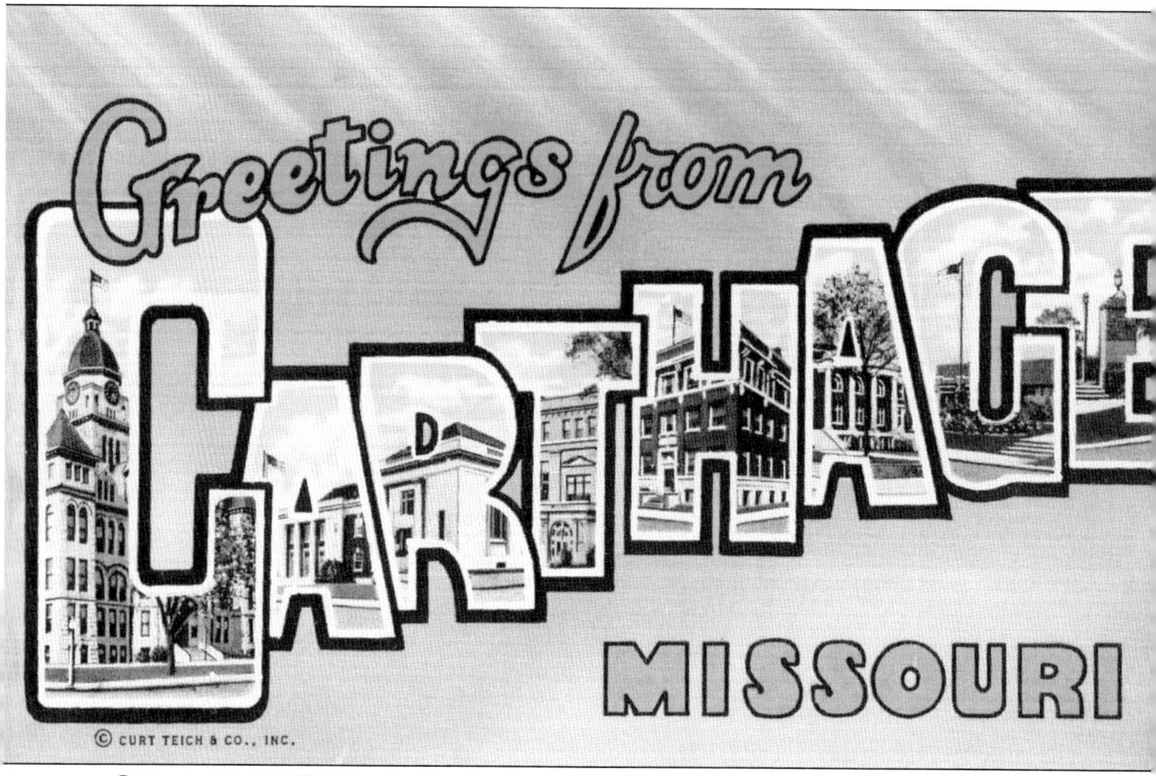

Greetings from Carthage. Popular during the 1930s–1950s, this "big letter" postcard features town scenes within the letters. The following structures are pictured, from left to right: Jasper County Courthouse (1894–1895), Memorial Hall (1924), Carthage Post Office (1909–1910), Carthage High School (1904–1905), YMCA at Sixth and Main Streets (1909), First Baptist Church (1924–1925), Bathhouse at Municipal Park Swimming Pool (1935), and Municipal Park entrance (1937). (Courtesy of Powers Museum.)

On the Cover: H.E. Williams Products, 100 South Main Street. See page 45 for more information. (Courtesy of H.E. Williams, Inc.)

IMAGES
of America

CARTHAGE
1940–1990

Wade Utter and Michele Hansford
for the Powers Museum

ARCADIA
PUBLISHING

ISBN 978-1-4671-1020-4

Published by Arcadia Publishing
Charleston, South Carolina

Printed in the United States of America

Library of Congress Control Number: 2013933150

For all general information, please contact Arcadia Publishing:
Telephone 843-853-2070
Fax 843-853-0044
E-mail sales@arcadiapublishing.com
For customer service and orders:
Toll-Free 1-888-313-2665

Visit us on the Internet at www.arcadiapublishing.com

This book is dedicated to all Powers Museum volunteers, interns, board members, and staffers during the museum's first 25 years of operation (1988–2013).

Contents

ACKNOWLEDGMENTS

This book has been a collaborative effort by many people. The authors and the Powers Museum wish to thank the following who have contributed to the production of this title: Matthew East, Brittany Golden, Stewart Johnson, Koral Martin, Darrel and Sheri Smith, Ann Haggard, John G. Hall, Lena Swoveland, Carl and Jane Crawford, Kathleen MacDonald Chick, Sue Joslen, David J. Eslick, Gwen Utter, Gary Hansford, Mark Elliff, Sally Armstrong, Erin Snyder, Donna Evans, Rev. John Davidson, Seth Colaw, H.J. and Patty Johnson, Lake County Museum (Illinois) and the Curt Teich Postcard Collection, Steve Weldon at the Jasper County Records Center, Lola Bove and Deb Haynes at the Carthage Public Library, and board members of the Powers Museum. The museum also thanks all who identified potential photographs on our social media outlets from December 2012 to March 2013.

Unless otherwise noted, the images found in this book come from the holdings of the Powers Museum. I thank all who loaned photographs and express additional appreciation to Crystal Manning, Terri Heckmaster, Kimberly Fullerton, Steve Beimdiek, Sharon Baird, Gloria Leeson, Lora Honey Phelps, Nancy Brewer, Pastor Chuck Davis, Rev. James Schnackenberg, and members of the Congregation of the Mother Co-Redemptrix for their extra efforts.

Items in this book from the museum were donated originally by Martha Horsbough, Nations Bank and James Bracht, Richard Ferguson, Mary Beimdiek, Jeanie Hill, David Wallace, Jack and Sue Vandergriff, Larry and Linda James, Robert Boots, Eleanor Coffield, Frances Pierce, the estate of Joe Craig, Carthage Chamber of Commerce and Max McKnight, Mercantile Bank and the former Home Federal Savings and Loan Association, Carthage R-9 Schools, Carthage Public Library, Rhoda Fairchild Chapter of the National Society of the Daughters of the American Revolution, Carthage Sportsmen's Protective League, anonymous donors, and the founding estate of Marian Powers Winchester.

Finally, the Powers Museum is grateful to the employees at Arcadia Publishing for their special considerations involved in the production of this book.

—Diane Sharits
President, Powers Museum Board

Unless noted otherwise, identifications of people are given from left to right throughout this book. Please consult www.powersmuseum.com/cupboard/arcadia2 for a full subject and name index for this book, along with caption updates, additional image source information, and identifications for multiperson images not printed in the book due to space limitations.

INTRODUCTION

It has been over a decade since the Powers Museum published its first Images of America book featuring Carthage from the late 1860s to the 1930s. On the occasion of its 25th anniversary, the museum wanted to issue another picture book; this time covering from 1940 to 1990.

With an aggressive municipal promoter in the form of the Carthage Chamber of Commerce along with several banking institutions as investment partners, Carthage survived the Great Depression in better fashion than many communities around her. Factories were not idle long before new occupants were found.

With the announcement of construction of the US Army's Camp Crowder (located in Newton County to the south) coupled with World War II industrial production and military-related travel on US Highway 66, Carthage experienced an economic boost and building boom during the 1940s. Modernization continued into the 1950s and 1960s challenging the Victorian-built environment from the 1890s to the 1910s as the city expanded. As new commercial hubs cropped up in the 1970s and 1980s, change also came to the heart of Carthage, the Courthouse Square Business District. Even America's "Mother Road," US Highway 66, was superseded by Interstate 44 south of town. These decades of challenge and change are the focus of this book.

The time frame was selected also because the museum was receiving increased requests for materials and information from these years; unlike when the museum first opened, most people were interested specifically in the Victorian period of Carthage's history. Whether this is the result of baby boomers reminiscing about their childhoods or just a general shift of interest to more contemporary history, the Powers Museum is proud to be involved in this project.

Most of the photographs in our first book came from the estate holdings of Marian Powers Winchester, which established the museum's collections and included items belonging to her parents Dr. Everett Powers and Marian Wright Powers as well as Marian's grandparents Curtis Wright and Nira Koogler Wright. This book, however, highlights selections from donations to the museum since its opening in June 1988. The museum is grateful to all donors who have added to the museum's collections these past 25 years.

Unfortunately, due to size limitations of the Images of America series, this volume cannot represent every business, church, school, or attraction built or in operation between 1940 and 1990. Selections were based in part on whether or not the subject was originally published in our 2000 book or included in another Arcadia title, *Route 66 in the Missouri Ozarks* by Joe Sonderman (2009).

Several images come from the museum's collection of Carthage High School yearbooks to honor *The Carthaginian*'s centennial this year. As inquiries for pictures of the 1950s through the 1980s grew, the museum discovered the advertising sections in the yearbooks held a treasure trove of images beginning with the late-1950s volumes.

So, enjoy your trip down memory lane, and please visit the Powers Museum in person or on the Internet.

—Michele Newton Hansford
Director, Powers Museum

One

Around the Square and Nearby

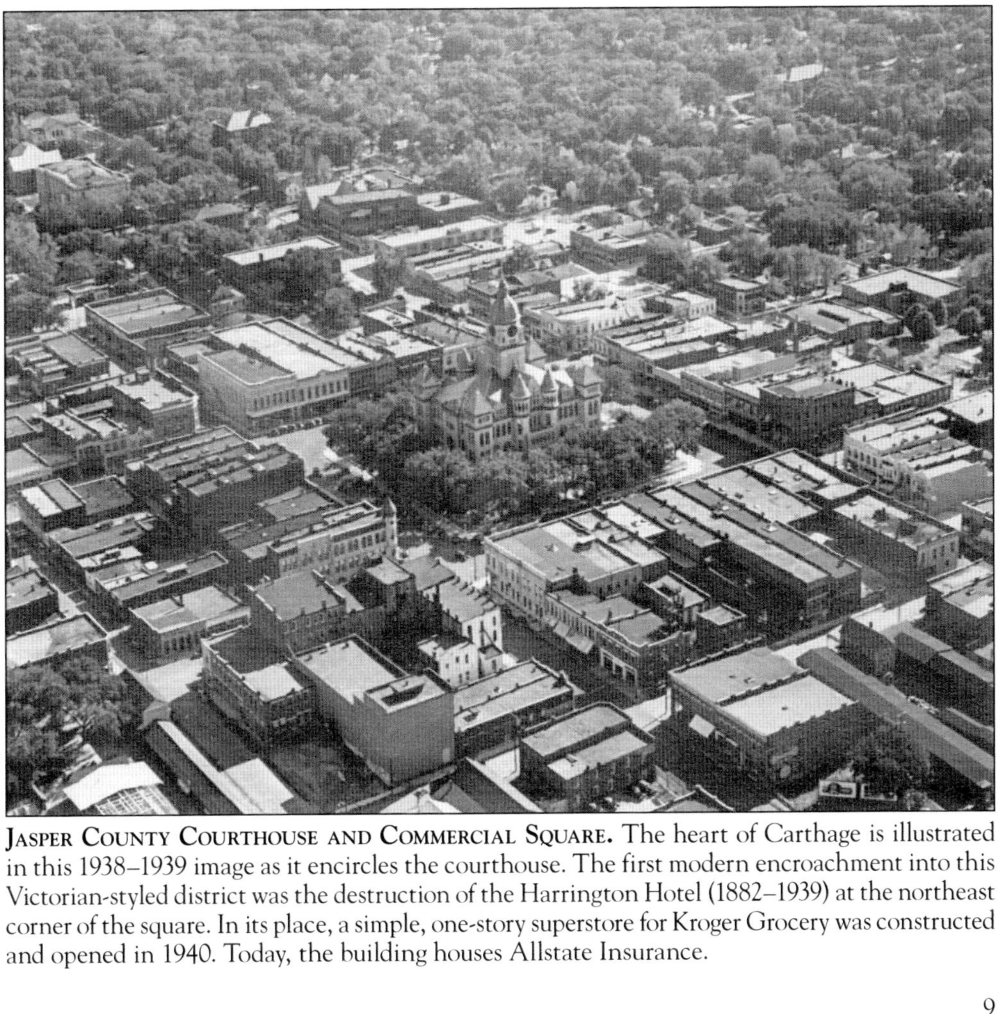

Jasper County Courthouse and Commercial Square. The heart of Carthage is illustrated in this 1938–1939 image as it encircles the courthouse. The first modern encroachment into this Victorian-styled district was the destruction of the Harrington Hotel (1882–1939) at the northeast corner of the square. In its place, a simple, one-story superstore for Kroger Grocery was constructed and opened in 1940. Today, the building houses Allstate Insurance.

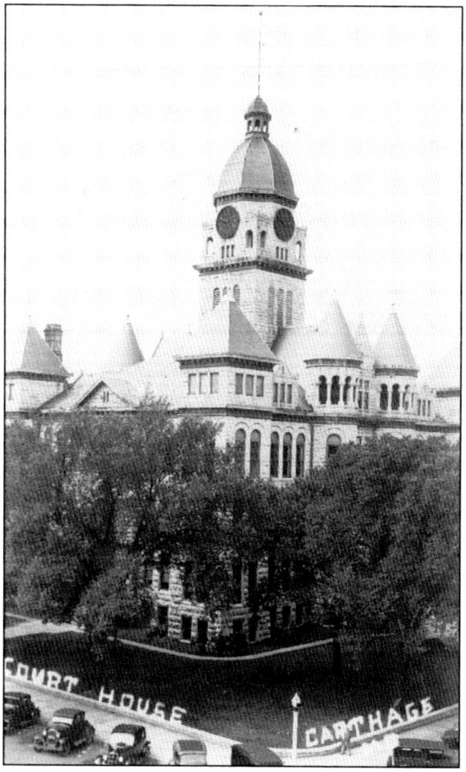

JASPER COUNTY COURTHOUSE. Built in 1894–1895, the Jasper County Courthouse was designed by M.A. Orlopp Jr. and was constructed with limestone from the Carthage Stone Company quarries, owned by Curtis Wright and partner William Logan. The original face of the tower's clock was dark, a tradition that continued until the 1950s, when its current white background was adopted. Also note the vehicles parked backwards.

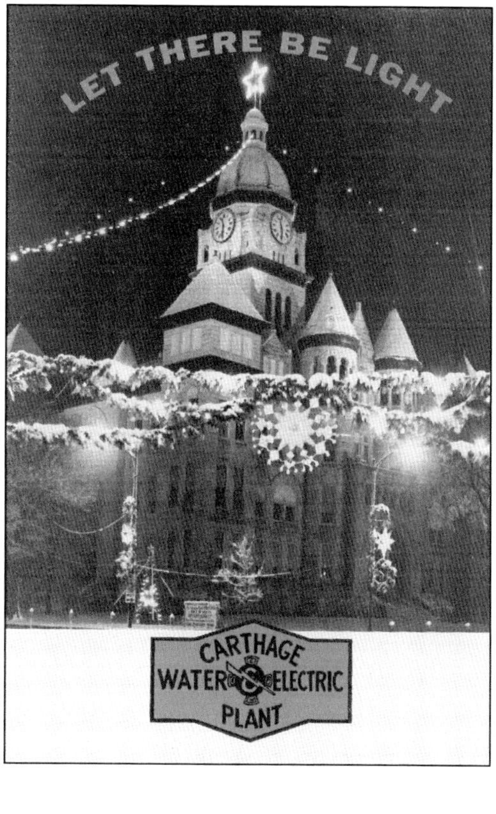

JASPER COUNTY COURTHOUSE. Decorated by Carthage Water and Electric Plant workers, the square and courthouse have been decorated each Christmas since 1916 when the first lighted Christmas trees were placed on the grounds of the courthouse. In 1958, architectural details of the courthouse were floodlighted for the first time to highlight the Romanesque Revival architecture of the structure.

Jasper County Courthouse. Ruth Kolpin donated the lighted star atop the courthouse tower. Called the Jasper County Star, it was dedicated on January 10, 1964, "to all mankind as a Guiding Star and a Star of Peace" as proclaimed by Governor Faubus of Arkansas, Governor Dalton of Missouri, Governor Bellmon of Oklahoma, and Governor Anderson of Kansas. Mayor Ralph Rhinehart presided over the ceremony.

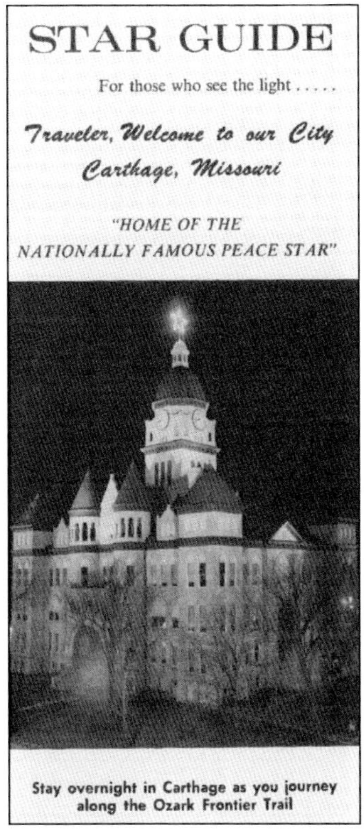

North Side of the Square, 100 Block East Third Street. Not only is the square a commercial center but also a social hub for community events, too. The end of a 1968 parade is seen here; however, the event sponsoring the parade is unidentified. Stores pictured include the former Reynolds Hardware, Barnes Jewelry, Baird News, Oklahoma Tire & Supply, Carthage Hardware, Browning Furniture, Carthage Sewing & Appliance Center, Carthage Cablevision, Boggess Agency, and Jasper County Title.

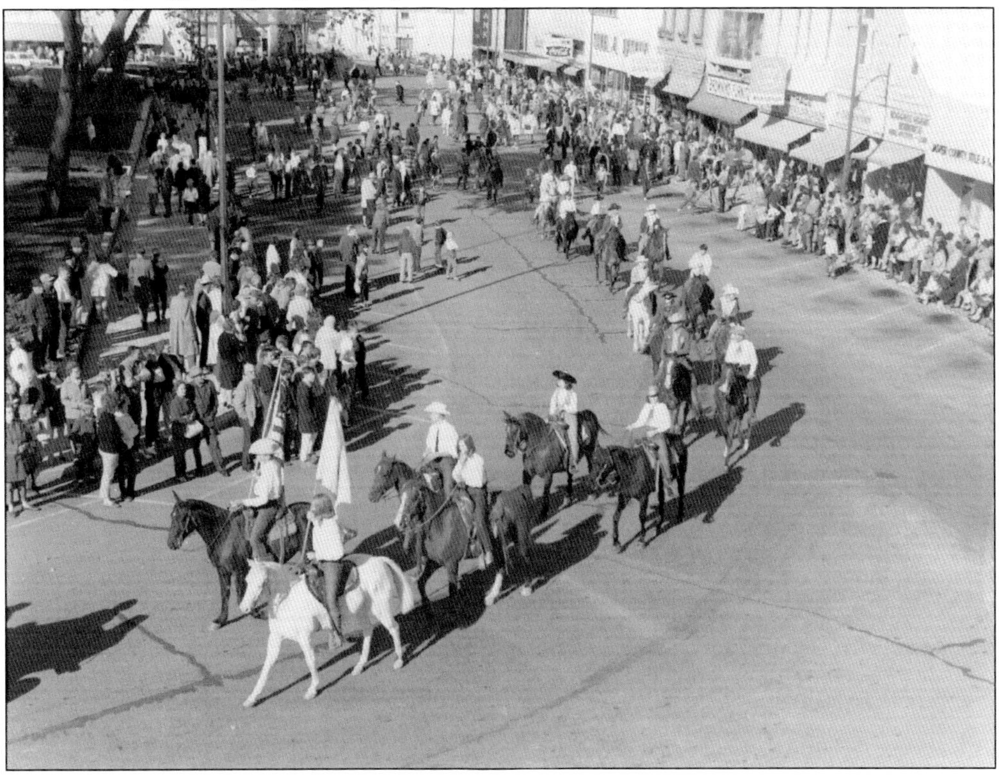

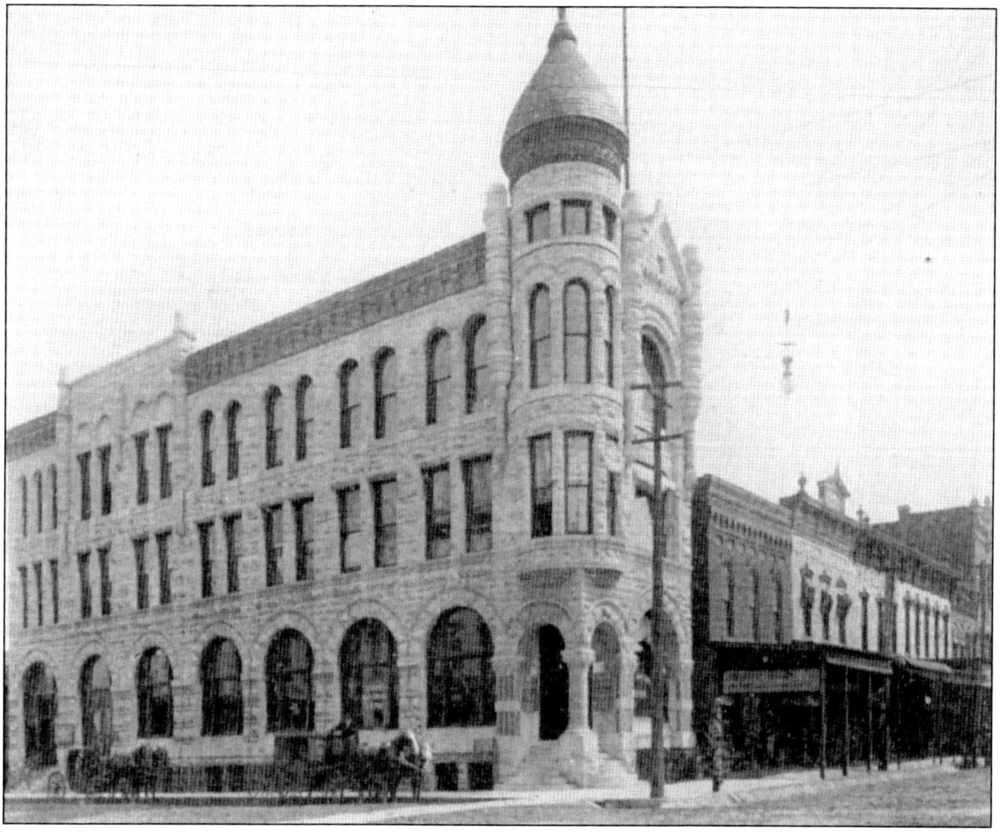

First National Bank, 300 Grant Street. In 1931, Central National Bank took over of the First National Bank and continued operations in First National's 1891 building. With the merger, Central National became the second-largest capitalized bank in town after the Bank of Carthage. By 1963, a new facility was needed, and one of the earliest buildings of local limestone was torn down.

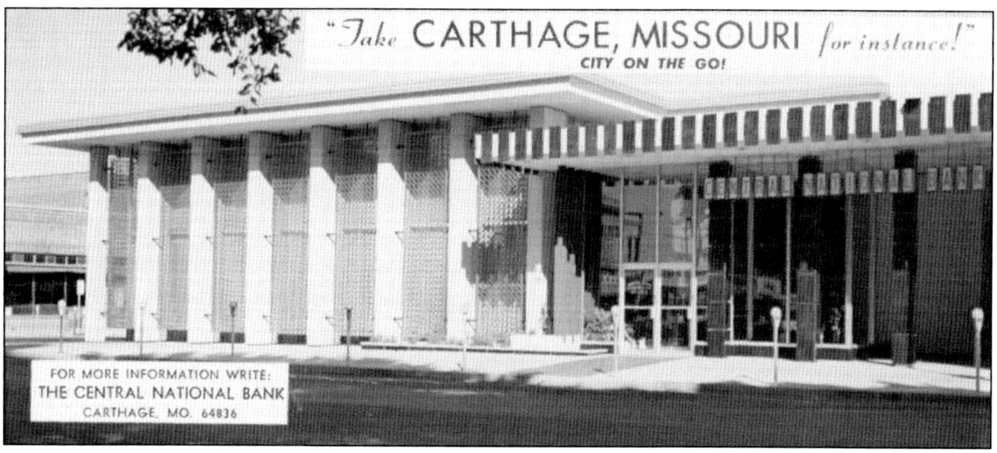

Central National Bank, 300 Grant Street. Central's new bank building opened in 1964 under bank president Ramon Evans. Designed by architect Richard Stahl, the building features glass-and-marble construction inside and out, including Ozark gray-veined stone quarried at Carthage Marble Corporation. In 1972, this structure became the United Missouri Bank and continues to operate today.

DOWNTOWN CAFÉS. From the 1940s to 1960s, many cafés where found on the square or within blocks of the downtown business district. This list from the 1951 telephone book illustrates the offerings available to serve the workers, shoppers, and tourists of Carthage.

Cafes

A & L Cafe
Steaks-Chicken Open 8 AM-Midnight
104 S Garrison---------------------3426
Alamo Cafe 305 S Garrison---------------3930
Beveridge Drive-In S of City--------------5504
Blue Lantern Cafe 500 S Main-------------4133
Blue Top Cafe 433 S Garrison--------------4934
Boots Drive-In Inc 120 S Garrison-----------2186
Buster Brown Inn NE of City---------------3970
(See Advertisement This Page)
C & W Cafe 115 E 3----------------------3988
Central Cafe 301 E Central----------------4917
Charley's Lunch 507 S Main---------------3915
Clover Inn Cafe
Mr & Mrs Norman Brown
N of City-------------------------4940
Fairlawn Cafe Fairlawn Dr----------------4951
Gene's Grill 332 Grant--------------------3956
Hello Cafe 1936 S Garrison----------------4922
John's Cafe 204 E 4----------------------4365
Ledford Bros Serv Sta & Cafe S of City-----6455
Maid-Rite Sandwich Shop 310 W 3----------3948
Main Street Cafe
Chas & Zoah Hogue-Owners
107 S Main------------------------4928
Red's Cafe
Open 6:00 AM Till 12 Midnight
323 W Central---------------------2051
Sunset Court & Cafe
Located 2 Mi E Hway 66
NE of City------------------------5411
Tommy's Drive-In SE of City-------------5353
Town House 1221 S Garrison--------------3105
Whisler's Lunch 116 W 4-----------------2403
White Rock Lunch
Open All Night—Hamburgers
502 S Main------------------------3921

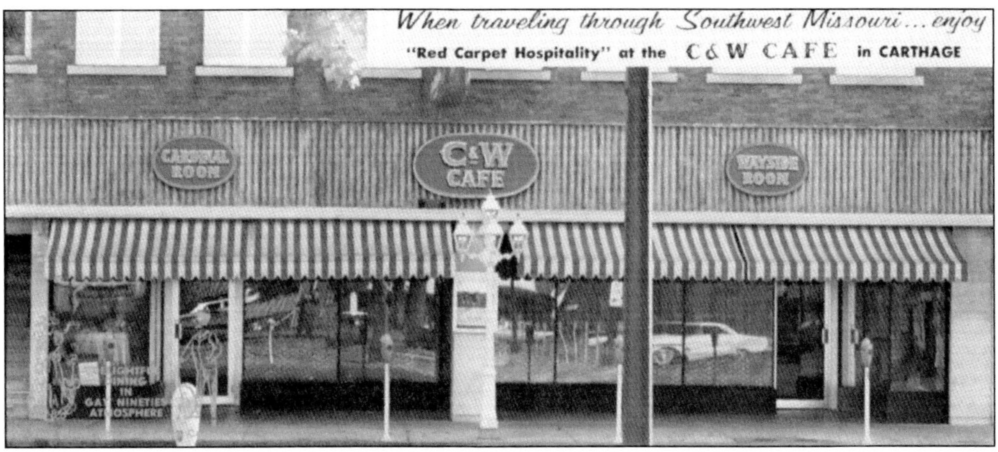

C&W CAFÉ, 342 GRANT STREET. Started on the square's north side in 1935 by Ray Carter and Albert White, the C&W moved to the Steadley Building in 1962. By then, Ray and Bonnie Carter solely owned it until 1975. It was then renamed the Gaslight Restaurant in 1977 by new owners Gerald and Betty Forest. A mural painted by Richard Rhine featuring the 1895 Southwest Missouri Electric Railway is still visible in the current store at this address.

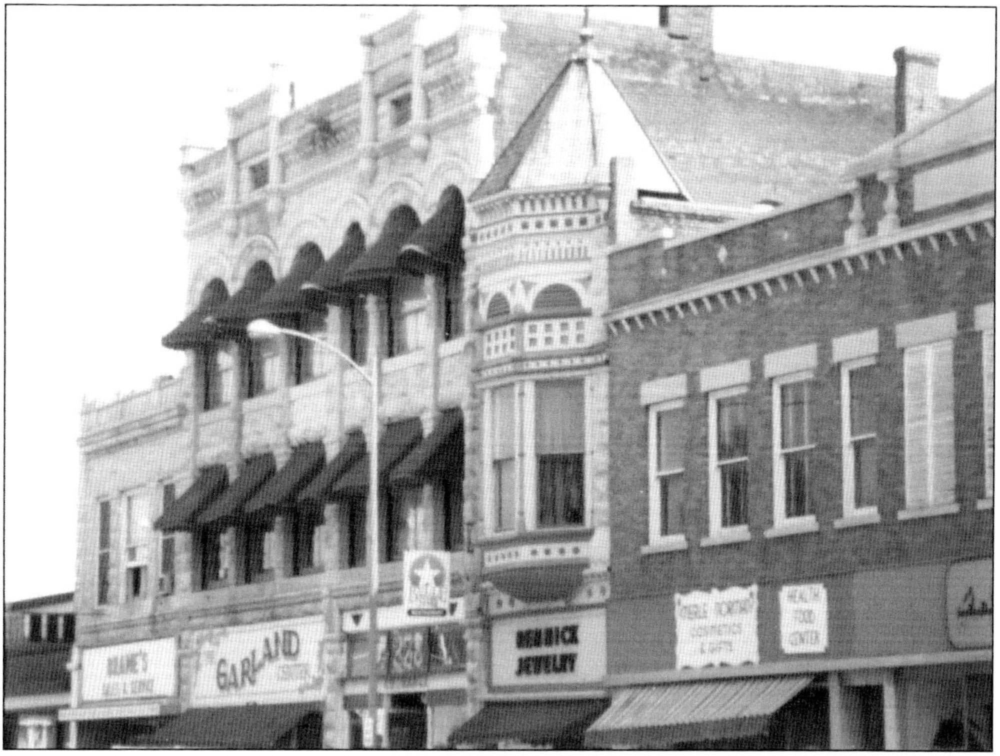

GARLAND CENTER, 328 GRANT STREET. The Garland Center sat mid-block along with Brane's Sales and Rennick Jewelry. Restoration of the 1892 limestone Garland and Myers structures by owners Lowell Davis, Bob DeBaca, and Tom Kingsbury began in 1980. A year later, the center opened, featuring stores on two levels and the Belle Starr Restaurant on the third floor. A fire in 1988 destroyed these four buildings, but not the Steadley Building on the right.

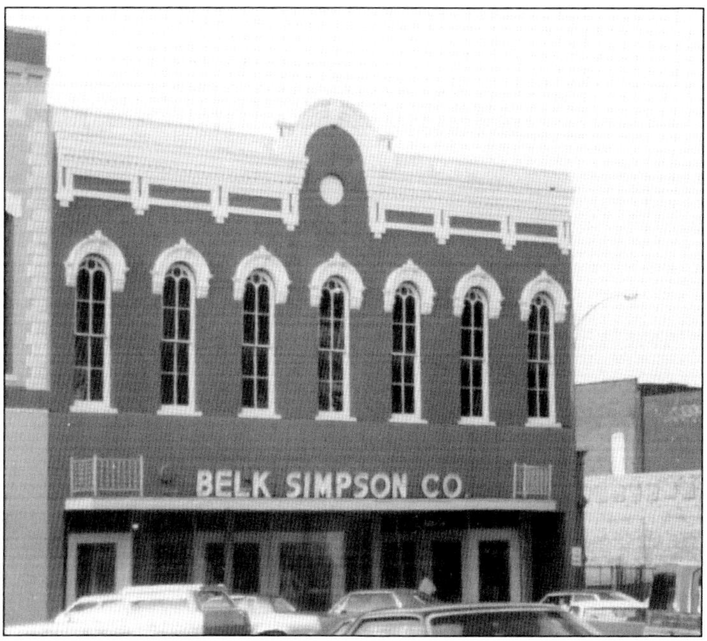

BELK-SIMPSON DEPARTMENT STORE, 136 EAST FOURTH STREET. Several department stores have occupied the storefronts below the former 1878 Burlingame and Chaffee Opera House. Among them were Scott (1941) and Burr (1947), which later combined to form Scott-Burr department store. Belk-Simpson, seen here in 1983–1984, operated in this building from the mid-1950s to 1988. Jack Norman moved his Ladies Peddler store to this address in 1989.

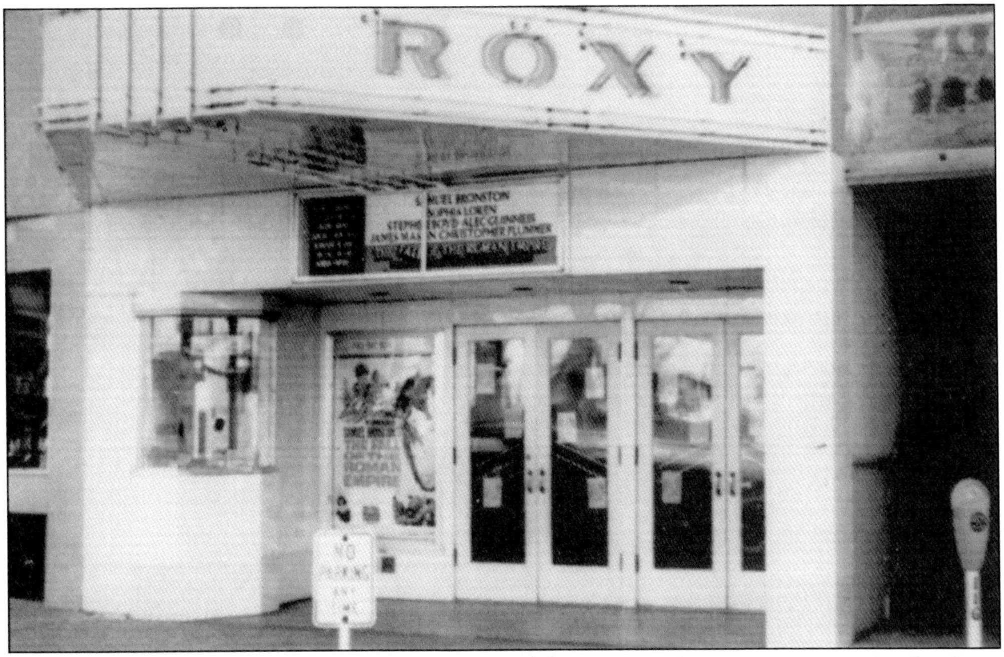

ROXY THEATRE, 124 EAST FOURTH STREET. One of three movie theaters near or on the Carthage Square in the mid-19th century, the Roxy, seen here in 1964, occupied the former Delphus Theater, which operated from 1908 to the late 1940s. William Bradfield and then Leroy Whitehead managed the Roxy. Fire hit the south side of the square in 1972, and three old structures, including the Roxy's building, were destroyed.

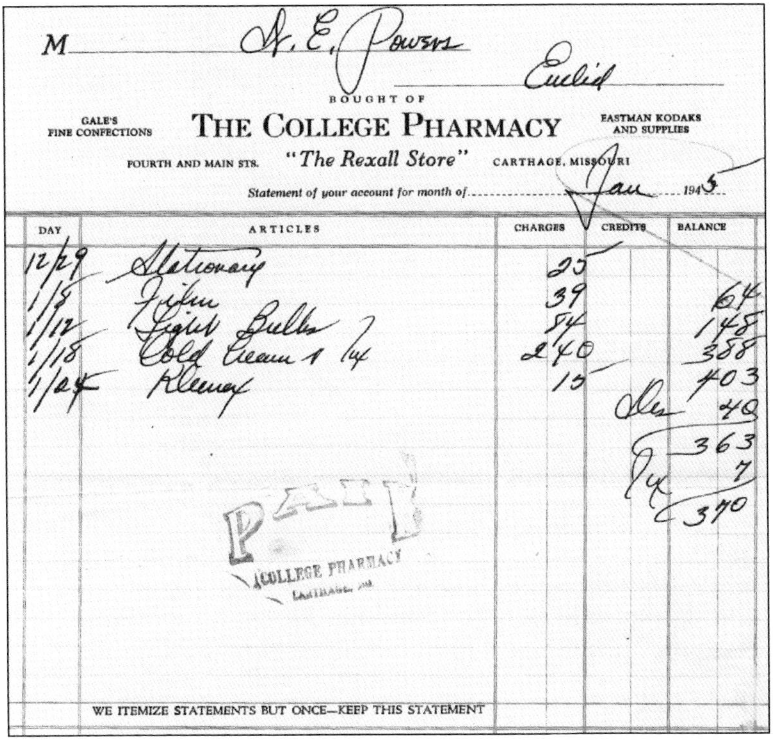

M N. E. Powers

Euclid

BOUGHT OF

GALE'S FINE CONFECTIONS — THE COLLEGE PHARMACY — EASTMAN KODAKS AND SUPPLIES

FOURTH AND MAIN STS. "The Rexall Store" CARTHAGE, MISSOURI

Statement of your account for month of Jan 1945

DAY	ARTICLES	CHARGES	CREDITS	BALANCE
12/29	Stationary	25		
1/5	Film	39		64
1/12	Light Bulbs	84		148
1/18	Cold Cream 1 ¼	240		388
1/24	Kleenex	15		403
				40
				363
				7
				370

PAID COLLEGE PHARMACY CARTHAGE, MO.

WE ITEMIZE STATEMENTS BUT ONCE—KEEP THIS STATEMENT

COLLEGE PHARMACY, 401 SOUTH MAIN STREET. Housed in the former Carthage National Bank Building, College Pharmacy was opened at this location in 1924 by Howard Gray. In 1972, his son William, who had been a partner since 1951, inherited the store and continued until 1999. This 1945 invoice for goods purchased includes 39¢ film and 84¢ lightbulbs.

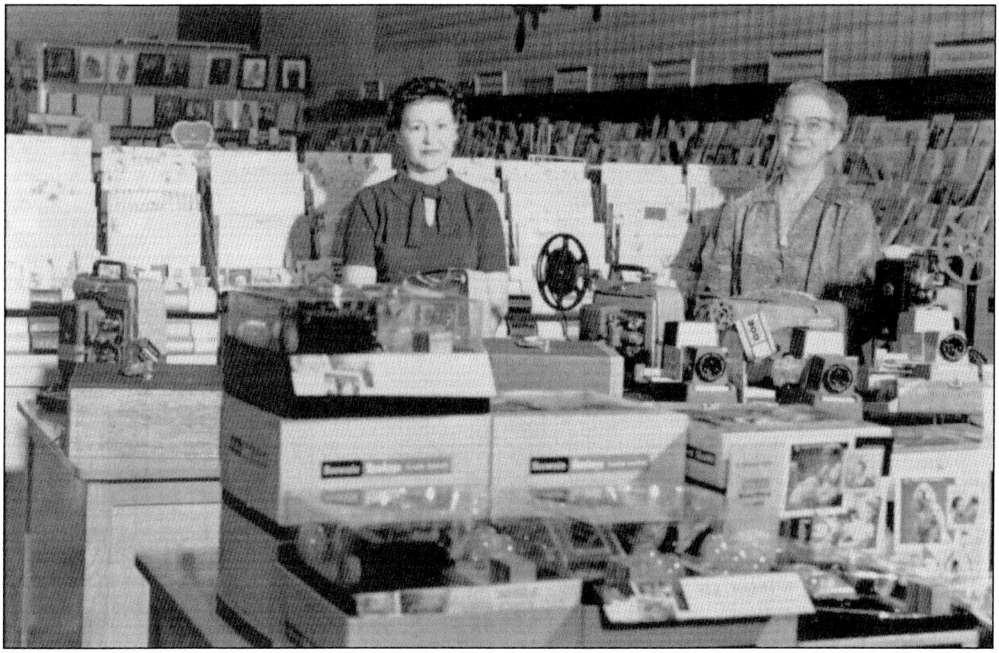

Steward Camera & Card Shop, 405 South Main Street. The Steward family not only owned one of Carthage's most popular photography studios but also a card store, frame shop, and camera supply house. Tending to the store in 1958 were Wilma Steward (left) and Georgia Steward (right).

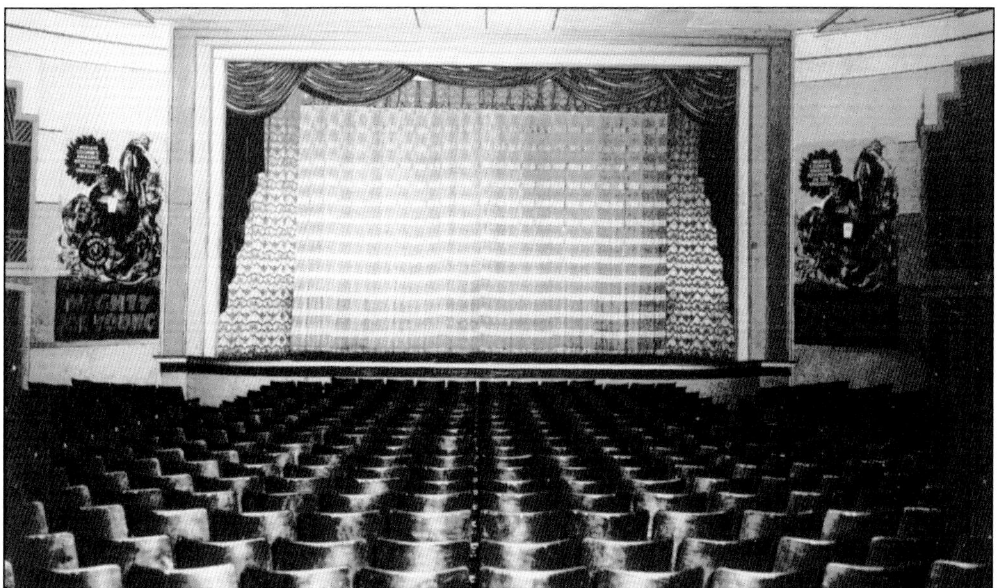

Tiger Theatre, 319 South Main Street. Banners on each side of the Tiger's stage advertised the 1949 film *Mighty Joe Young.* The Tiger operated on the square's west side until 1954, when a second fire in the Center Building's history closed the theater. Other stores occupying the Center Building in 1954 were Jaffe's Shoes and Murray-Duncan Drugs, with professional offices above on the second floor.

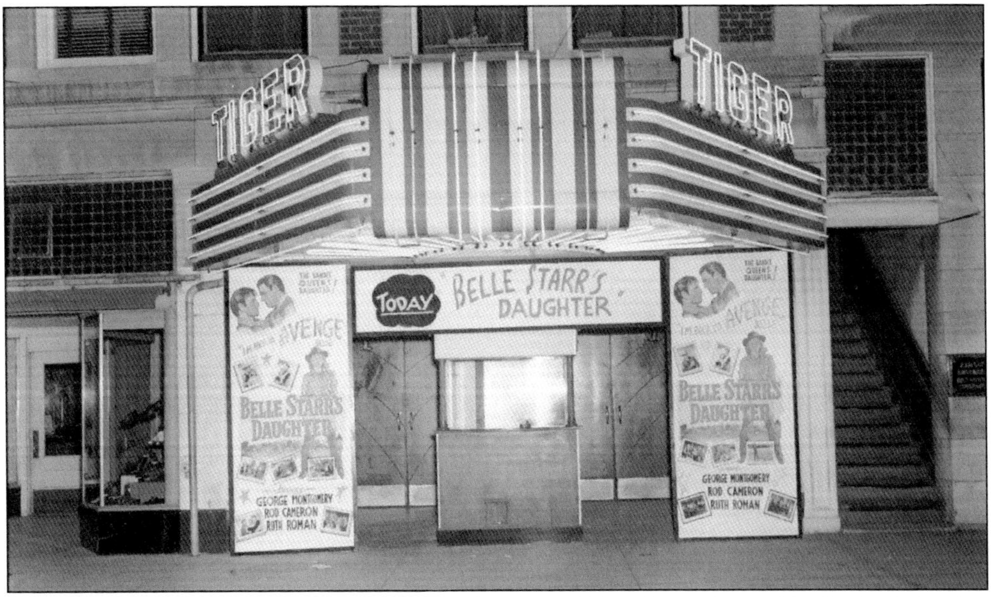

Tiger Theatre. *Belle Starr's Daughter* debuted in late 1948 and was directed by Lesley Selandar, who was noted for Westerns. William Riley Burnett, considered one of Hollywood's most famous screenwriters, wrote it. Movies with a connection to former Carthage resident Myra Belle Shirley, who was later known as Belle Starr, always attracted viewers.

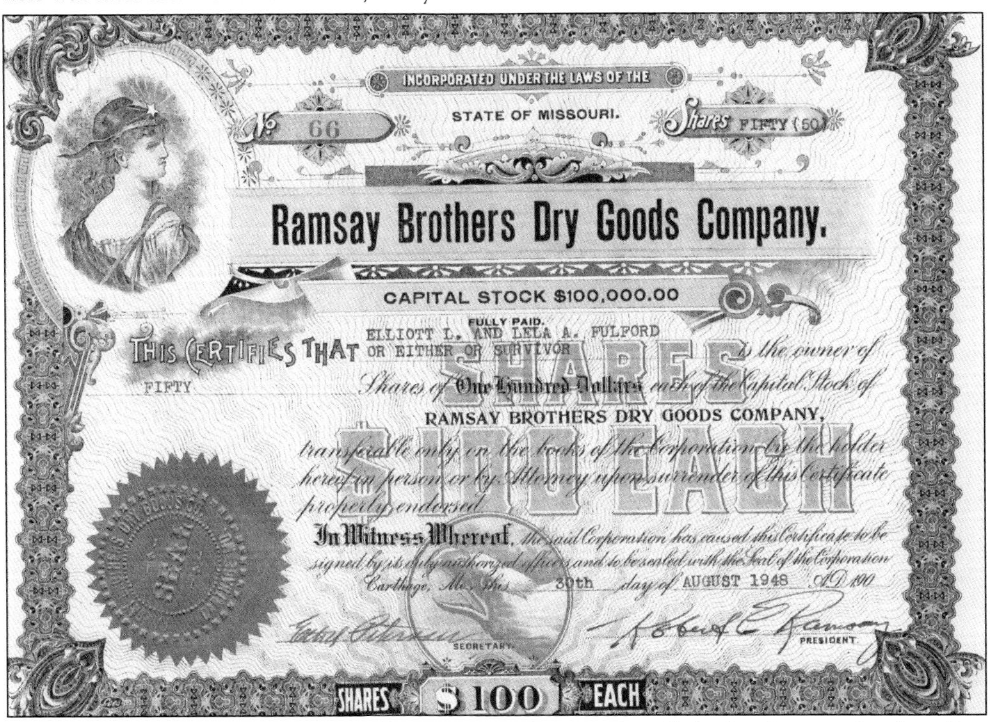

INCORPORATED UNDER THE LAWS OF THE STATE OF MISSOURI.

No. 66 Shares FIFTY (50)

Ramsay Brothers Dry Goods Company.

CAPITAL STOCK $100,000.00

FULLY PAID.

This Certifies That ELLIOTT L. AND LELA A. FULFORD OR EITHER OR SURVIVOR is the owner of FIFTY Shares of One Hundred Dollars each of the Capital Stock of RAMSAY BROTHERS DRY GOODS COMPANY, transferable only on the books of the Corporation by the holder hereof in person or by Attorney upon surrender of this Certificate properly endorsed.

In Witness Whereof, the said Corporation has caused this Certificate to be signed by its duly authorized officers and to be sealed with the Seal of the Corporation Carthage, Mo. this 30th day of AUGUST 1948 A.D. 190

SECRETARY. PRESIDENT.

SHARES $100 EACH

Ramsay's Department Store, 311 South Main Street. Established as Ramsay Brothers Dry Goods Company in 1895 by A.A. Ramsay and his brother Robert, this business served Carthage shoppers until 1975. In 1962, the Fulfords purchased additional stock in the company, as seen from Ramsay's stock book now in the collection of the Powers Museum.

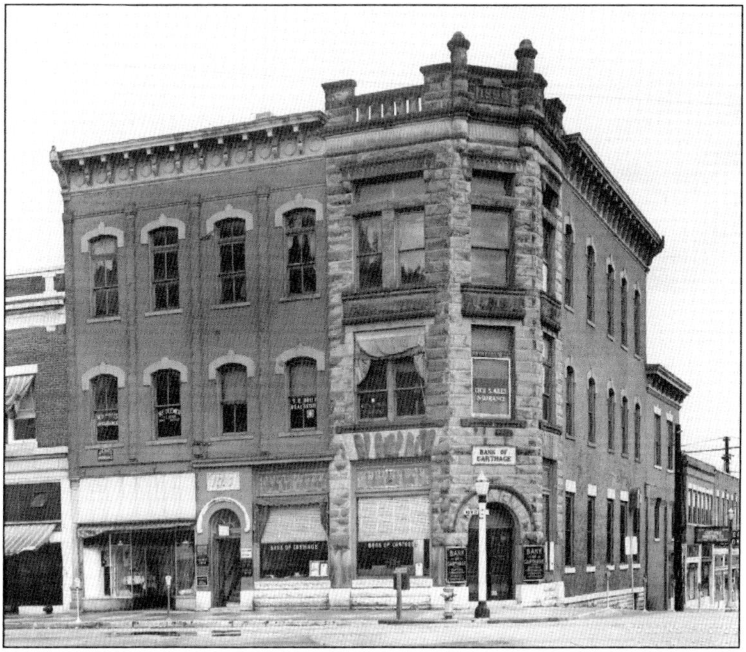

BANK OF CARTHAGE, 301 SOUTH MAIN STREET. Organized in 1868, this was the first bank started in Carthage after the Civil War. By 1947, when photographed by Gordon Rollins, the bank's president was Walter Carter and vice presidents were John Marsh and C. Rex Carter. The second floor housed offices for professionals, and the third floor originally was the Independent Order of Odd Fellows lodge.

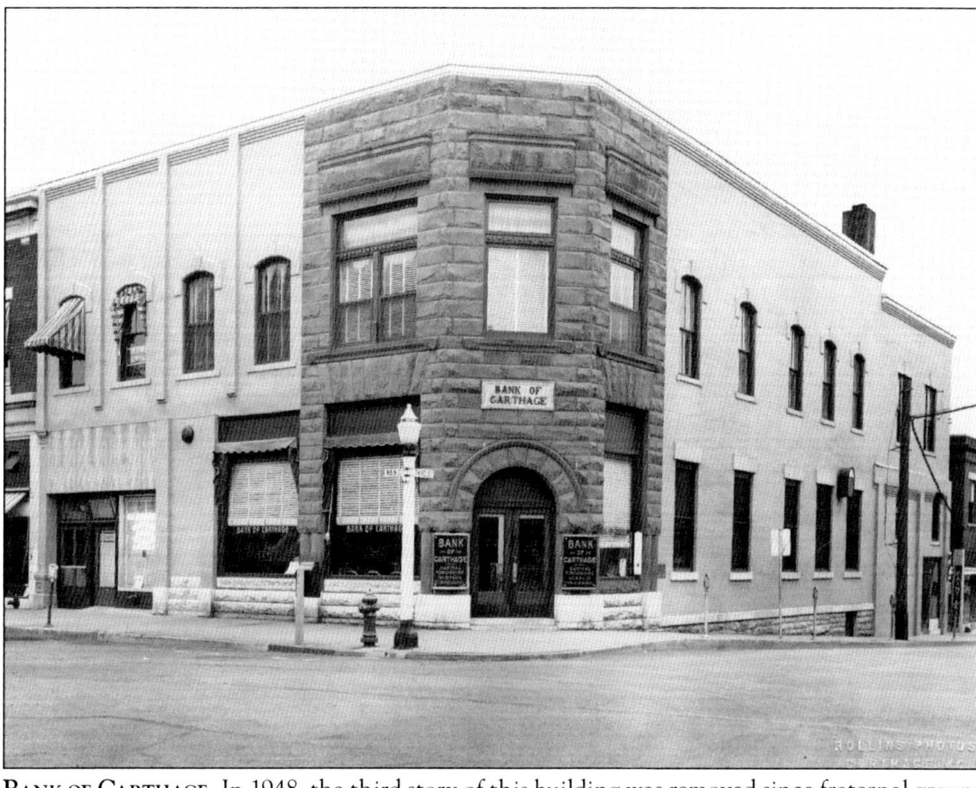

BANK OF CARTHAGE. In 1948, the third story of this building was removed since fraternal groups no longer used it. The building, constructed in 1884 as two stories, was expanded to three floors in 1890 and remodeled again in 1910. One of the longest leased offices above the bank was the Cecil Miles Insurance Agency. Dr. Everett Powers also had his office on the second floor.

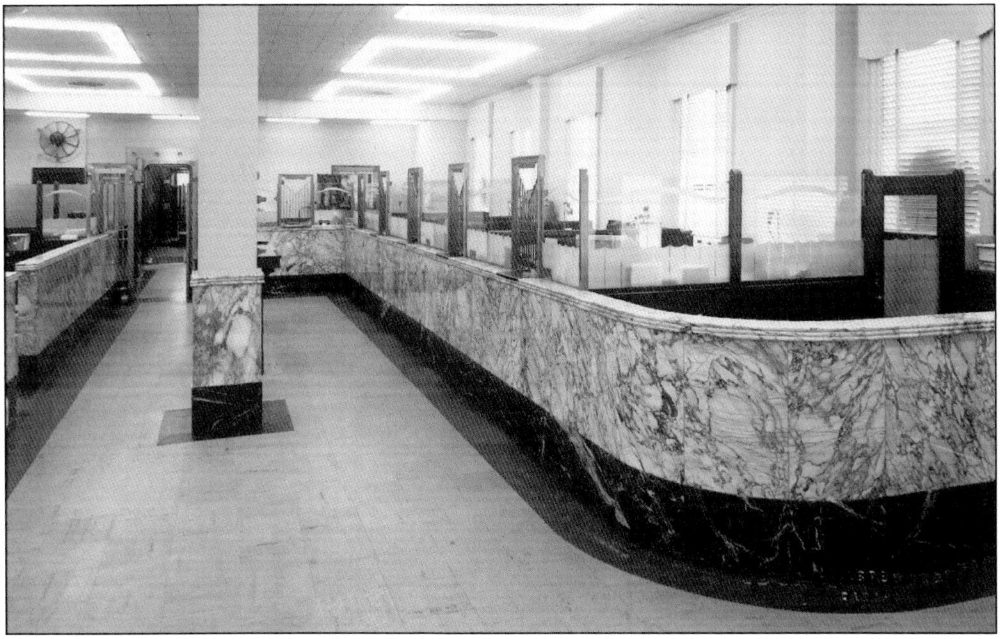

BANK OF CARTHAGE. Over the years, the bank's interior also was remodeled several times. This late 1930s view displays the results of Depression-era redecorating, undertaken to help the unemployment situation of the time. An ornate ceiling was covered with acoustic tile and old bronze grilles on the counters were removed, although the marble counters and wainscoting remained.

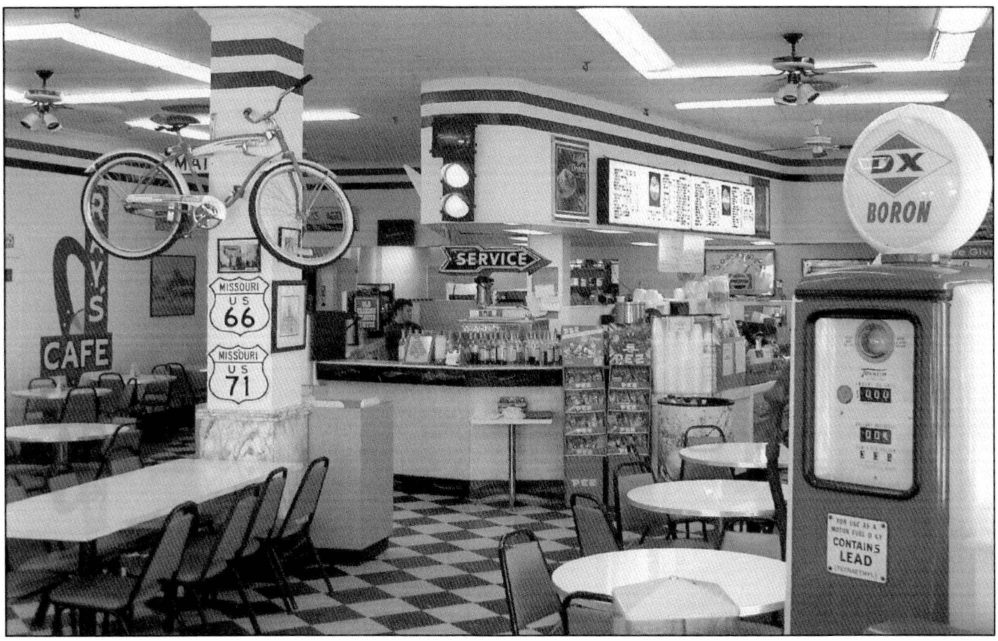

CARTHAGE DELI, 301 SOUTH MAIN STREET. After the bank moved in 1961, the building became the Gray-Krummel Drugstore until 1988, when it merged with College Pharmacy. Then, Tom and Corrine Candela moved their Carthage Deli up from 321 South Main Street to this address and decorated the interior with Carthage memorabilia still visible today under current deli owner Chris Brown. (Courtesy of and © Chris Brown.)

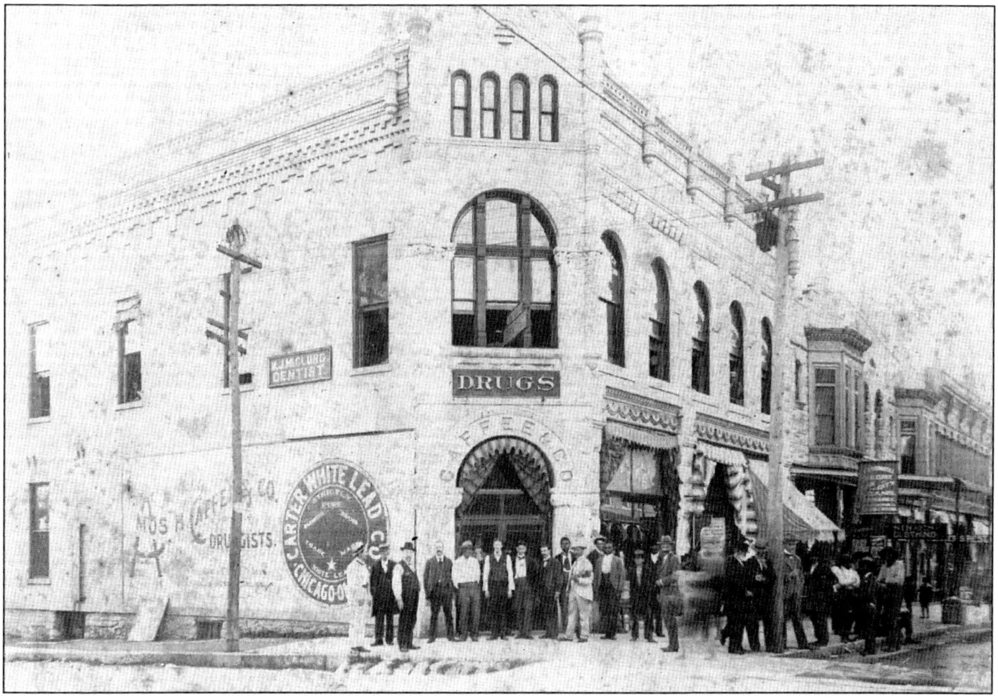

CAFFEE BUILDING, 231 SOUTH MAIN STREET. By 1959, the Bank of Carthage desired a new location. It acquired the Caffee Building across the street and tore down the structure. Amos Caffee's wholesale drug business had occupied the corner from 1866 until 1924, when Howard Gray and Edwin Seaver opened a drugstore in the space.

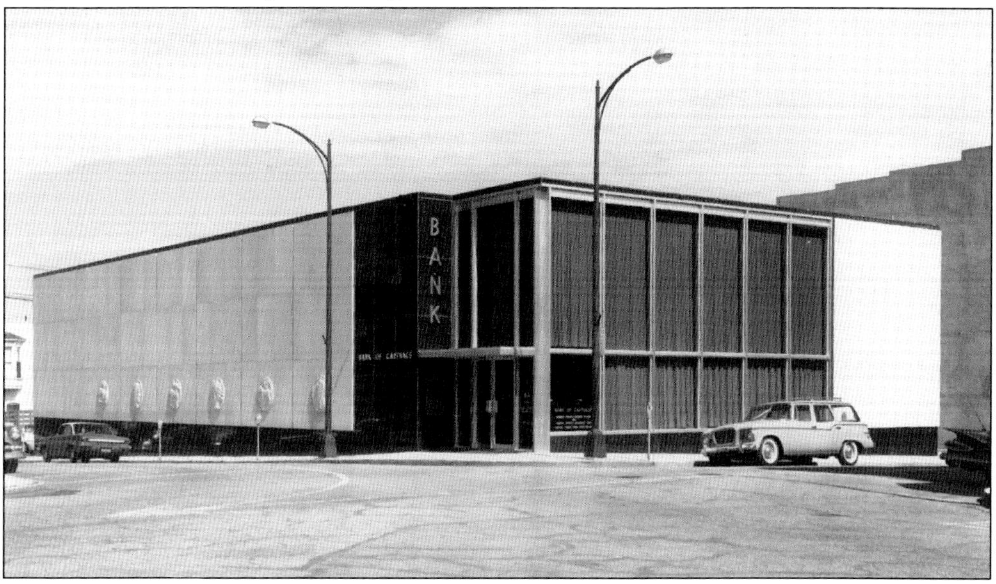

BANK OF CARTHAGE, 231 SOUTH MAIN STREET. Designed by architect A.C. Esterly and built by M-P Construction, this building's exotic granites and marbles, used inside and out, were supplied by Locarni Marble. Carthage Marble Corporation provided additional limestone, and the building was described as having "clean architectural lines of forward thinking." Mills Anderson was president, and Carl Sanders was the first depositor in 1961.

The story of the coins

No one knows who made the first coins, but since the first known state was Lydia in Asia Minor it is thought that coins originated there or in Greece. The Greeks, in fact, were probably the first to have coins that were made of a standard shape, a standard size, a standard content and a standard value established by a state. Coinage started there in the seventh century B.C. and for the first 2,000 years of coin history production was by hand. It was not until about 1500 A.D. that the first coinage machinery came into use in Italy and spread slowly through Europe.

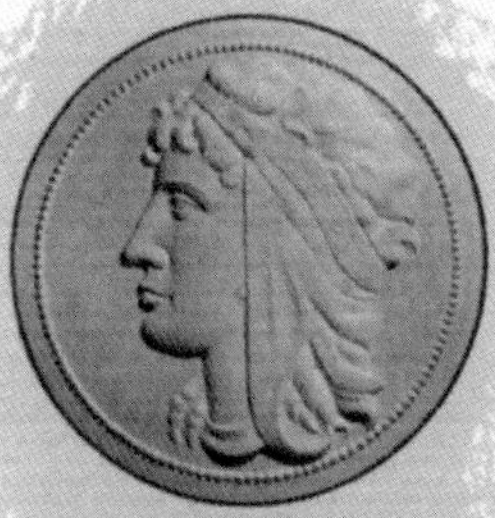

No. 1

The front of a Silver Stater, dating from about 350 B.C., representing the head of a goddess.

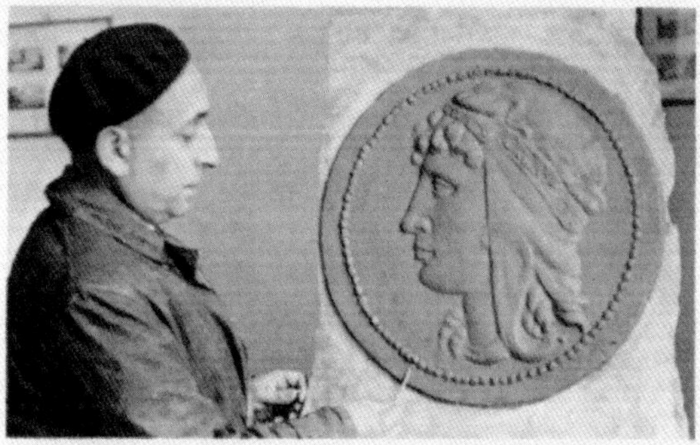

The Italian craftsman, Senor Piccini, puts the finishing touches on a clay model, to scale, of coin No. 1.

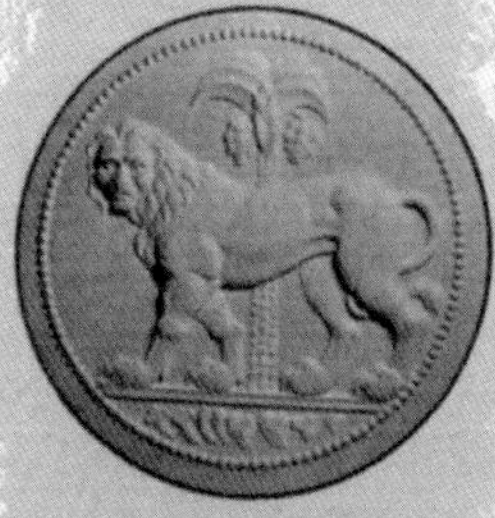

No. 2

The back of Coin No. 1 showing a lion in front of a date palm tree.

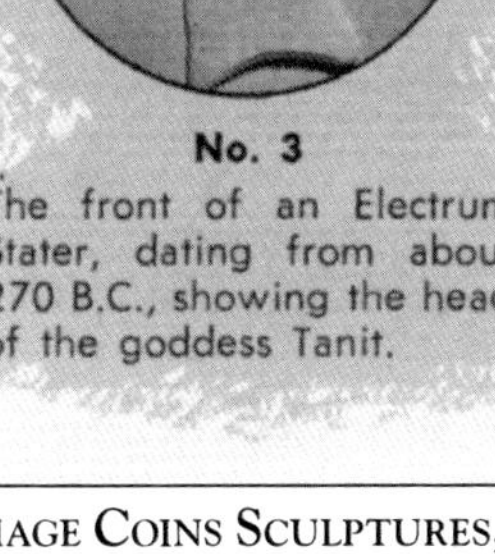

No. 3

The front of an Electrum Stater, dating from about 270 B.C., showing the head of the goddess Tanit.

The replicas of the coins of ancient Carthage, which are mounted on the outside south wall of the new building of the Bank of Carthage, at Carthage, Missouri, are backed by a romantic era of colonization, commerce, adventure, war and eventual destruction.

Ancient Carthage, founded by the Tyrians around 814 B.C. and destroyed by the Romans in 146 B.C., was the richest of the Phoenician colonies. The Phoenicians themselves were an ancient people of Asia Minor, famous for their phenomenal skills in seafaring and trading and for their development of an alphabet.

In those days north Africa was fertile farmland, with rich fields, gardens, orchards and vineyards. The Carthaginians sailed through the Pillars of Hercules (Straits of Gibraltar) and then along the Atlantic coasts of Europe and Africa. They also traded inland for elephants, slaves and precious metals. As they conquered the islands and coasts, they extracted fabulous tributes. Carthage, the great commercial city-empire, had a population of some 250,000 and 220 magnificent docks. The great city also had impressive temples and stunning public buildings, including a treasury and a mint. The coins of ancient Carthage were based on Greek models and the Carthaginians also used leather strips with various denominations stamped on them, the forerunners of paper money. These were freely accepted throughout the empire — a convincing indication of flourishing business and sound government.

Carthage Coins Sculptures, 100 Block of West Third Street. Unique to the Third Street facade of the Bank of Carthage building (now the Jasper County Courthouse Annex II) are six sculptures of ancient Carthage coins, which were crafted in Italy and installed by Carthage Marble personnel. During the 1950s through the early 1970s, Carthage had an informal sister-city relationship with the Tunisian city.

. . . as sculptured on the south wall of the Bank of Carthage building.

The idea of incorporating replicas of coins of ancient Carthage into the building design of the building of the Bank of Carthage was originated by the architect and bank officials and the liaison details with the producing marble works in Carrara, Italy were handled by the Carthage Marble Corporation of Carthage, Missouri. The marble used is Aurisina Chiara, quarried near Trieste, quite similar in color to Missouri's Carthage stone.

The inherent artistic talents of Italian craftsmen were put to work on the replicas. Research was necessary to locate actual coins to be used as models and in one case only one coin was found, a slightly damaged specimen finally traced to the Museum of Archeology of Siracusa, Sicily. From it the producers were allowed to make a plaster mold from which the clay model was made.

In the actual sculpturing process clay models are first made and approved, then transposed to the rough marble and sculptured by a combination of hand work and power equipment. Some of the fittings for the air hammer used in the production of the coin replicas are designed for rough cutting, while others are for fine finish work.

Each of the coins is 3'6" in diameter, with a thickness of 4" and each has a weight of 500 lbs. They have been carefully installed by skilled artisans of the Carthage Marble Corporation.

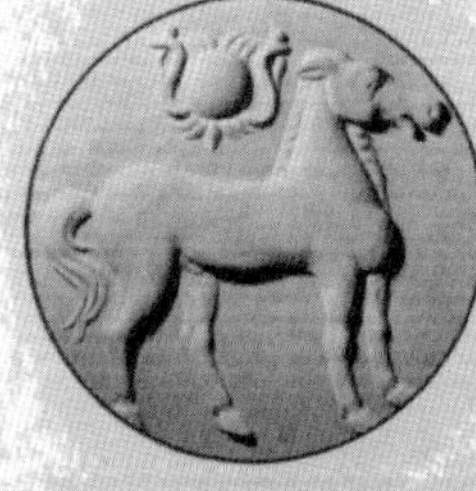

No. 4
The back of Coin No. 3 showing a horse and sunburst with serpents.

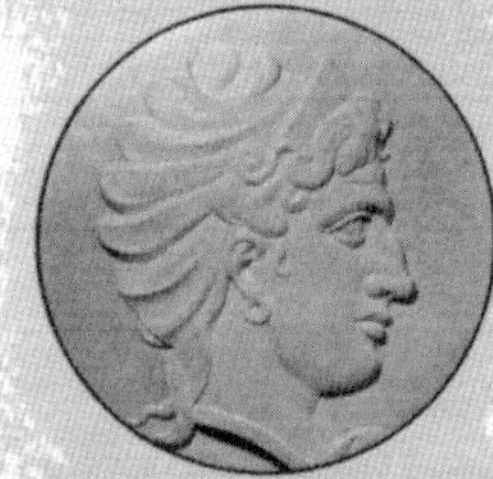

No. 5
This coin shows a female head, about 350 B.C. It is a great rarity among ancient coins.

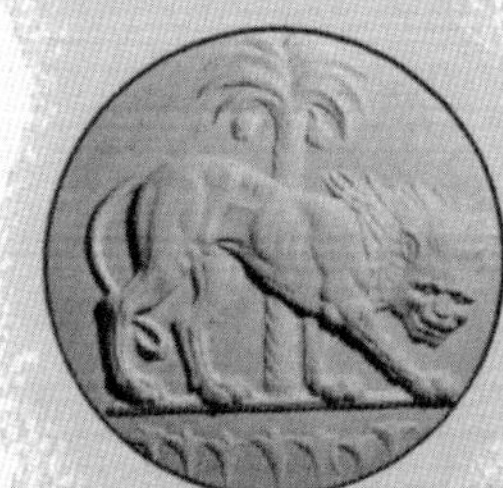

No. 6
The back of Coin No. 5 shows a lion in front of a date palm tree.

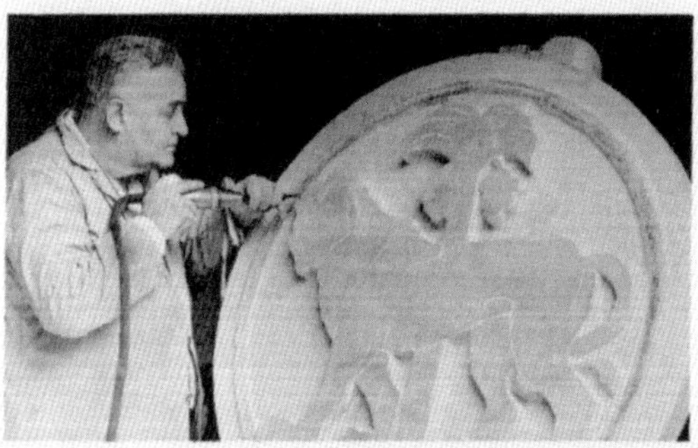

Professor Ciardelli, teacher at the Art School of Marble at Carrara, Italy is shown here using power equipment in the sculpturing of one of the coin replicas for the Bank of Carthage.

You are cordially invited to inspect these works of art at your convenience. They are indeed unique. In the growing community of Carthage, Missouri, they serve as monuments to the peoples and the works and the progress of another Carthage . . . ancient Carthage, home of Hannibal the Great, on the shores of the Mediterranean . . . founded by aggressive Phoenicians . . . destroyed by aggressive Romans.

Story by Richard F. Ferguson

CARTHAGE COINS SCULPTURES. Richard Ferguson, who authored the Bank of Carthage's 1968 history booklet to celebrate its 100th anniversary, wrote the text for "The Story of the Coins." In 1997, when the bank was purchased by a larger regional banking system, the bank's archive of historical material was donated to the Powers Museum.

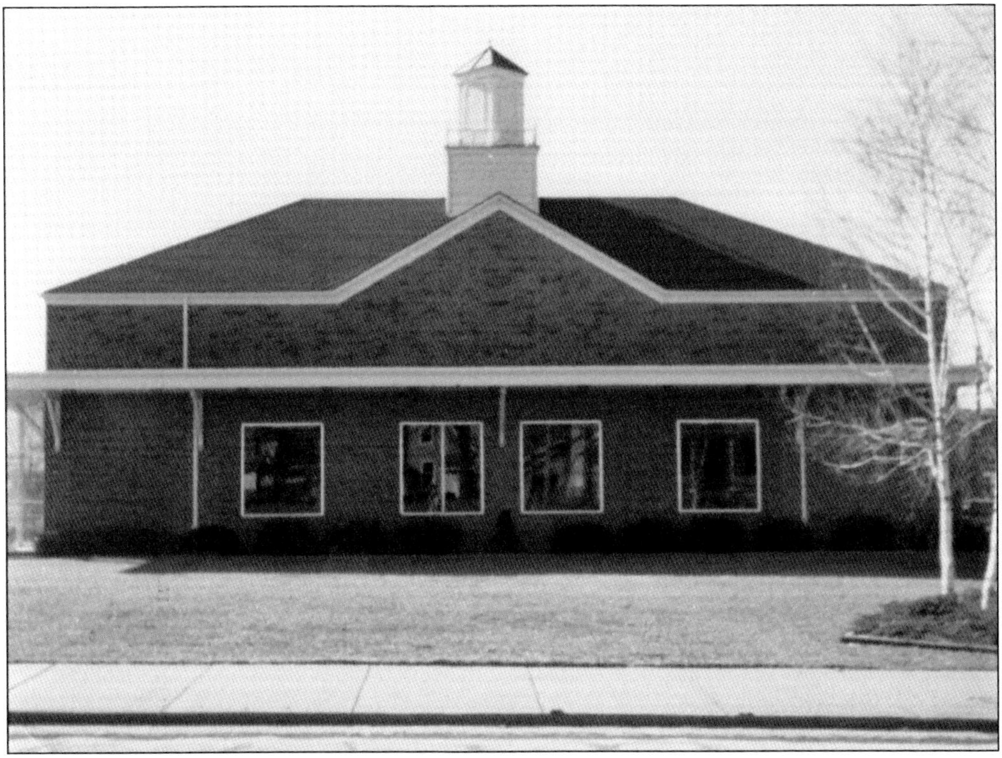

Southwest Missouri Bank, 300 West Third Street. Formed in 1979 by local investors, this bank is still locally owned today. It acquired the 1940s former A&P Grocery building for its operations and has expanded the facility numerous times. Garry Denney was the bank's first president and executive officer. (Courtesy of Southwest Missouri Bank.)

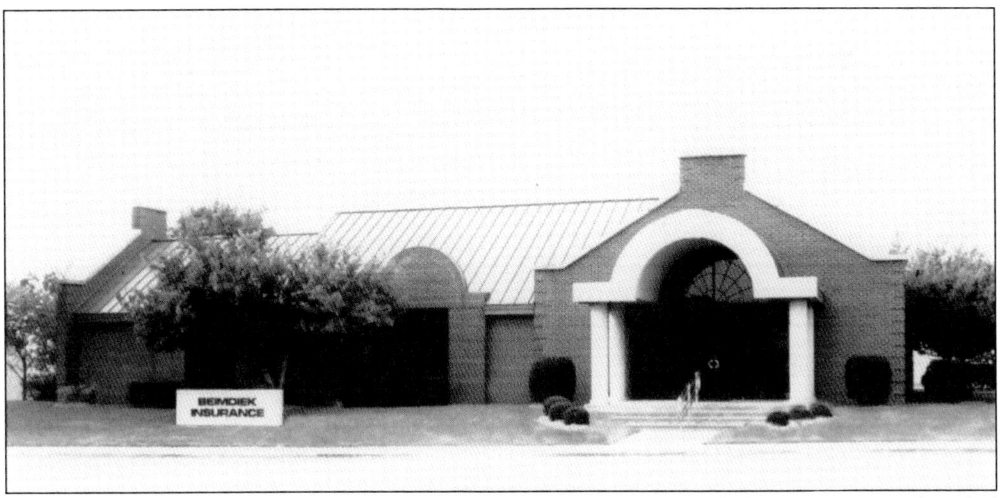

Beimdiek Insurance Agency, Inc., 303 West Third Street. Beimdiek Insurance was founded in 1936 when George S. Beimdiek started the business from scratch. George S. Beimdiek sold his ownership in 1976 to his son George S. "Steve" Beimdiek III, who incorporated the company as Beimdiek Insurance Agency, Inc. Its new office building was completed in 1990. (Courtesy of Beimdiek Insurance Agency.)

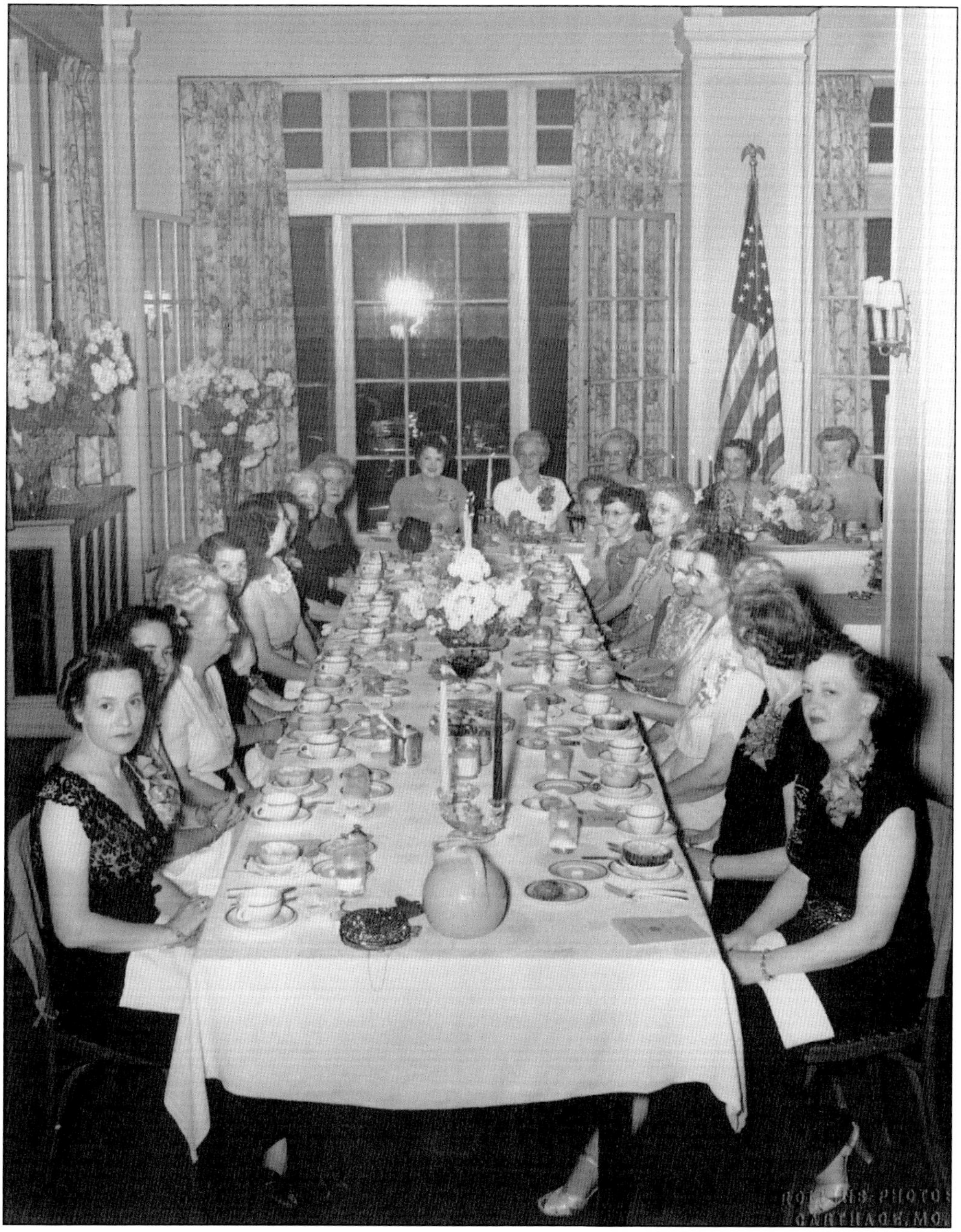

DRAKE HOTEL, 406 HOWARD STREET. Unlike smaller hotels in Carthage, the Drake served Carthage in many ways, including being a meeting center, as evident in this double view. These unidentified Soroptimist ladies and their guests are banqueting in the beautiful lobby of the hotel, which was retained when the structure was converted to apartments in 2006.

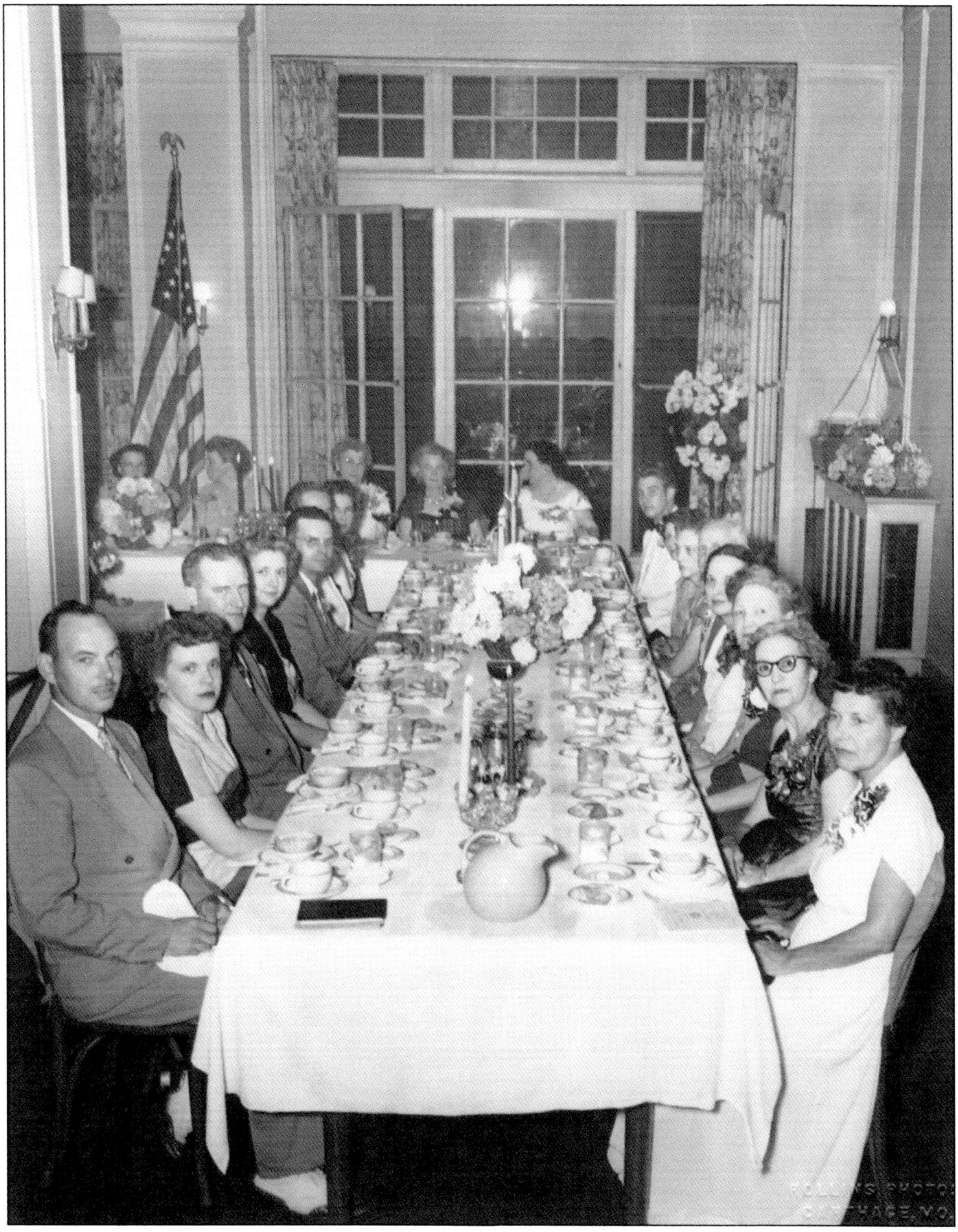

DRAKE HOTEL. Constructed in 1922, the hotel also was the site of the chamber of commerce during the 1960s. The Drake's all-you-can-eat Sunday chicken dinner cost $1 in the late 1940s and early 1950s and was favored by Dr. Everett Powers, who usually sat at a certain table to view artwork of the Grand Canyon. Later, the piece was presented to him and now is part of the museum's collection.

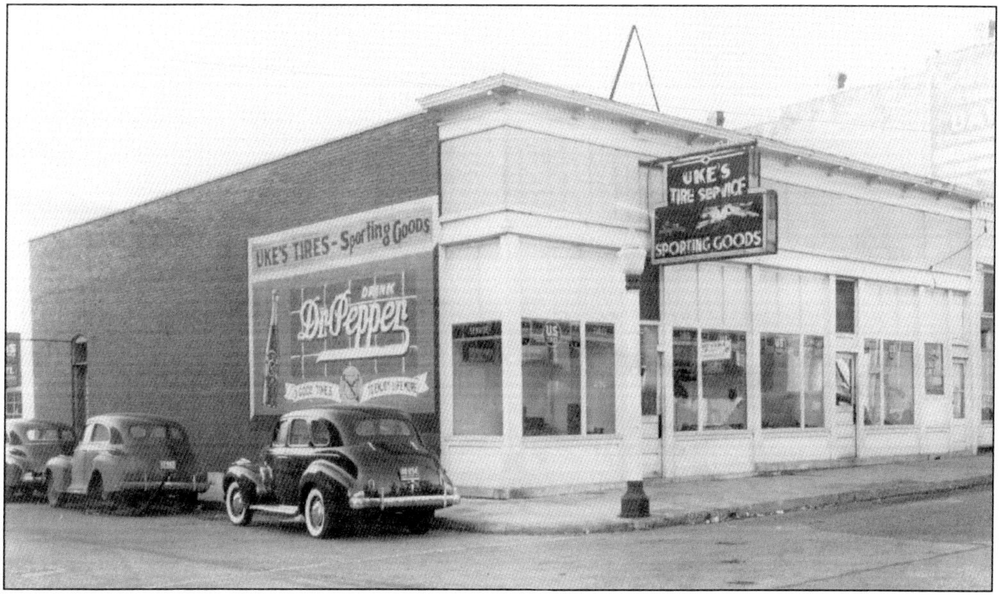

Uke's Tires & Sporting Goods, 230 East Fourth Street. Located across the street from the Drake Hotel was this popular store for car owners, athletes, and outdoor enthusiasts, opened by Euclid "Uke" M. Haughawout in 1934. By 1955, Uke and son Bill moved the store to 122 Grant Street to the former Harris Motor Company, where it remained until the late 1980s. The store, pictured around 1950, was torn down in the mid-1960s.

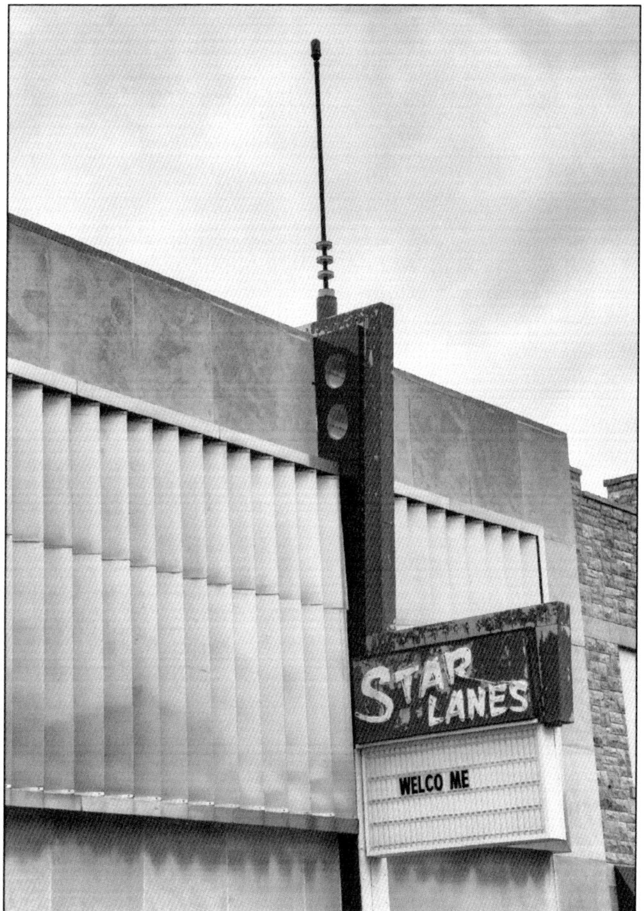

Star Lanes Bowling, 219 East Third Street. This building was the former Crane Theatre (also known as the Fox Theatre), where movies and occasional live shows were offered from the late 1920s to 1959. Russell Newport and Gene Fain opened the bowling alley, Star Lanes Bowling, in 1961, and it continues to operate today. (Photograph by Koral Martin.)

Two

Crossroads of America

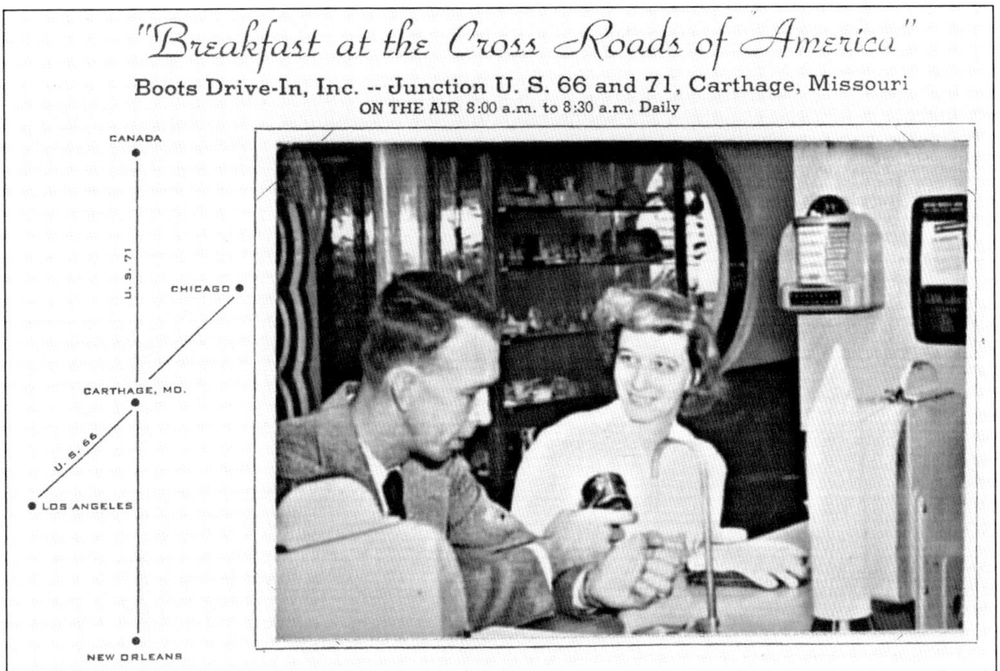

Breakfast at the Crossroads of America. Located on Garrison Avenue where US Highway 66 and US 71 Highway converged, Boots Drive-in was the site of a live radio show hosted by Lee Crocker of KDMO Radio. Crocker would interview travelers visiting Boots Drive-in, including this unidentified woman, who was photographed by Jean Goff around 1950. (Photograph by Jean Groff; courtesy of Chris Brown.)

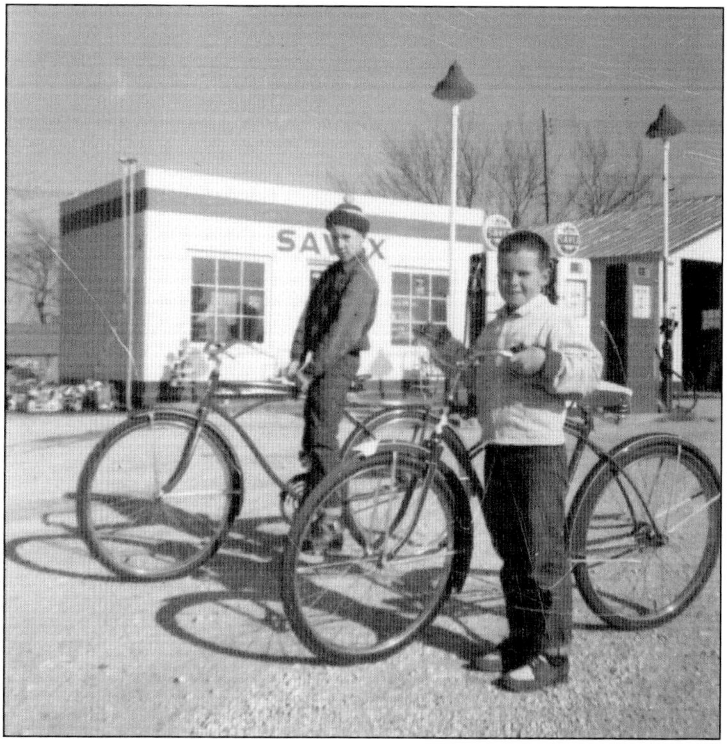

SAVEX Filling Station, US Highway 66, East of Carthage. Even with the large number of filling stations in the city limits, there were stations located up and down Route 66 in rural areas. This SAVEX station and garage was built by David Utter in the 1940s. It is pictured around 1960 here, with the station owner's son Bob (in foreground) and his friend Eddie Joyce. (Courtesy of Wade Utter.)

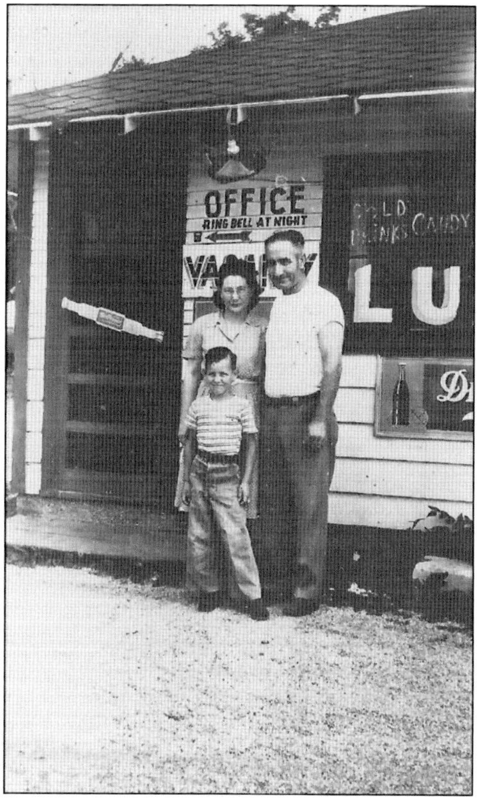

Sunset Café, Cabins & Drive-in, US Highway 66 East. Ann and Clyde Leeson operated the Sunset Café after World War II on the original alignment (now Old 66 Boulevard). As customers waited in their cars for food, cartoons and short films were shown on a small screen in the yard. By 1949, a full-scale drive-in movie theater was opened, operating until the early 1970s. Son Bud Leeson is pictured in front with his parents. (Courtesy of Gloria Leeson.)

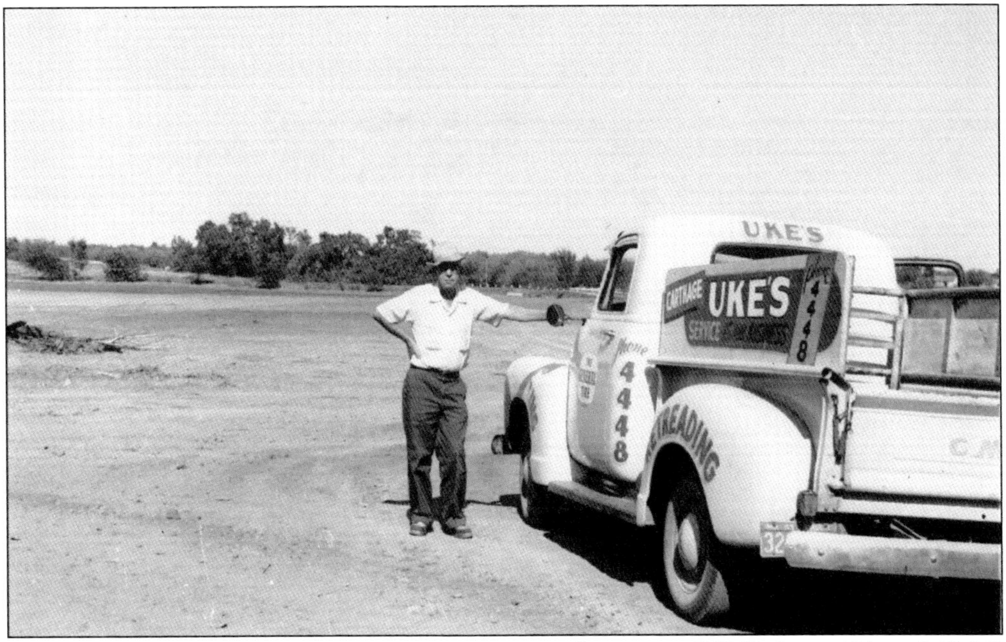

FUTURE US HIGHWAY 66 AND KELLOGG LAKE. A new alignment of US Highway 66 (now MO 96) into Carthage from the east was started in 1953. Here, the roadbed is under construction while Uke Haughawout and his truck sit in the area of Kellogg Lake's future development. Haughawout was one of the lake's most ardent supporters, once the Carthage Sportsmen's Protective League created it after the highway was completed.

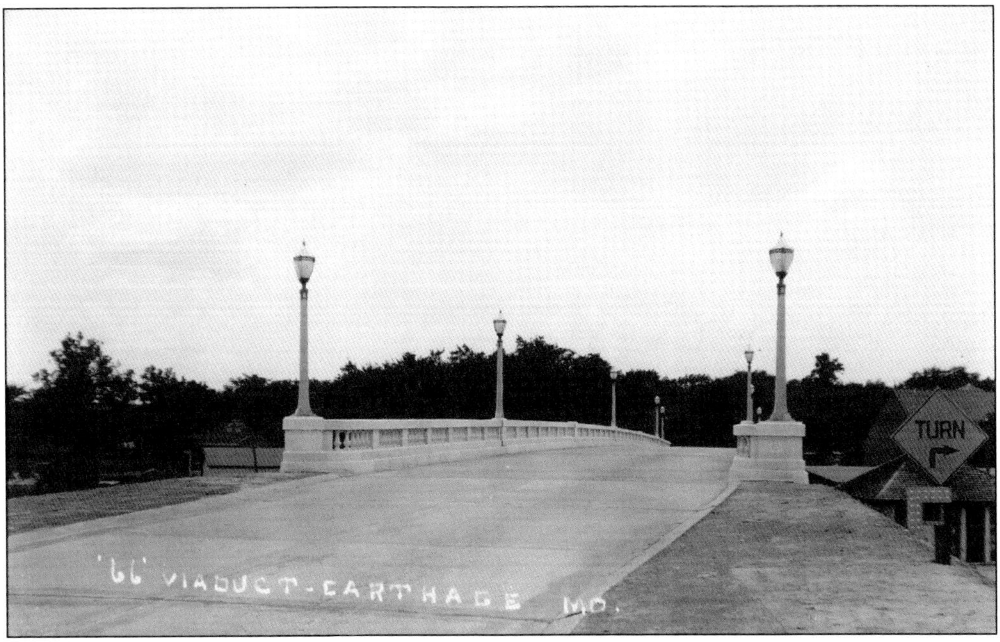

RAILROAD VIADUCT, US HIGHWAY 66 EAST. Constructed in 1934 to provide passage over the Missouri Pacific and St. Louis & San Francisco Railroads, this bridge was constructed of concrete supports and limestone sides finished by Carthage Marble Corporation. Only a few of the original light fixtures, paid for by the City of Carthage, remain atop the sides.

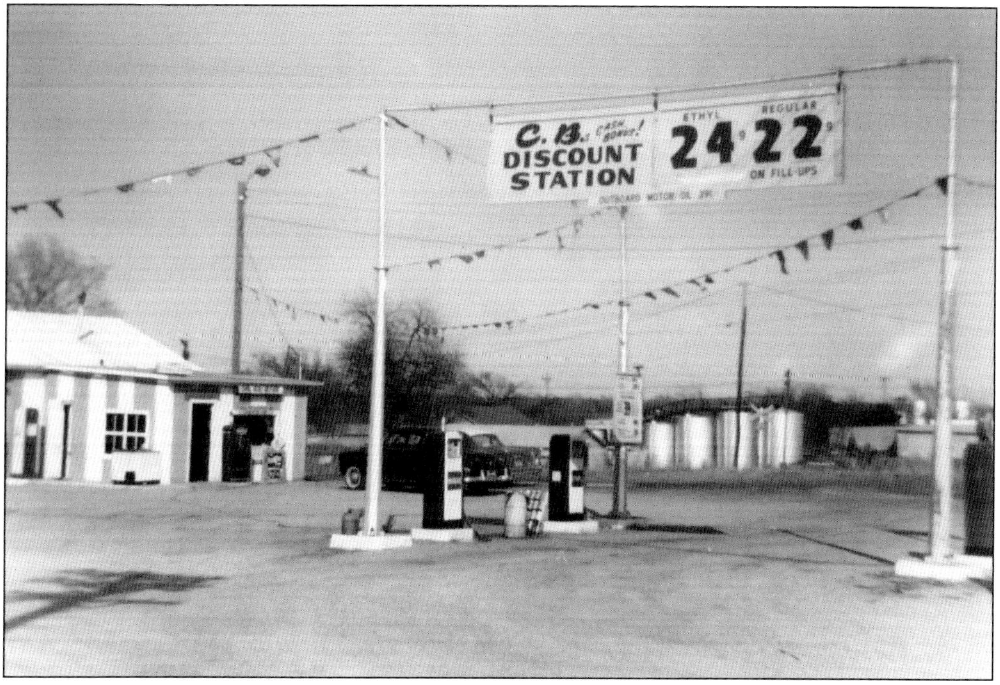

Bud's Bait & C.B. Discount Station, 803 East Central Avenue. Bud Leeson and wife, Gloria, opened a bait shop in 1962 and sold gasoline for Fike Oil Company. Wanting to be closer to Kellogg Lake, the couple moved their store near the Spring River Bridge on US Highway 66 in 1969. Now run by Gloria and son-in-law David Shumaker, Bud's Bait Shop and Canoe Rental celebrated its 50th anniversary in 2012. (Courtesy of Gloria Leeson.)

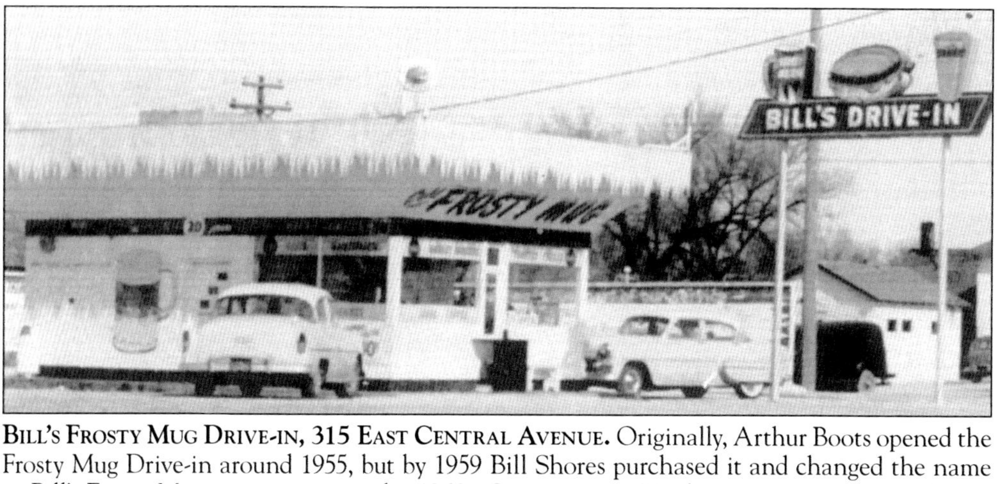

Bill's Frosty Mug Drive-in, 315 East Central Avenue. Originally, Arthur Boots opened the Frosty Mug Drive-in around 1955, but by 1959 Bill Shores purchased it and changed the name to Bill's Frosty Mug, operating into the 1960s. Starting in 1972, the next operator was Harvey Still. Next door, in 1962, the Guest House Motel was opened by Frank Shagets, and although remodeled, it remains today while the pictured property is now site of a Snak-Atak store.

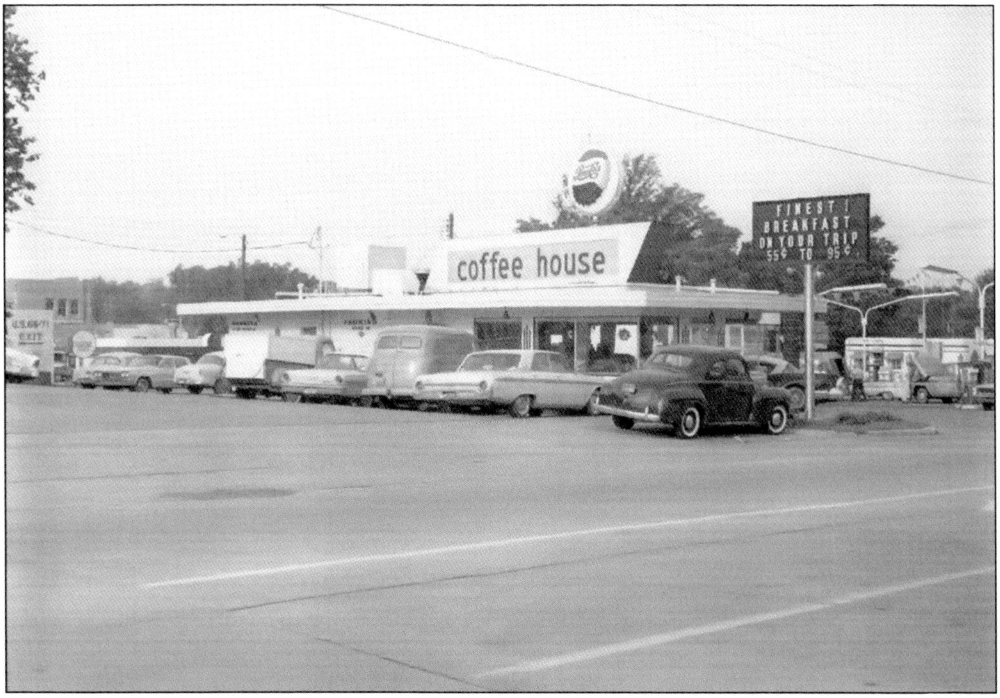

COFFEE HOUSE, 411 WEST CENTRAL AVENUE. One of Arthur Boots's other businesses along US Highway 66 was this café. Opened as the Burger N' Shake around 1959, Boots changed it to a breakfast format around 1964 renaming the business Coffee House. It operated until 1971. In this image, Boots's earlier businesses, Boots Drive-in and Boots Court can be seen in the background.

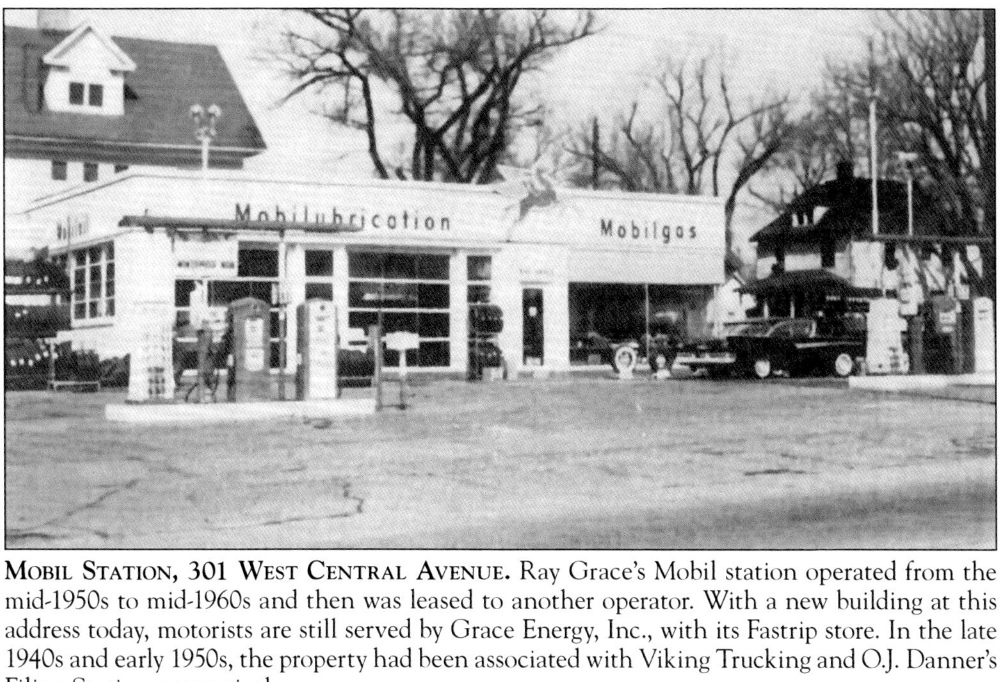

MOBIL STATION, 301 WEST CENTRAL AVENUE. Ray Grace's Mobil station operated from the mid-1950s to mid-1960s and then was leased to another operator. With a new building at this address today, motorists are still served by Grace Energy, Inc., with its Fastrip store. In the late 1940s and early 1950s, the property had been associated with Viking Trucking and O.J. Danner's Filing Station, respectively.

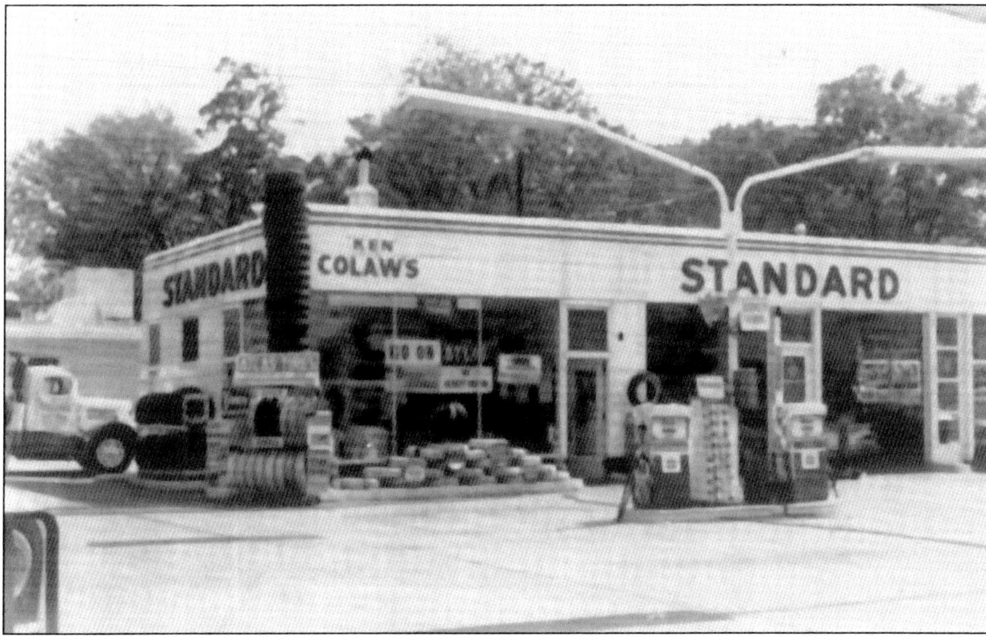

COLAW'S STANDARD STATION, 328 WEST CENTRAL AVENUE. This location had been occupied by a gas station since 1928, and Kendall Colaw operated this particular station from 1940 until 1977. By the 1950s, there were 32 gas stations in Carthage, most located on Garrison or Central Avenues. At the height of US 66's popularity, Colaw's and others were open 24 hours a day.

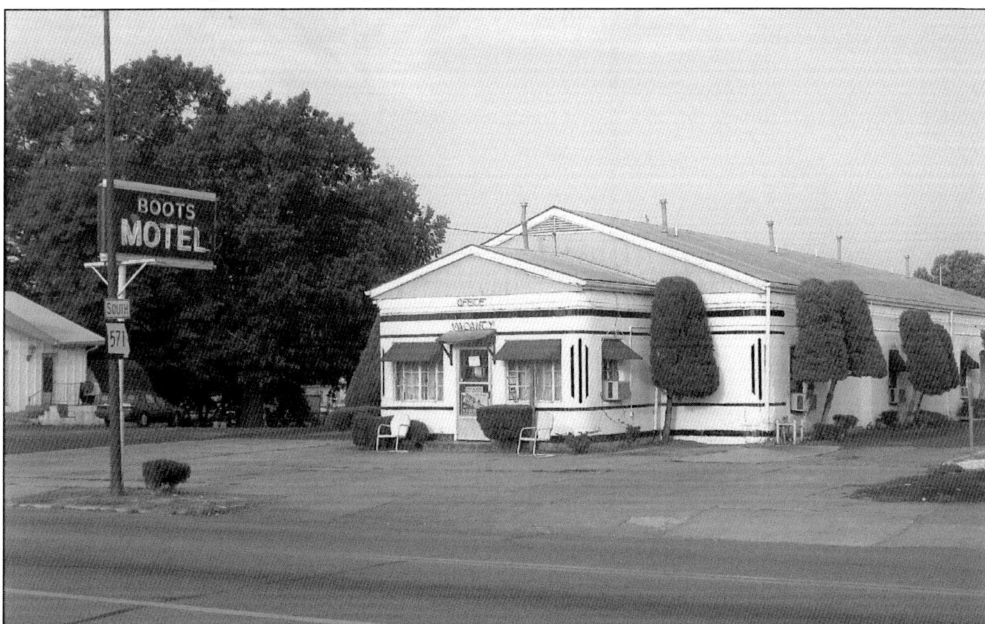

BOOTS COURT, 107 SOUTH GARRISON AVENUE. In 1939, Arthur Boots deliberately selected a location at two major highways to build a motor court but first opened the Red Horse Service Station. By 1942, after rooms had been constructed, some additional furnishings were purchased from the Muehlebach Hotel in Kansas City, Missouri, including brass spittoons. Cleaning them was a job for son Robert, who says the task was "character building." (Photograph by David J. Eslick.)

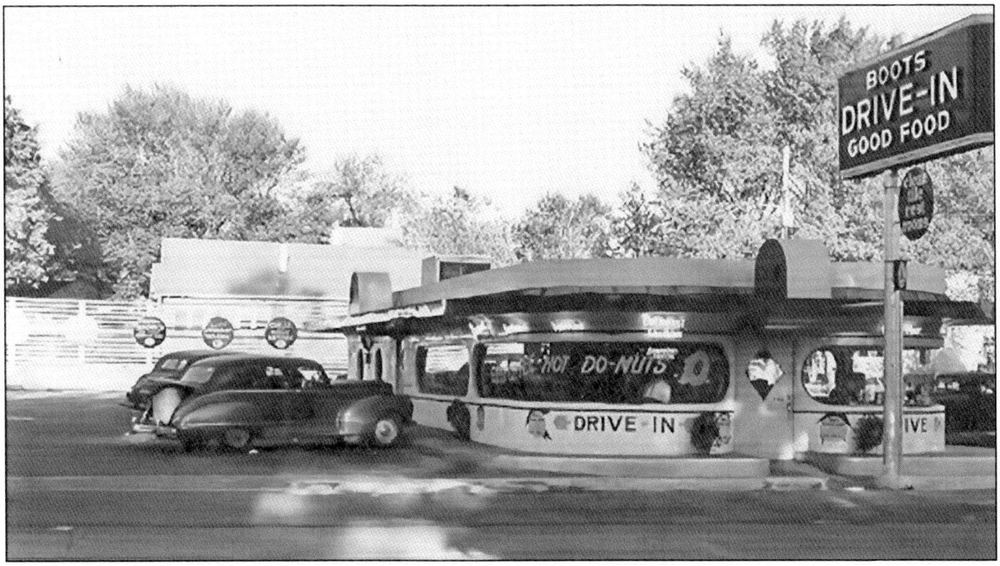

Boots Drive-in, 120 South Garrison Avenue. Opened in 1947 by Arthur Boots and his son Robert, the eatery quickly became an icon for tourists traveling US Highways 66 and 71 as well as being a hangout for Carthage teenagers. It offered breakfast, along with fountain service, sandwiches, and "frosty malts," at any hour. The building is now occupied by Great Plains Credit Union.

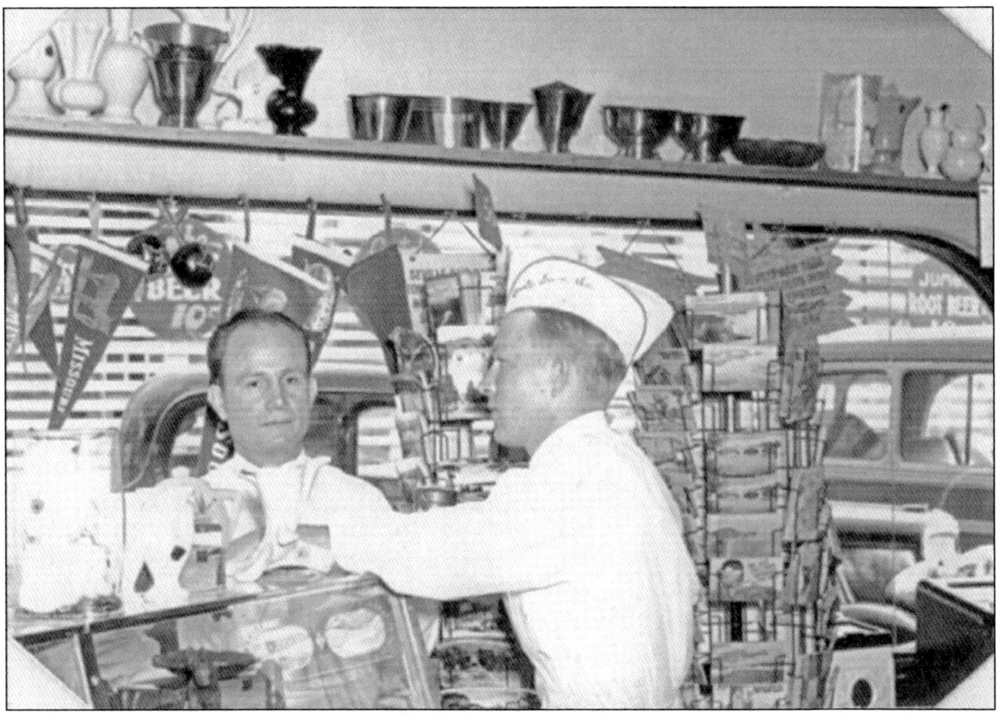

Boots Drive-in. The drive-in also was a gift shop selling souvenirs such as postcards, pennants, and pottery, as seen behind Robert Boots (right) and C. Jude Arney (left). Arney was substituting for Lee Crocker of "Breakfast at the Crossroads" the day photographer Jean Goff made this image. Arney was one of the drive-in's later owners along with Herbert Olson and Billy and Shara Shores. It closed in 1971.

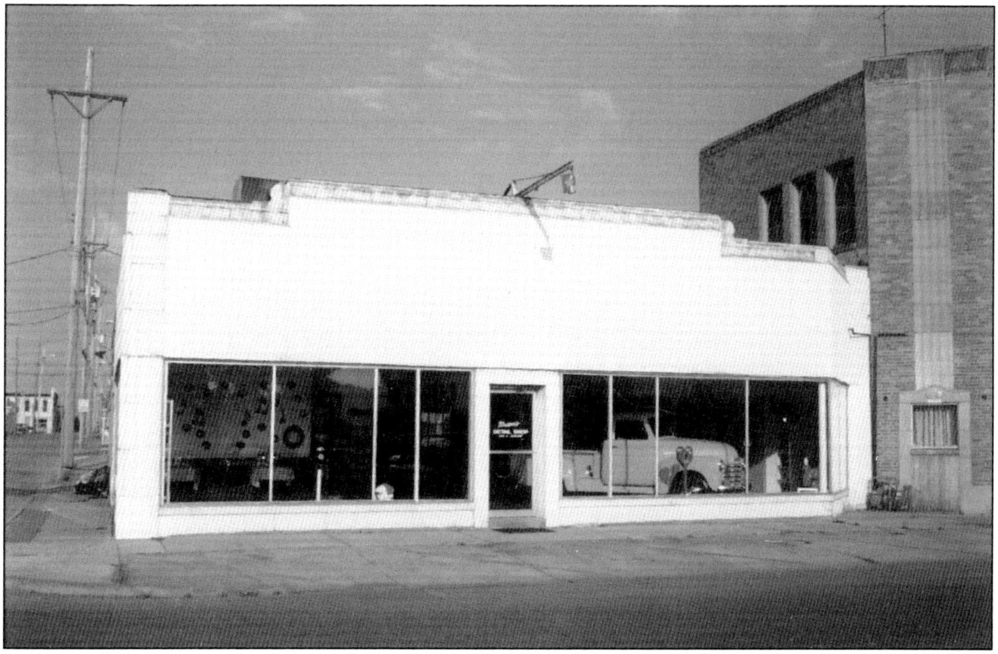

Darrow Garage, 200 South Garrison Avenue. Started as a gas station in the 1920s, a showroom was added to a previous structure in 1935. Since then, the building has been associated with various automobile-related businesses, such as Jones Tire (1947), Myers Motor Supply (1957), O&S Supply (1960s–1970s), and finally Mason's Detail Shop, prior to the building being torn down.

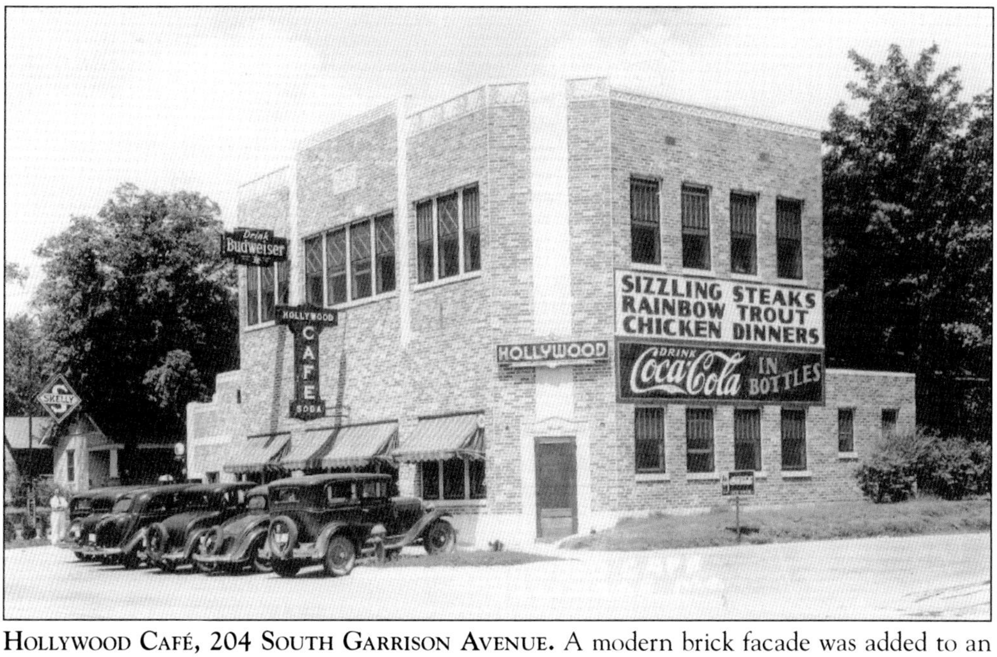

Hollywood Café, 204 South Garrison Avenue. A modern brick facade was added to an old residence and became the new Hollywood Café, moving from the square's south side. Later, Lee's Steak House operated here until the building was converted into offices in the 1960s for professionals, such as engineer Frank Hoblick and others. Like the Darrow Garage, this building no longer stands.

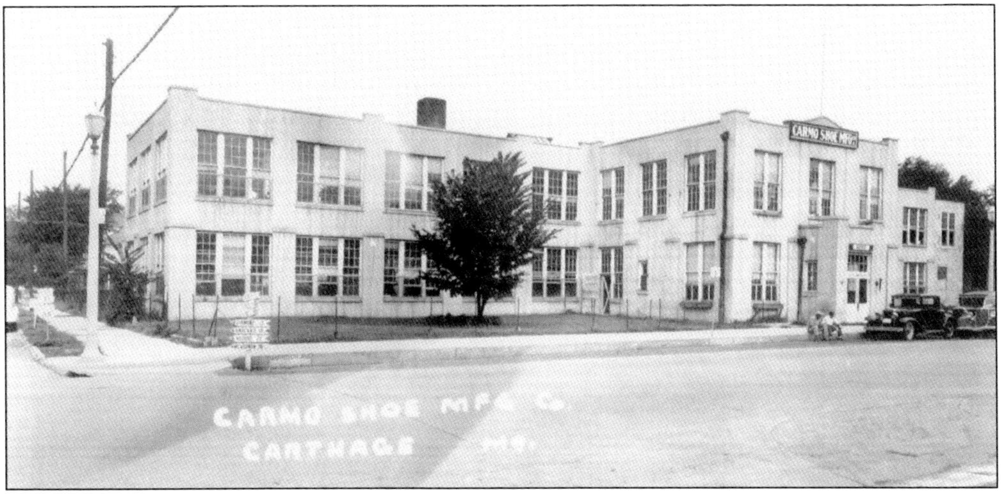

Carmo Shoe Company, 321 South Garrison Avenue. Since World War I, Carthage has had a long tradition of manufacturing shoes. Carmo operated in this building until the late 1930s, and during the 1940s, another shoemaker used the building for a short period. By 1961, the factory was torn down, and the property was used for Ted and Terry Brust's Used Cars for many years. Today, it is the site of Braum's Ice Cream.

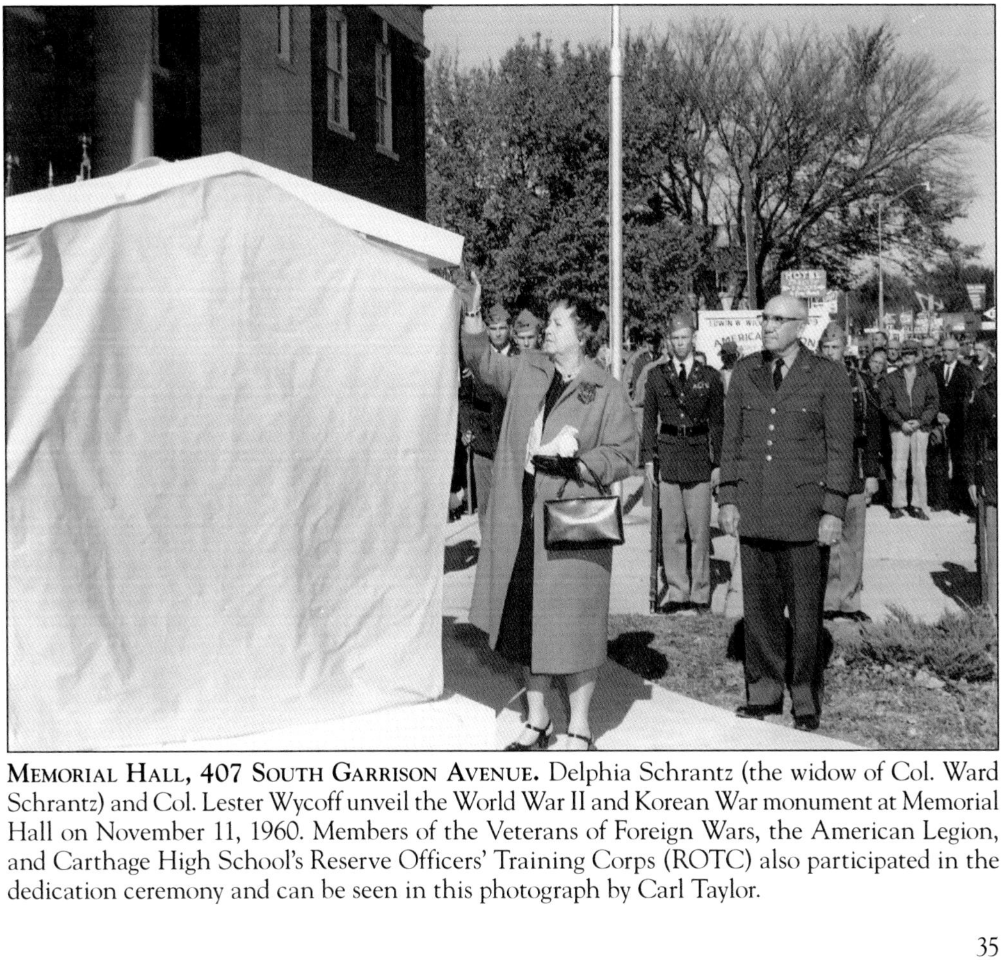

Memorial Hall, 407 South Garrison Avenue. Delphia Schrantz (the widow of Col. Ward Schrantz) and Col. Lester Wycoff unveil the World War II and Korean War monument at Memorial Hall on November 11, 1960. Members of the Veterans of Foreign Wars, the American Legion, and Carthage High School's Reserve Officers' Training Corps (ROTC) also participated in the dedication ceremony and can be seen in this photograph by Carl Taylor.

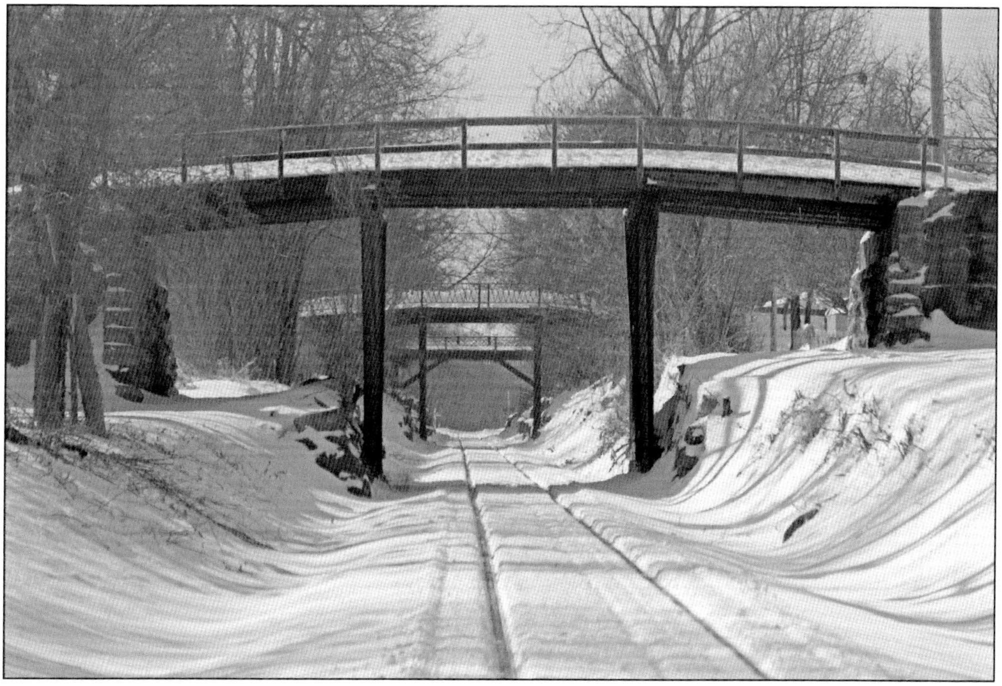

Oak Street Bridge, 600 Block of Oak Street. Nicknamed "wee hill" or "tickle tummy hill," this wooden structure continues to serve Carthage, although some alteration of the bridge is expected in the future. A bridge has been at this location since the Missouri Pacific Railroad made the first cut to lay track through the neighborhood in the late 1870s.

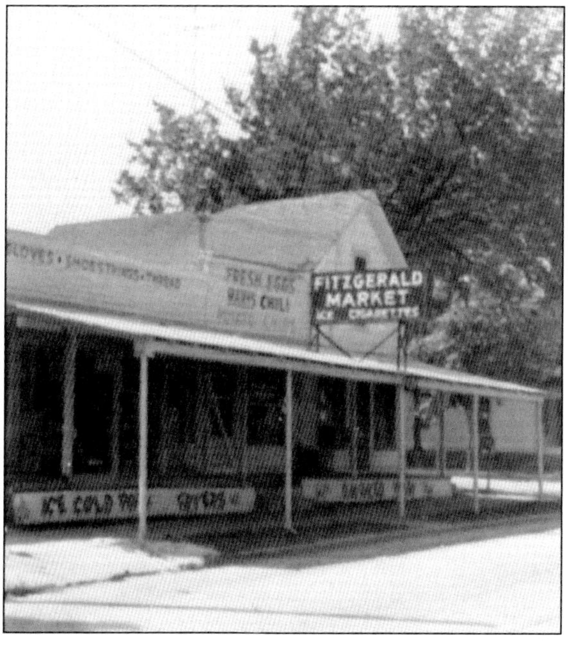

Fitzgerald Market, 732 Oak Street. Representative of neighborhood groceries throughout Carthage before large grocery chains, the Fitzgerald served not only local families but also those traveling US Highway 66 in the 1960s. Older existing structures that served as groceries along Oak Street were Earle's Grocery at 1001 Oak Street and Byrd's Grocery at 1002 Oak Street.

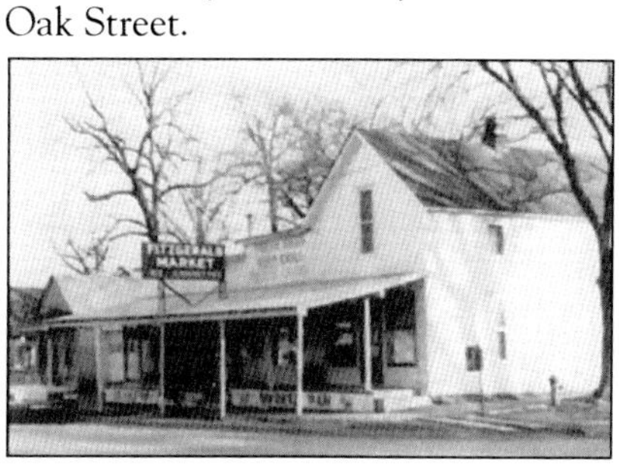

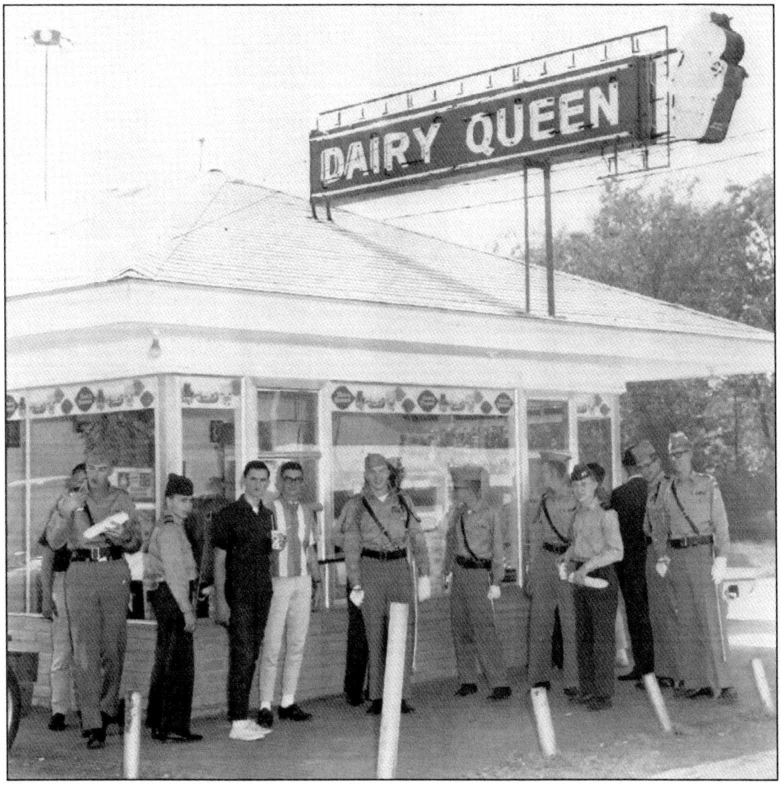

DAIRY QUEEN, 1220 OAK STREET. Once franchises were offered, Carthage soon was home to a Dairy Queen in the late 1940s. The store became one of the longest-operating businesses along this stretch of old US Highway 66 closing in 1994. Today, Boomer's BBQ operates in the former DQ Brazier Building. In the mid-1960s, on the back lot was a model railroad store called the Boomer Shack.

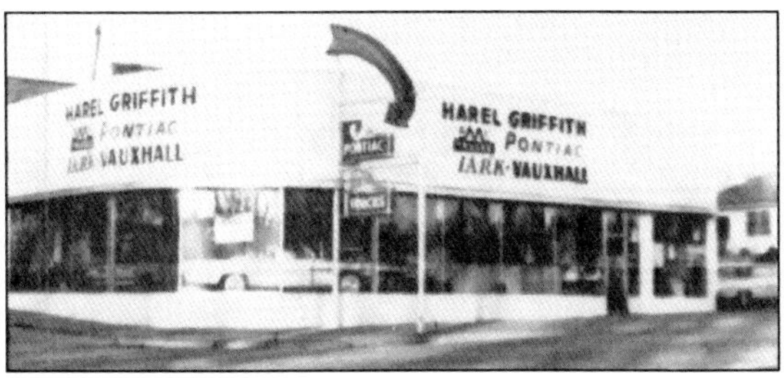

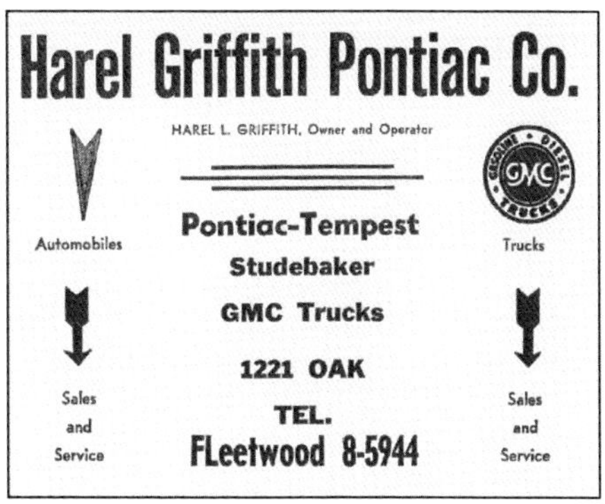

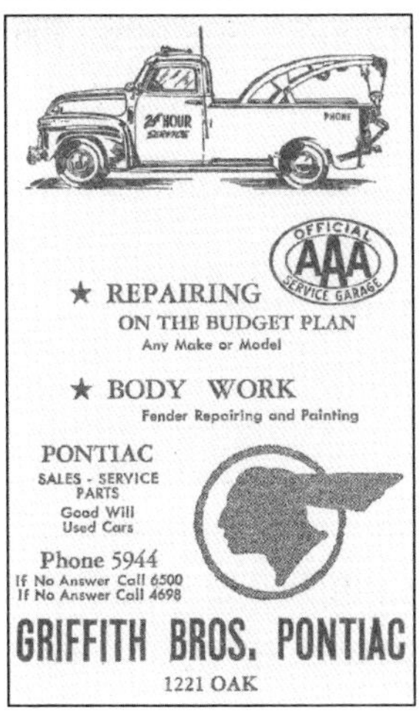

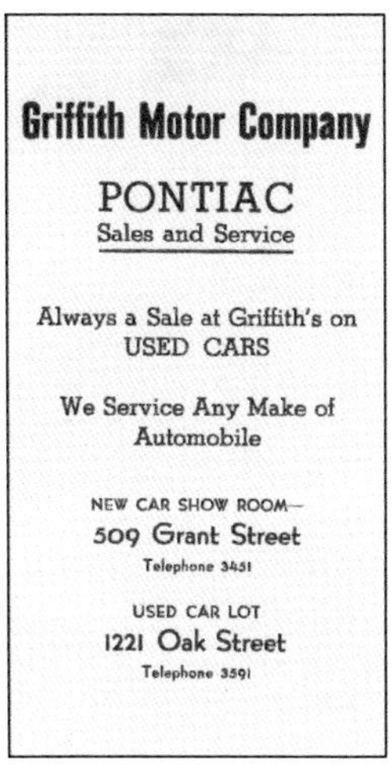

HAREL GRIFFITH AUTO, 1221 OAK STREET. From the 1940s until closing at this location in 1991, Harel, and later his sons, sold new and used cars at this address and across the street. Continuing down US Highway 66 beyond the western city limits, Herb Griffith also maintained an auto salvage yard and towing service. The Art Moderne building, used as an auto show room and garage, was damaged in an ice storm and was torn down in 2006.

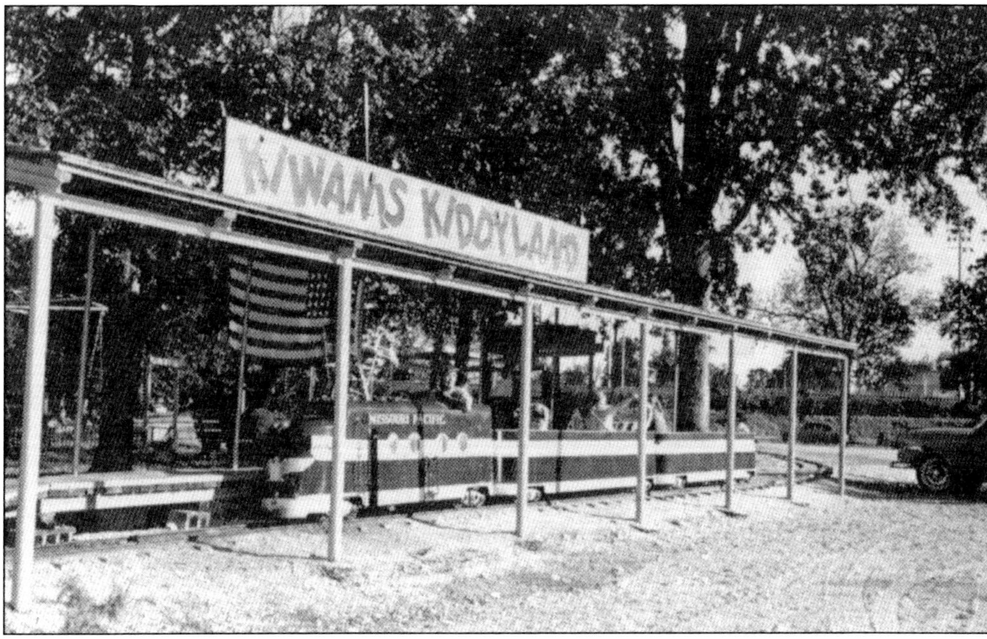

KIDDIELAND, MUNICIPAL PARK, WEST OAK STREET. From surplus US Army World War II materials, the Kiwanis Club built several children's rides in 1948. Four years later, track for a mini-train was added, and today the complex, including a carousel added in 2012, is operated (weather permitting) from Memorial Day to Labor Day on Saturday and Sunday afternoons.

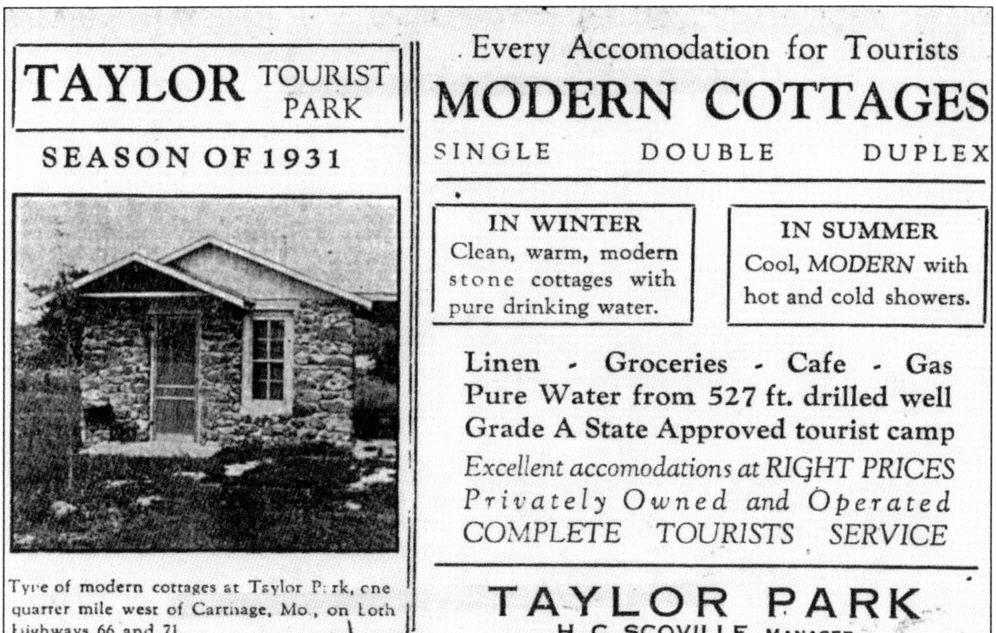

TAYLOR TOURIST PARK, 1617 OAK STREET. Constructed by Dr. C.B. Taylor as one of the first tourist courts in Carthage in the late 1920s, this property later became known as Parkview Motor Court and Café, since it was situated across from Municipal Park. The abandoned tourist cabins were torn down in 1987 to become the location of the Powers Museum in 1988.

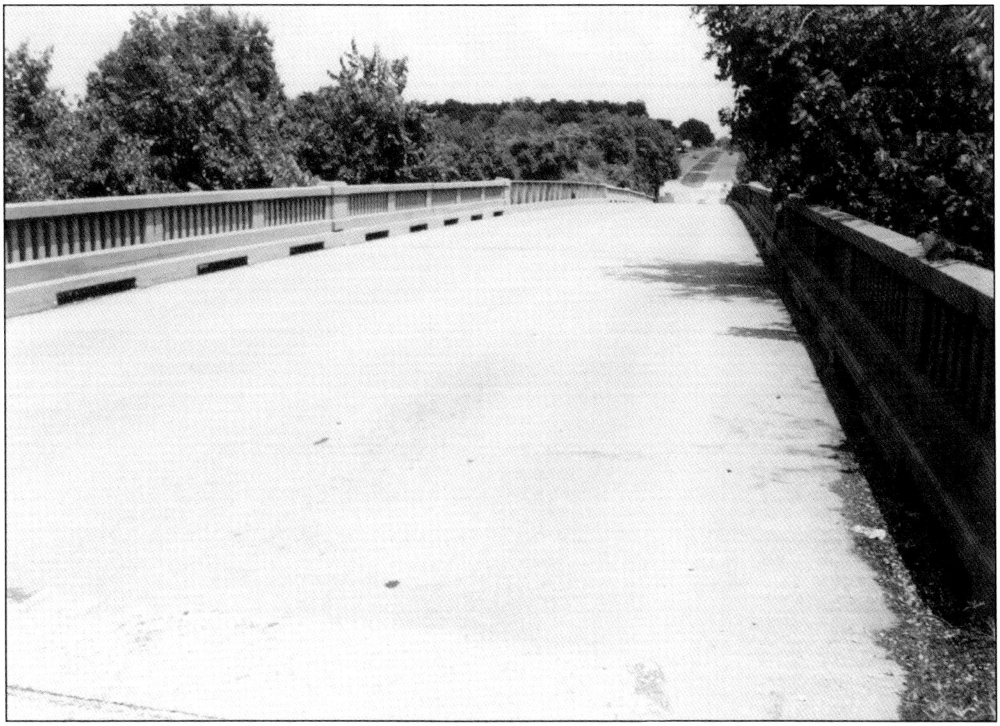

US HIGHWAY 66 WEST BRIDGE. Dedicated with Municipal Park in 1937, this bridge was constructed in 1935 and represented a relocation slightly north from an earlier alignment (signed as Historic 66 Byway today). Now cut off by Highway MO 171, this 1935 alignment continued to what is now Leggett & Platt's headquarters west of town. The Route 66 roadbed east of Leggett & Platt can still be seen.

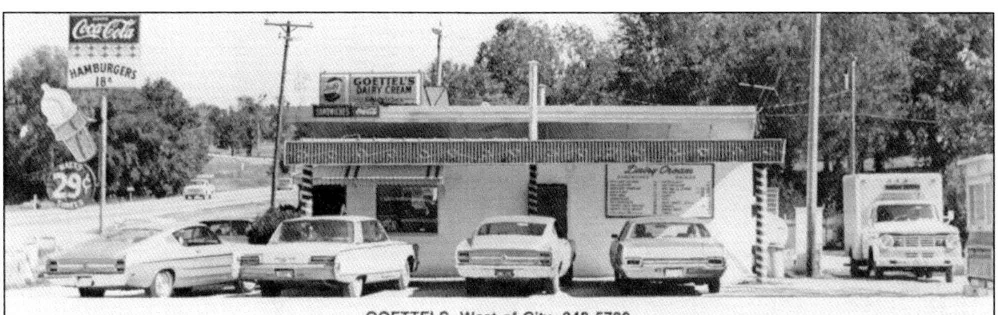

GOETTLE'S DAIRY CREAM DRIVE-IN, US HIGHWAY 66 WEST. Goettle's was located west of Municipal Park's golf course and was operated by Ben and Betty Goettel until 1984. Like several drive-ins in the city, this business became a popular teenage hangout. The drive-in no longer stands.

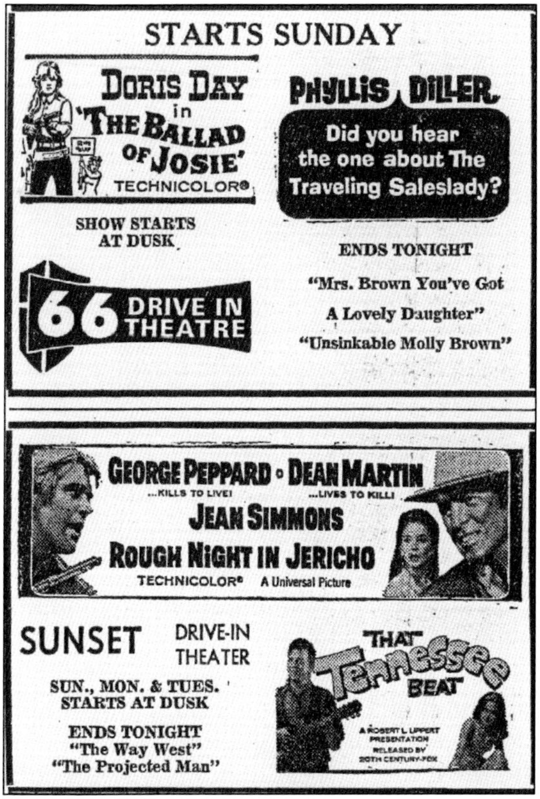

66 Drive-in, US Highway 66 West. Like Kiddieland using surplus war material, 66 Drive-in began its operation in 1949 with surplus movie projectors from Camp Crowder. Movies were shown here until 1985, when the parking area became a salvage yard. The drive-in was restored in 1997, and movies are offered weekends from April to early September. Pictured are 1968 advertisements for both the 66 and Sunset Drive-ins. (Courtesy of *Carthage Evening Press.*)

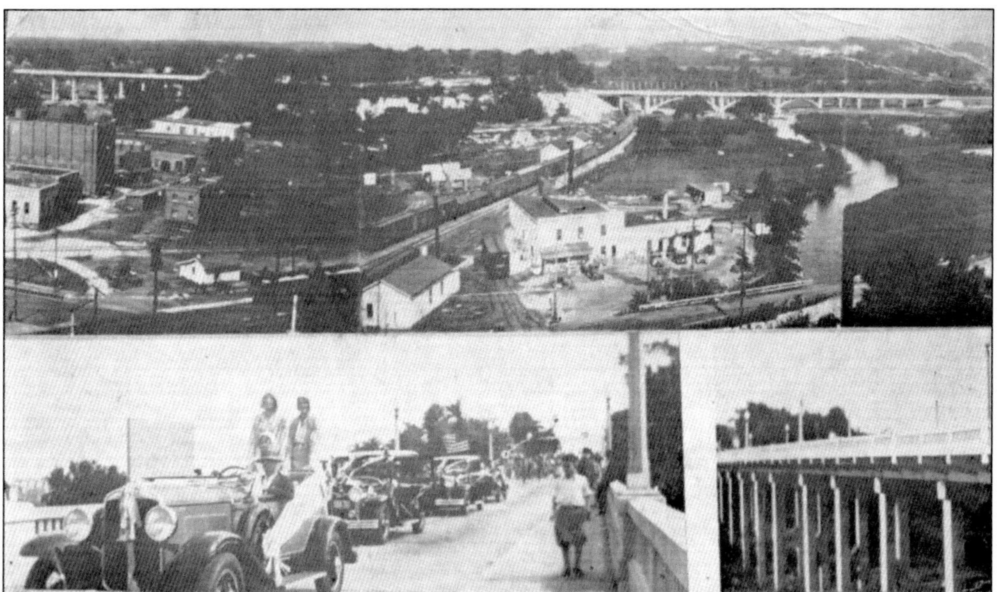

US Highways 71 and 66 Bridges. US Highway 71 replaced the Jefferson Highway auto trail that entered Carthage on North Main Street. These three bridges, spanning one mile in length, were constructed in 1930 for $205,000. US Highway 66 also used the "new mile," connecting by current County Road V to Route 66 northeast of Carthage.

Mr. Quick, 125 North Garrison Avenue. US Highway 71 entered Carthage through a residential neighborhood until it joined US Highway 66 at Central Avenue. Over the years, commercial development at that intersection crept farther north on Garrison Avenue. One example was Mr. Quick Hamburgers, constructed in 1970. The building is now used by Carthage Family Restaurant.

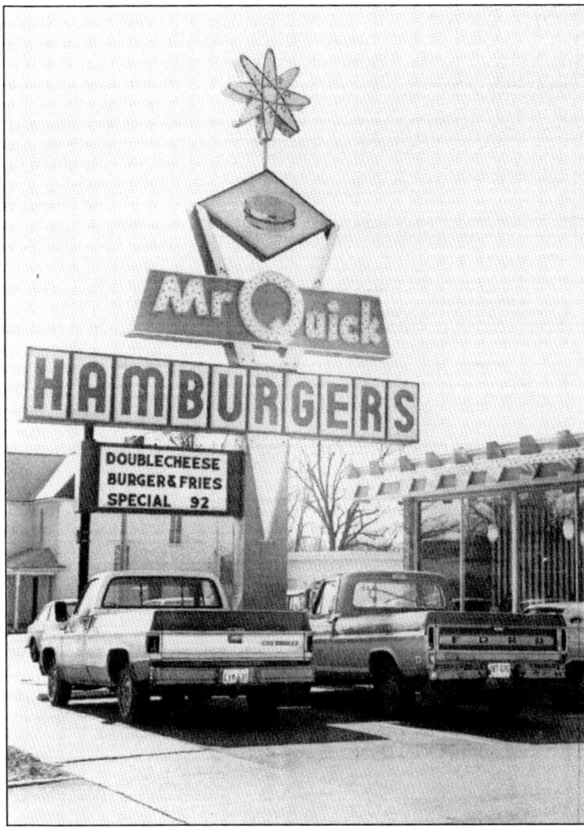

Whisler's Drive-up, 300 North Garrison Avenue. Whisler's hamburgers have been sold at many locations including downtown and on Route 66. By the mid-1950s, the store settled where it operates today. Charles Whisler began in 1922 with the White Rock Café at 502 South Main Street, where he sold hamburgers for 5¢ each. Upon retirement, his son Charles L. took over for several years until Jesse and Violet Whitesell purchased the business. (Photograph by Koral Martin.)

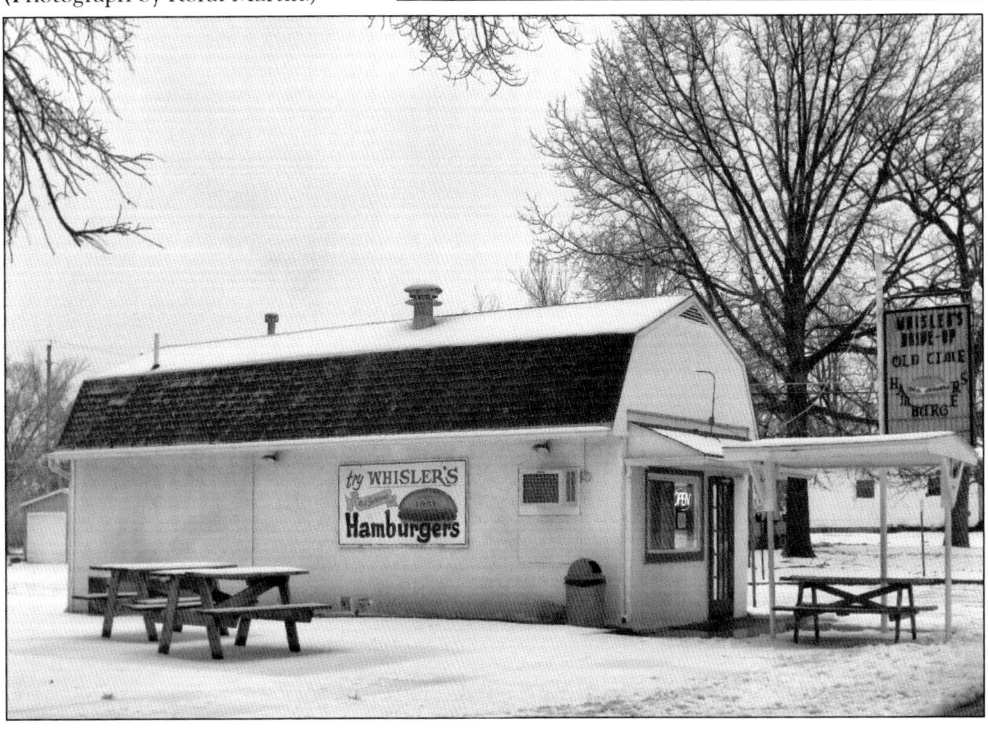

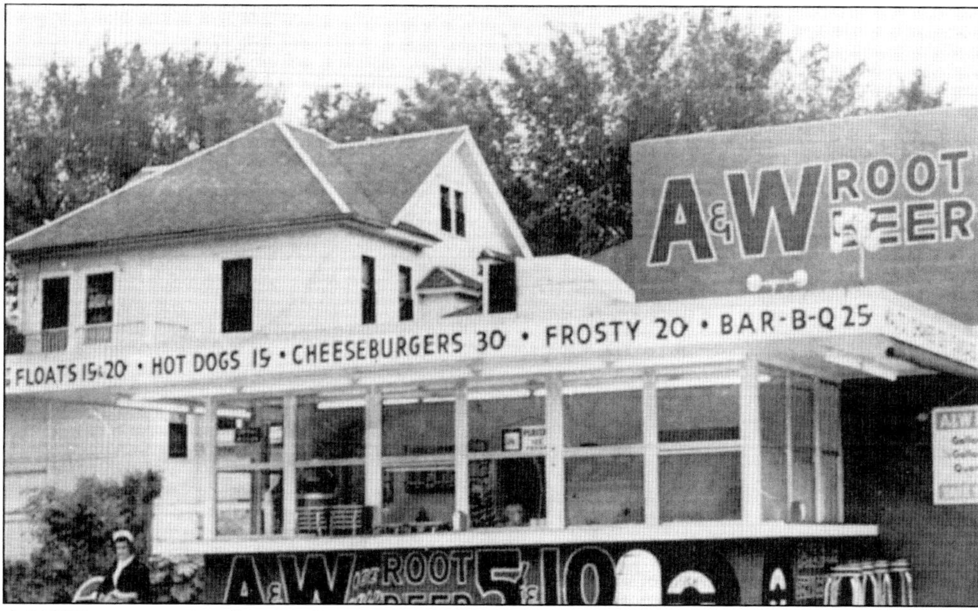

A&W Drive-in, 502 South Garrison Avenue. As franchising of food establishments became popular, Carthage saw its share of these businesses. The A&W opened in 1955. A&W's competitor Dog 'N' Suds Drive-in on West Oak Street near Municipal Park was open a few years before the US Highway 71 Bypass took its property. A&W continued until 1984, and today the building houses The Mercantile.

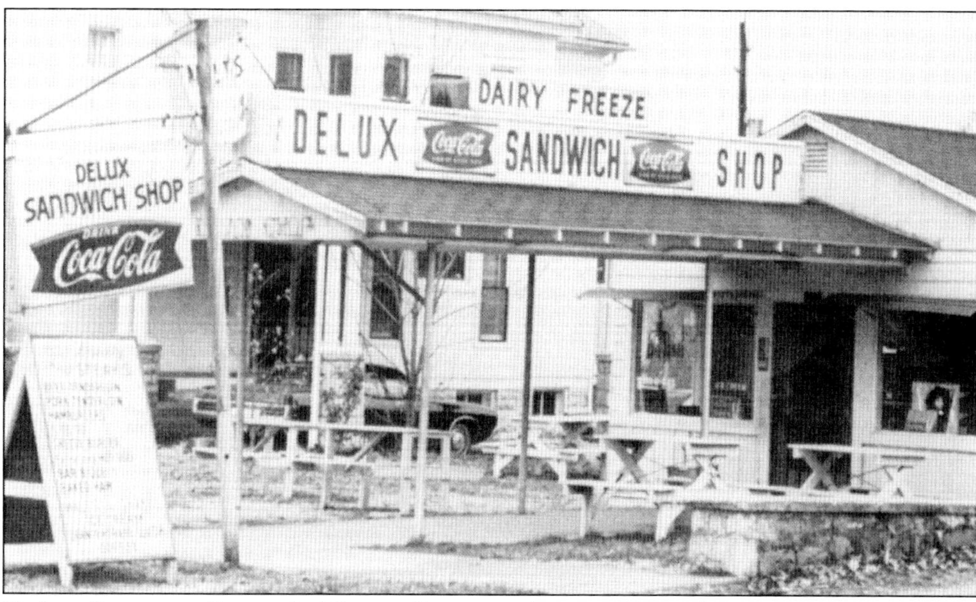

De Lux Sandwich Shop, 1215 South Garrison Avenue. US Highway 71 continued through town as Garrison Avenue, which, for the most part, was residential. There were occasional commercial niches such as at Macon Street. Here, in 1967, were the Brown Derby Service Station, De Lux (owned by Norval and Essie Lehman), and Clarence Taylor's Why Not? Restaurant. Recently, the De Lux was the Lilly Pad gift shop until 2012, when the property opened as the Deluxe Creamery.

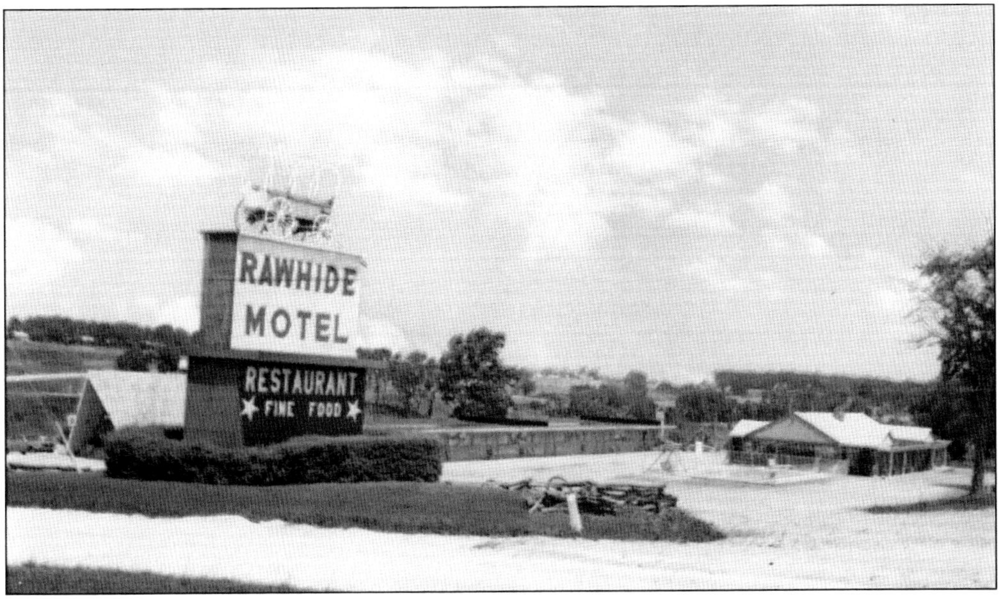

Rawhide Motel, US Highway 71 and Interstate 44. In the early 1960s, with the construction of Interstate 44 completed, many travelers bypassed US 66. However, US 71 continued to be the main artery through western Missouri. Where it intersected the interstate, travel services that were once found in town sprang up. Among them were Rawhide Motel and Restaurant, Ozarkland, Phillips 66 Gas, Coachlight Restaurant, and others. In 2012, US Highway 71 was upgraded to Interstate 49.

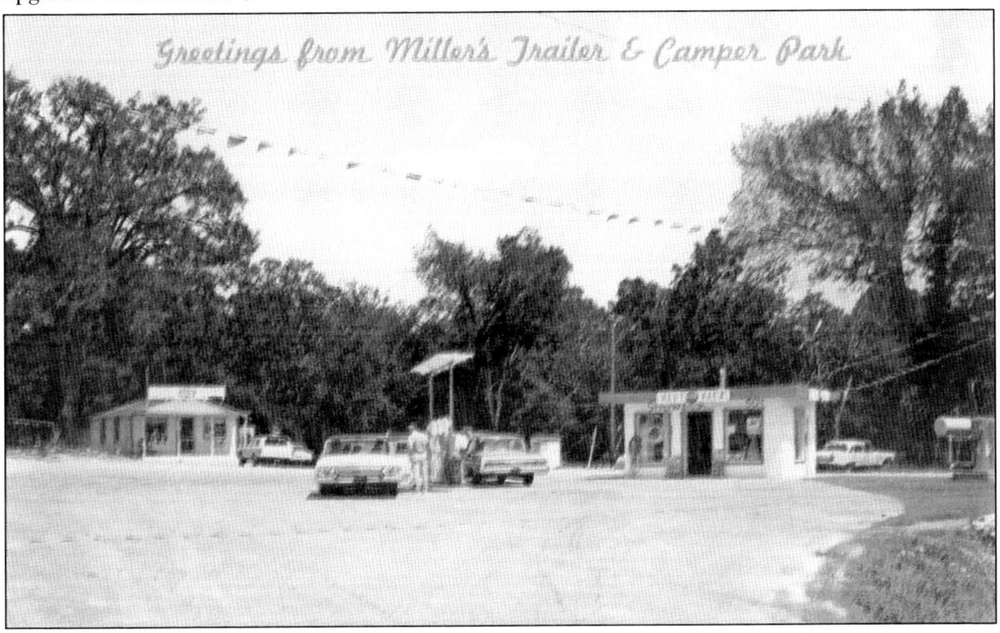

Miller's Trailer Park, US Highway 71 and Interstate 44. Located south of the interstate's interchange was Miller's (now Ballard's Campground) for those with campers or recreational vehicles. When Coachlight Restaurant burned in 1967, the northwestern quarter of the 71/44 interchange became a business hub for sellers of these vehicles starting with Martin Lown's Coachlight Trailer & Camper Sales.

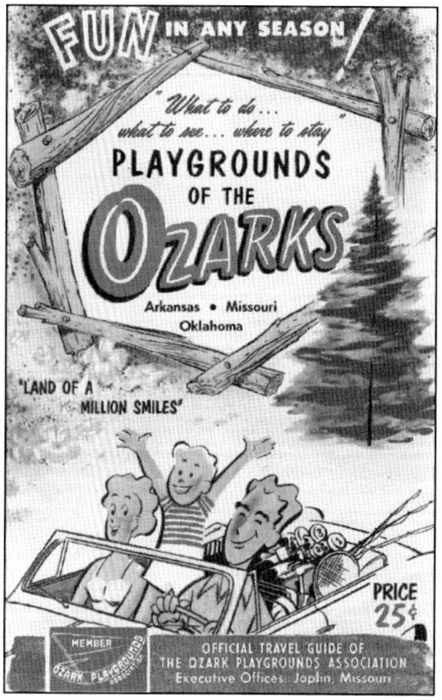

OZARK PLAYGROUNDS ASSOCIATION. Founded in 1919 to promote the area as a tourist destination, the Ozark Playgrounds Association is considered one of the first regional tourism groups in the nation. It continued into the early 1970s and was based in Joplin, Missouri. Here, Jasper County attractions are highlighted for 1955 when Carthage was considered one of the "Gateway Cities" to the "Playgrounds of the Ozarks."

Missouri Gateway Cities to The Playgrounds of the Ozarks

. . . a different phase of The Playgrounds, where larger cities serve as gateways and transcontinental highways bound or traverse the area.

Schifferdecker Park in Joplin has excellent displays of Tri-State minerals.

At Diamond, near Joplin, is the nation's newest National Monument dedicated to George Washington Carver, the great Negro scientist.

Near Sarcoxie are some of the world's largest peony fields.

At Carthage on the banks of Spring River are located quarries that produce marble of "Italian" quality. Also important state managed trout areas (Indian and Capps Creek). Pulaskifield is a quaint Polish village on State Highway 97. Nearby is Jolly Mill, at what was once the town of Jollification.

JOPLIN (B-4) U. S. 66, 71 & 166, Mo. 43 & 57. Jasper Co. City pop. 38,717, metropolitan pop. 50,631. Alt. 1,010. "The Crossroads of America" and 4th market of Missouri. Metropolis of great agricultural district and tri-state lead and zinc field. Marketing, manufacturing, entertainment and shopping center. Headquarters of the Ozark Playgrounds Association.

CONNOR HOTEL—Southern Missouri's largest hotel. Headquarters for conventions or trade groups. 400 fireproof rooms. Refrigerated air-conditioned. Cordially welcome to visit the ever-popular Rendezvous. Headquarters for comfort during your Ozark or cross-country trip. Write Box PG. Ph. MAyfair 3-5100.

JOPLIN MOTEL—U. S. 66 West edge of city. Rest in the best. Private tile tubs and showers. Refrigerated air-conditioned, furnace heat, Beautyrest mattresses on all beds. Modern furniture. Garages. Children's playgrounds. Parklike. Near cafe, golf course and drive-in theater. Ph. MAyfair 4-4805. Write Rt. 3, Box 352-PG.

KORONADO COFFEE SHOP—1717 W. 7th, U. S. 66 West of Main Street at Koronado Kourts. Attractive, modern, air-refrigerated restaurant, good food. Open daily 6:30 a. m. to 9 p. m.

BOB MILLER'S RESTAURANT—Third blk. north on Main St. from U. S. 66 & 166. District's newest, most modern, air-conditioned restaurant. Be Sure It's "Bob Miller's." 419 Main, Box PG.

WAUGH & FERGUSON BIRD FARM—Birds of all kinds. Talking and singing birds our specialty. Normals, rares. Wholesale, retail. Ship anywhere. Live arrival guaranteed. Cages, supplies. 115 E. 6th, 1 blk. north on Virginia Ave. off 7th St. on city routes U. S. 66-71-166. Ph. MAfair 3-9218.

WILDER'S RESTAURANT—Famous for good things to eat and drink. K.C. steaks and southern fried chicken. Free parking lot. Air-conditioned. 1216 Main St., Joplin, Box PG.

MOUNT VERNON (B-5) U. S. 166 & Mo. 39. Lawrence Co. seat. Pop. 2,057. Alt. 1,480. Frisco Lines. Important agricultural and dairying community. Missouri State Sanatorium. Chesapeake Fish hatchery nearby.

CARTHAGE (B-4) U. S. 66 & 71. Jasper Co. Pop. 11,188. Alt. 1,007. Historical. Civil War battleground. Rare display art objects from ancient Carthage. Home of Carthage Marble. Municipal Park swimming, golf, tennis, picnic grounds. 28-acre fishing lake and recreational park. Excellent tourist accommodations. Sightseeing tours. Famous for agriculture and industry.

KEL-LAKE MOTEL—½ mile East of Carthage on U. S. 66 & 71 by-pass. By beautiful Kellogg Lake. New, modern brick construction, air-conditioned, tile baths, steam heat, radios, AAA recommended. Family and commercial rates. Open all year. Ph. 9947. Write Rt. 1, Box PG.

LAKE SHORE MOTEL—East U. S. 66 and Lake Kellogg. It's new! And complete from ceramic tub and shower baths to private telephones, Broadloom rugs from wall to wall. Also beautiful lobby. Enjoy good fishing in Lake Kellogg. It costs you no more. Write Box 37-PG.

SARCOXIE (B-5) U. S. 166, Mo. 37. Jasper Co. Pop. 1,042. Alt. 1,088. Ample modern tourist accommodations and good restaurants. Artesian water. Dairying, farming, strawberries and poultry. Juvenile Shoe Corp., home of world famous peony fields and nurseries.

SARCOXIE NURSERIES—(Wild Bros. Nursery Co.). One of Missouri's oldest and largest nurseries. Established 1875. Display gardens open to public. Famous Peony fields blooming in May. Growers of acres of evergreens, shrubs, trees and flowers. Catalog on request, Box PG.

WEBB CITY (B-4) U. S. 66 & 71, Mo. 57. Jasper Co. Pop. 7,000. World famous lead and zinc mines. Industries: Webb Corp., Smith Brothers Mfg. Co., Elder Mfg. Co., Rex Metallic Casket Co., Tri-State Chemical Co. Important shipping point for road ballast, explosives, etc.

Three

Business and Industry

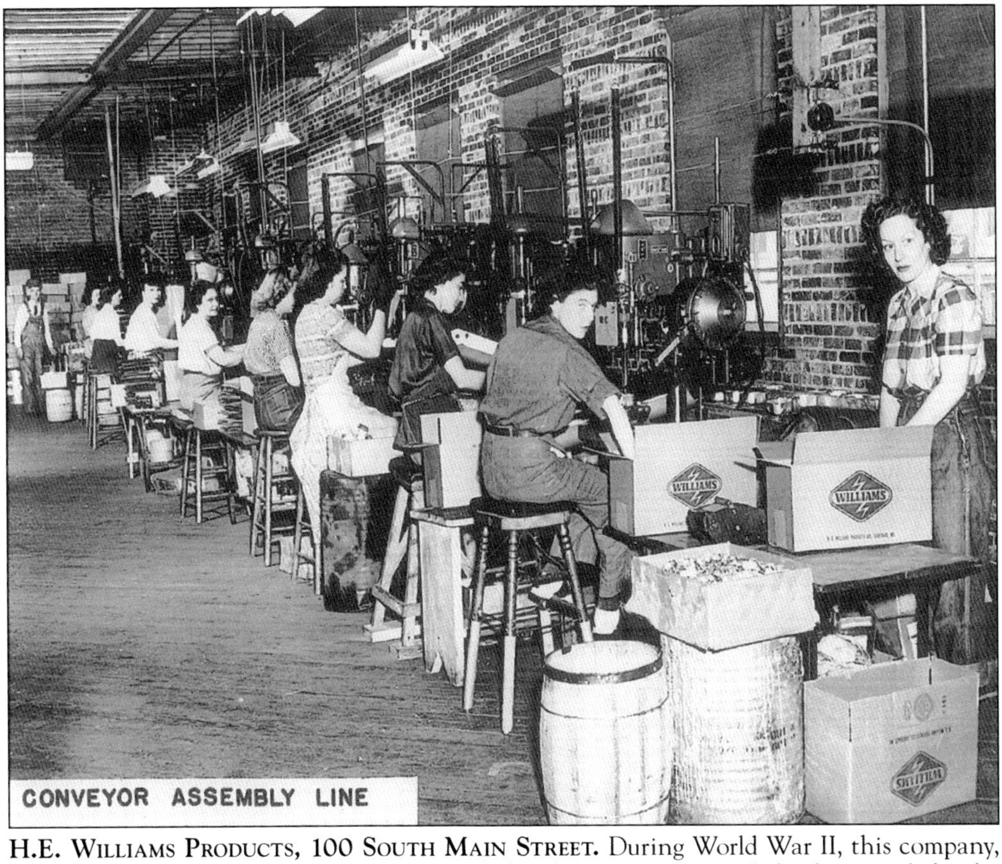

H.E. Williams Products, 100 South Main Street. During World War II, this company, founded by Harold E. Williams in 1921, made bomb support clips and the framework for the bubble canopies for military aircraft. During this time, when steel was rationed and difficult to procure for light fixture reflectors, Williams created a way to use treated masonite instead. With many local men serving in the military, women replaced them on production lines. Employee Joyce Canfield is on the far right. (Courtesy of H.E. Williams, Inc.)

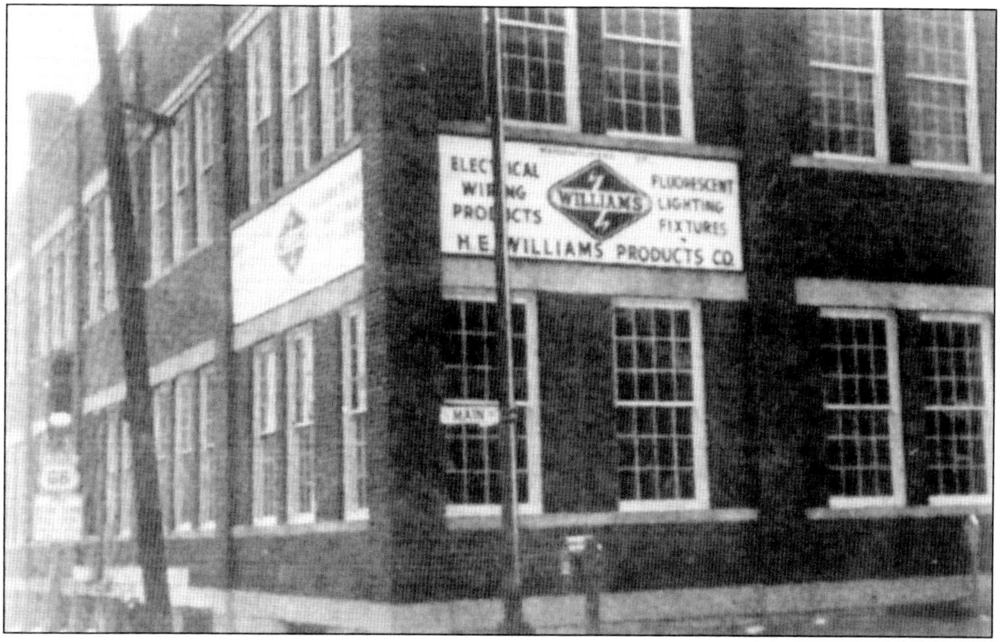

H.E. Williams Products. The company moved to this building located at Central Avenue (US Highway 66) and Main Street in 1929. It had been the Juvenile Shoe Company, but once Williams moved in, manufacturing of various steel items such as potato mashers continued along with the first production of automobile accessories. By 1939, after the commercial introduction of fluorescent technology, the company began to design and produce light fixtures and other miscellaneous electrical components.

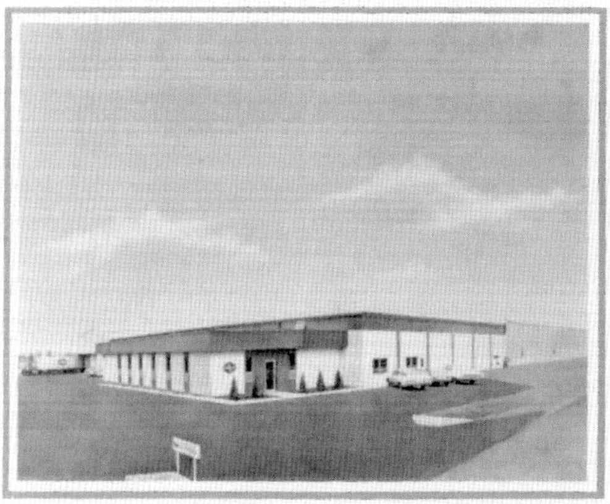

We take this opportunity to invite you to inspect our new offices and manufacturing facilities, located at 831 West Fairview . . . and to help us observe our 50th Anniversary year, 1921-1971.

H. E. WILLIAMS PRODUCTS CO.

Carthage, Missouri 64836

Refreshments • Guided Tours

H.E. Williams, Inc., 831 West Fairview Avenue. After the war, expansions to the Main Street plant were made in 1948 and 1963 as production increased, but by late 1970 the company moved to this location under H.E. Williams's direction. John Williams, son of the founder, succeeded his father in leading the company with H.E. Williams remaining as chairman of the board. The third generation of family leadership began when grandson Mark Williams joined the company, and today he is chief executive officer. (Courtesy of H.E. Williams, Inc.)

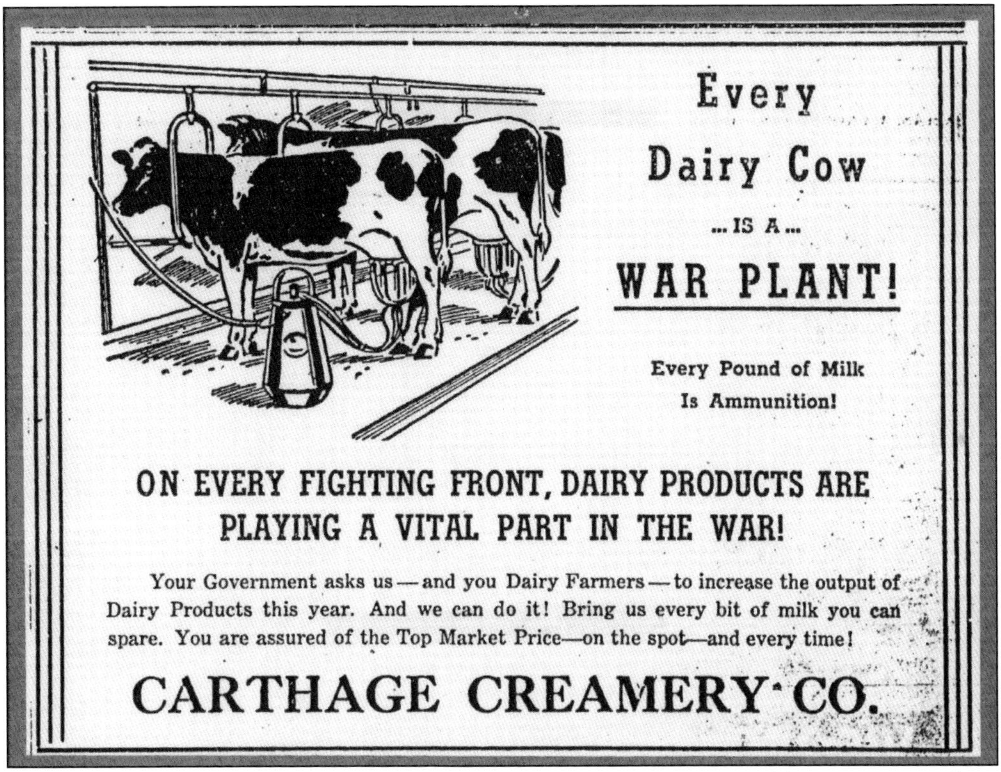

CARTHAGE CREAMERY COMPANY, 545 NORTH MAIN STREET. During World War II, "every dairy cow [was] a war plant," supplying local military camps with dairy products. Owned by the Jensen family, Carthage Creamery made cottage cheese and ice cream in addition to milk and butter under various labels, including the Spring River Brand. The creamery closed in 1972. (Courtesy of *Carthage Evening Press*.)

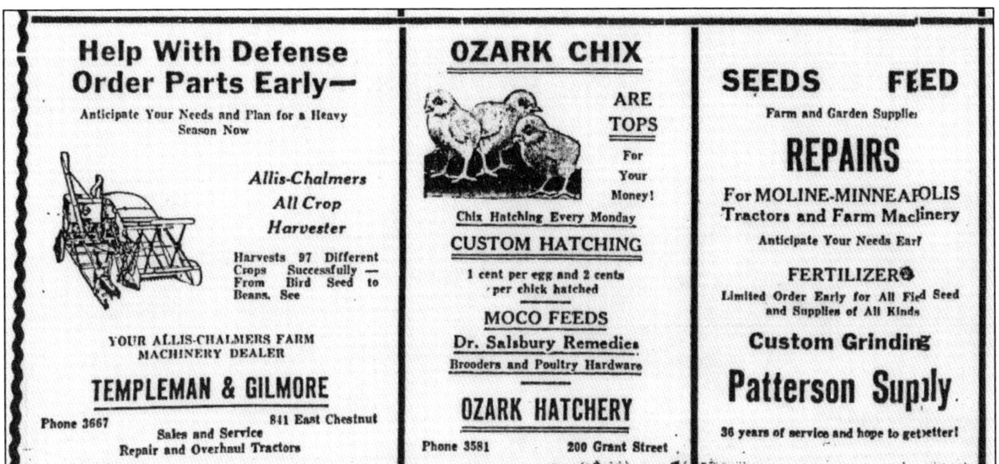

NATION'S FARMS ADVERTISEMENT. Farms were the "front lines of defense," and "farmers were the men behind the men behind the guns," boasted this World War II advertisement. Many local businesses were willing to help farmers overhaul equipment and increase their production. (Courtesy of *Carthage Evening Press*.)

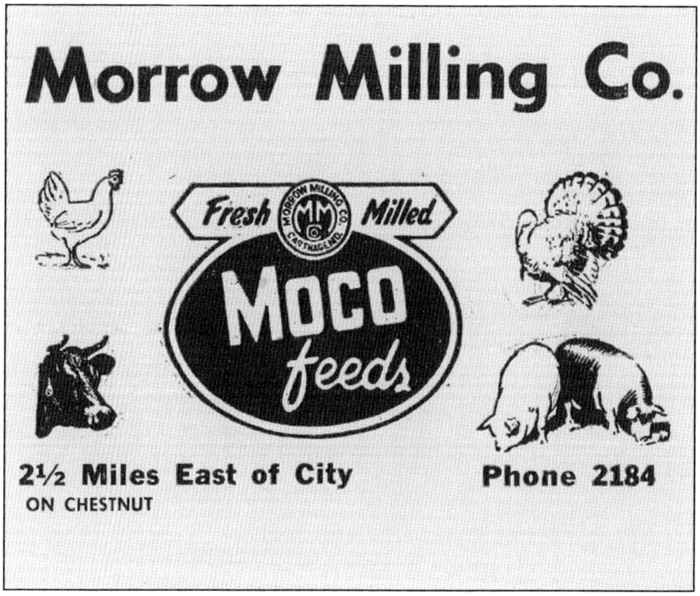

MORROW MILLING COMPANY, EAST OF CARTHAGE. Sitting on one of the oldest mill sites in Jasper County, the Morrow family acquired the mill in 1884. S.R. Morrow Sr. became the sole owner after World War II, and in the next decades, when sons Tom, Joe, and S.R. Morrow Jr. entered the business, the company produced Moco Feeds for livestock and added a poultry breeder, hatchery, and growing operation. Operations continued to 1972.

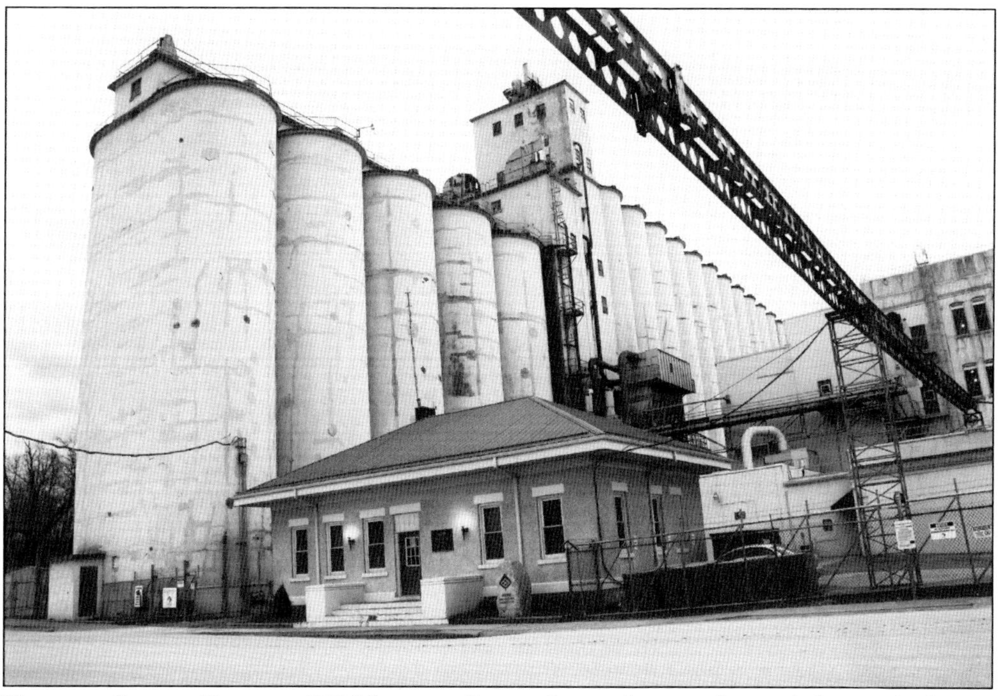

NATIONAL BISCUIT COMPANY, 323 MERIDIAN STREET. Located in a modernized plant at the former 1895 McDaniel Mill, National Biscuit operated from the 1930s until 1984, when current-day successor, ADM, Inc., took over. Historically, the area the mill sits in has been one of the main industrial areas of Carthage since the early 1870s. (Photograph by Koral Martin.)

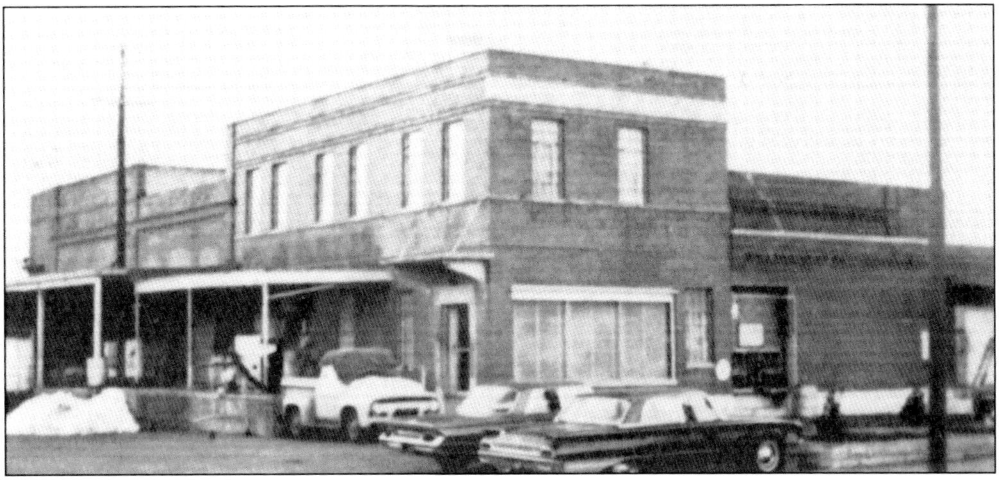

Carthage Ice & Cold Storage, 501 North Main Street. Owned by the Spradling family, this company (later Refrigerated Services, Inc.) started as an icehouse in 1927 and then moved into refrigerated storage, liquid-freeze processing, and food distribution. The company also enticed other businesses to Carthage. Among the latter was Bowman & Company (later Standard Brands at 510 North Main Street), which processed egg products.

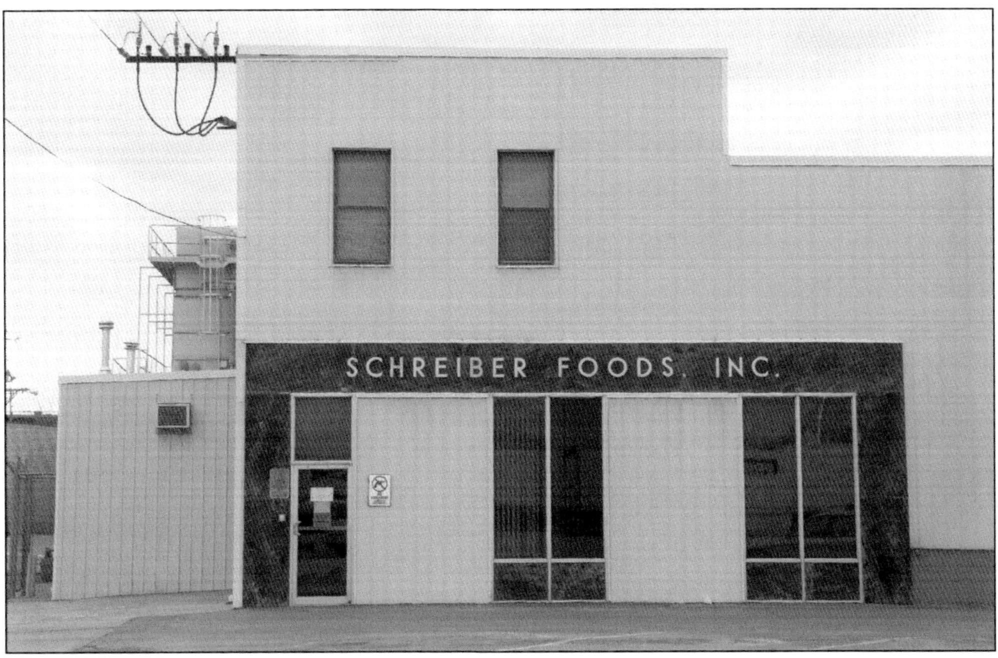

Schreiber Foods, Inc., 127 Claxton Avenue. When L.D. Schreiber Cheese wanted to expand production with a Missouri-based plant, it purchased Standard Brands' Cheese Division in 1950, managed by Frank Claxton. Claxton became a corporate vice president, and the plant's street name was changed to honor his leadership. (Photograph by Koral Martin.)

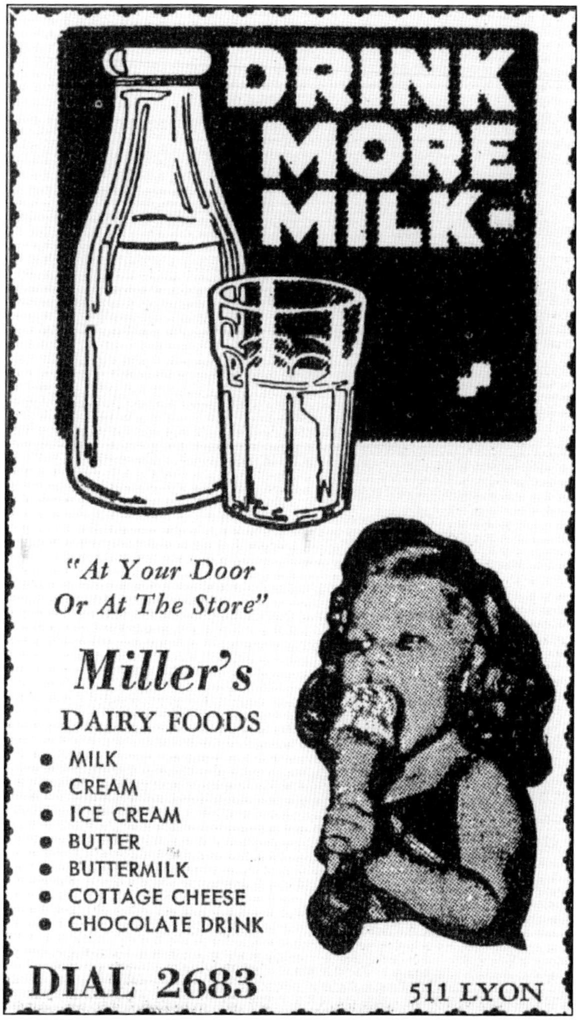

MILLER'S DAIRY, 511 LYON STREET. Local dairies were not only supplying milk to local food processors, they were also making products to sell to Carthage residents. Among the numerous commercial dairies during the 1940s through the 1960s were Lundy, JaRu (selling the Golden Guernsey label), Elliott's Modern, Periman, Egan, Hartley & Sons, and Carthage Dairy.

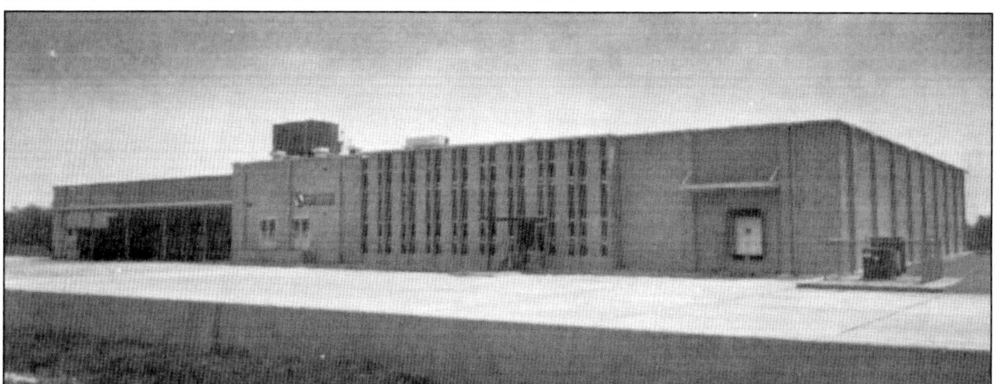

SAFEWAY, INC., CHEESE DIVISION, 1112 WEST FAIRVIEW AVENUE. In 1958, Safeway began processing cheese at 209 East Vine. Ten years later, after a favorable vote to approve over $1 million of industrial development bonds, this facility was built in 1968–1969. Safeway's manager at the time was George Pamperin. Later, Schreiber Foods took over the facility in 1994.

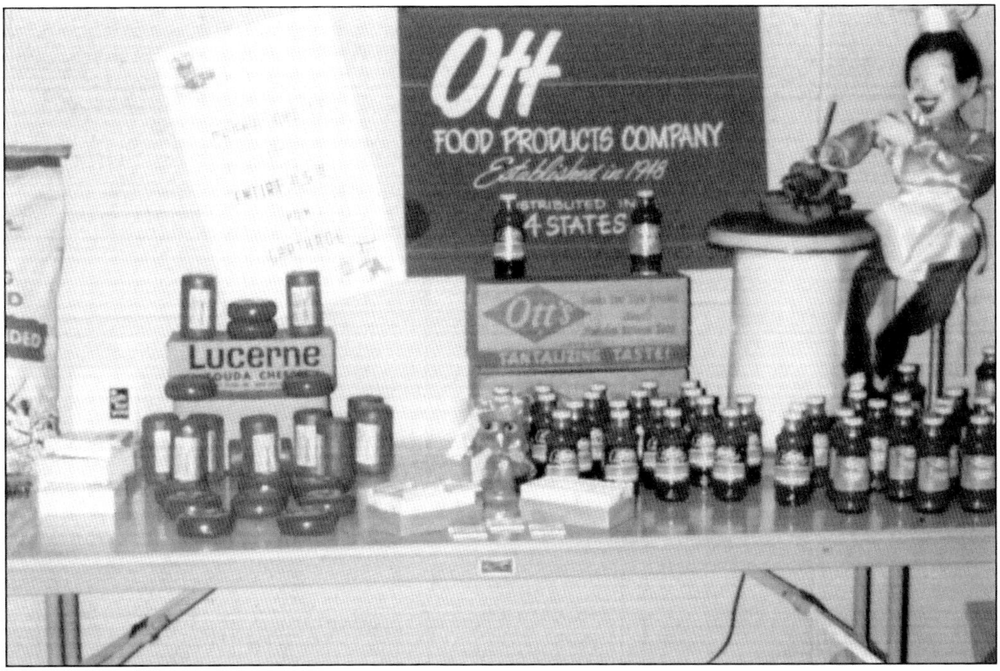

SAFEWAY & OTT FOOD PRODUCTS DISPLAY. The Carthage Chamber of Commerce has sponsored Business Expos for many years, and this c. 1975 display features products of both Safeway and Ott Foods at Memorial Hall. On the box of Ott's salad dressings is its early advertising slogan: "Tantalizing Taste."

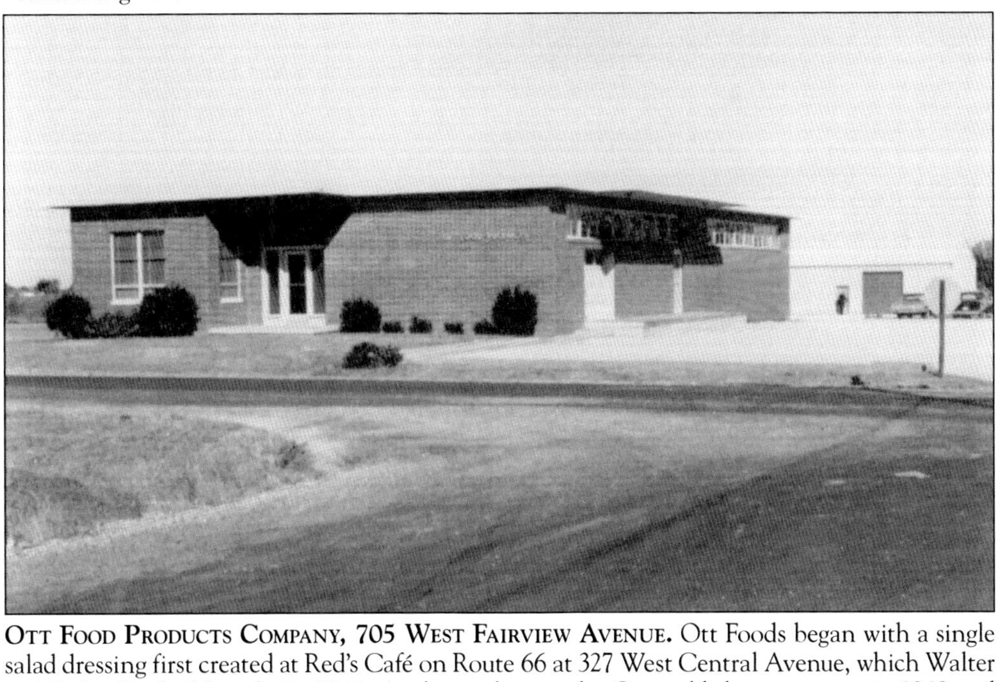

OTT FOOD PRODUCTS COMPANY, 705 WEST FAIRVIEW AVENUE. Ott Foods began with a single salad dressing first created at Red's Café on Route 66 at 327 West Central Avenue, which Walter and Ruby Ott had bought in 1946. As demand grew, the Otts sold the restaurant in 1948 and started this factory in 1954 to handle expanded production that had outgrown its 531 Oak Street factory.

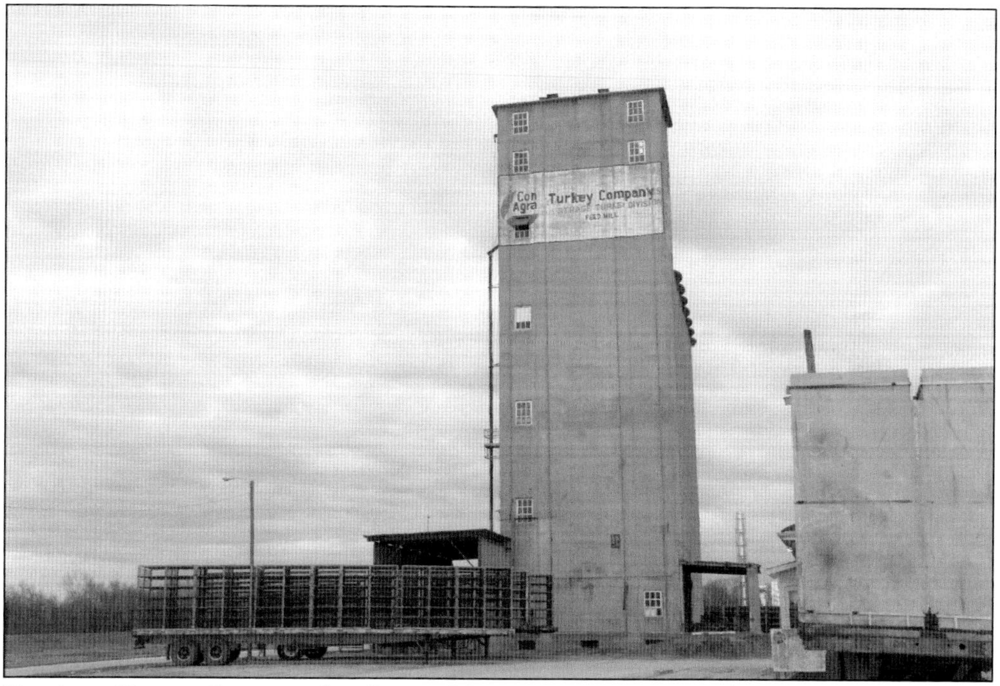

CONAGRA TURKEY COMPANY, 500 BLOCK, NORTH MAIN STREET. Turkey processing operations were conducted at 411 North Main Street, but the feed grain operation of ConAgra was a short distance away in the historic Cowgill and Hill mill complex. ConAgra began production in Carthage in 1973 in the former Morrow Foods Poultry plant, which ConAgra expanded in the mid-1980s. (Photograph by Koral Martin.)

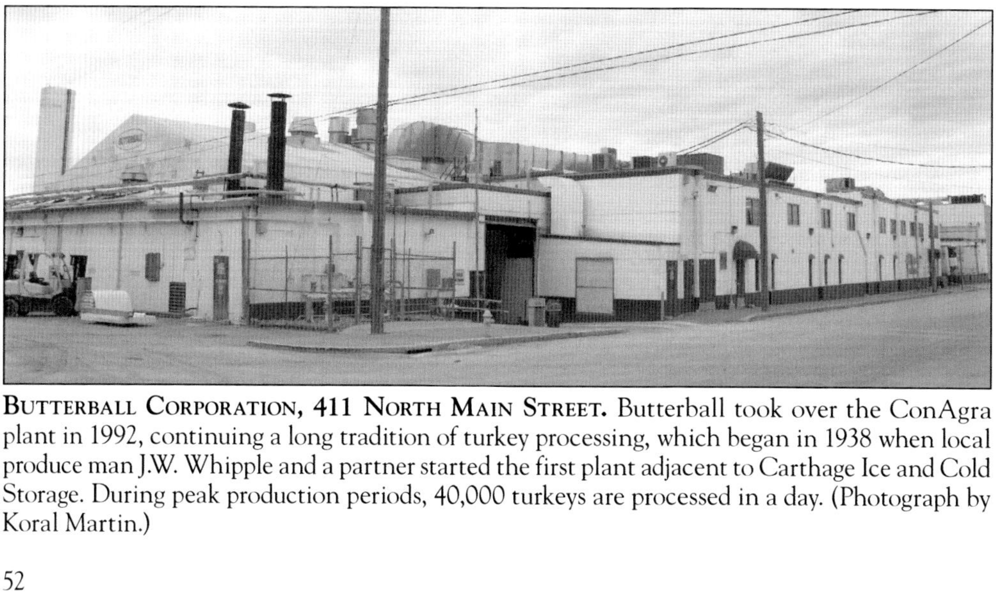

BUTTERBALL CORPORATION, 411 NORTH MAIN STREET. Butterball took over the ConAgra plant in 1992, continuing a long tradition of turkey processing, which began in 1938 when local produce man J.W. Whipple and a partner started the first plant adjacent to Carthage Ice and Cold Storage. During peak production periods, 40,000 turkeys are processed in a day. (Photograph by Koral Martin.)

YOUR FIRM'S EXPANSION TO CARTHAGE WILL PUT YOU IN

GOOD COMPANY!

Balanced industry and rich farm land provide stability to this Southwest Missouri community; its products are distributed and sold throughout the nation. Manufacturing firms already here include:

- **ATLAS CHEMICAL INDUSTRIES - Agricultural Chemicals**
- **BECK CASKET CO. - Caskets**
- **CARTHAGE CORD CO. - Furniture Components**
- **CARTHAGE CREAMERY CO. - Margarine & Butter**
- **CARTHAGE CRUSHED LIMESTONE CO. - Construction Materials**
- **CARTHAGE FOUNDRY & MACHINE CO. - Milling Equipment**
- **CARTHAGE MARBLE CORP. - Domestic & Imported Marbles**
- **CARTHAGE POULTRY CO. - Poultry Processing**
- **CENTRAL WOODWORKING CO. - Custom Woodwork**
- **FLEX-O-LATORS, INC. - Automotive & Furniture Components**
- **FOX DELUXE FOODS - Packaged Consumer Foods**
- **FRANK-RHINE CO. - Bank Construction**
- **GENERAL IRRIGATION CO. - Irrigation Systems**
- **GOODMAN MFG. CO. - Extracts**
- **HARMON WOODWORKING CO. - Custom Woodwork**
- **HERCULES POWDER CO. - Commercial Explosives**
- **HOKANSON & SONS, INC. - Agricultural & Commercial Tanks**
- **INDEPENDENT GRAVEL CO. - Construction Materials**
- **JACKSON PRINTING CO. - Commercial Printing**
- **KNOST ENGINEERING CO. - Custom Designers**
- **LEGGETT & PLATT, INC. - Bedsprings & Furniture**
- **LOCARNI MARBLE CORP. - Domestic & Imported Marbles**
- **MORROW MILLING CO. - Livestock & Poultry Feeds**
- **NATIONAL BISCUIT CO. - Flour Processing**
- **NORRIS GRAIN CO. - Grains & Feeds**
- **ORBIT PRODUCTS CO. - Farm Equipment**
- **OTT FOOD PRODUCTS CO. - Salad Dressing & Barbecue Sauce**
- **PARTY STEAK CO. - Packaged Meats**
- **REFRIGERATED SERVICES, INC. - Cold Storage & Warehousing**
- **SAMPSON MFG. CO. - Farm Equipment**
- **SAFEWAY CHEESE PLANT - Cheese**
- **SCHREIBER CHEESE CO. - Cheese**
- **SMITH BROS. MFG. CO. - Work and Casual Clothing**
- **STEADLEY CO. - Bedsprings & Furniture Constructions**
- **U. S. ART MARBLE CO. - Precast Terrazza Products**
- **WILLIAMS PRODUCTS CO. - Fluorescent Lighting Fixtures**

CARTHAGE INDUSTRIES, C. 1967. Through the decades, Carthage's diversification of industries and businesses has always been one of the most important promotional tools used by government and chamber officials.

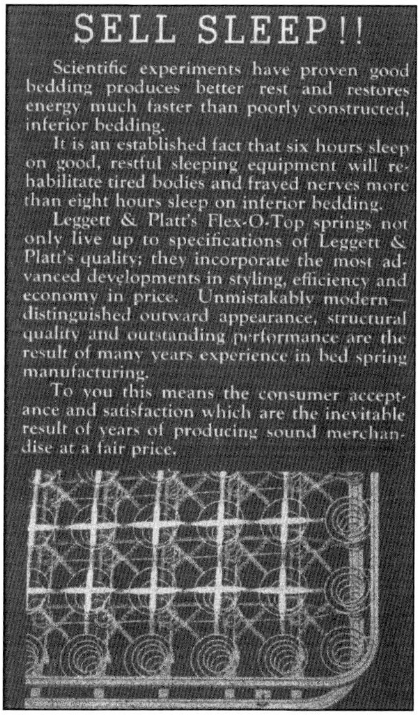

LEGGETT & PLATT, INC., 602 WEST CENTRAL AVENUE. Joseph Leggett received a patent in 1885 for his 1883 invention of the steel coiled bedspring. Partnering with Cornelius Platt, a business was started that grew in the first half of the 20th century to include plants in Louisville and Winchester, Kentucky, as well as Ennis, Texas. Bedding components, including "the most perfect spring bed in the world today," were the company's focus.

LEGGETT & PLATT-ARMCO WIRE MILL, 1225 EAST CENTRAL AVENUE. After working through World War II defense contracts, Leggett & Platt began a period of diversification and expansion over the next decades. One example was this wire mill, designed by Frank E. Ford Jr. and opened in 1970. The plant's machines provided 90 percent of the company's wire used in manufacturing. The factory also contained Carthage's first antipollution equipment. (Courtesy of Leggett & Platt, Inc.)

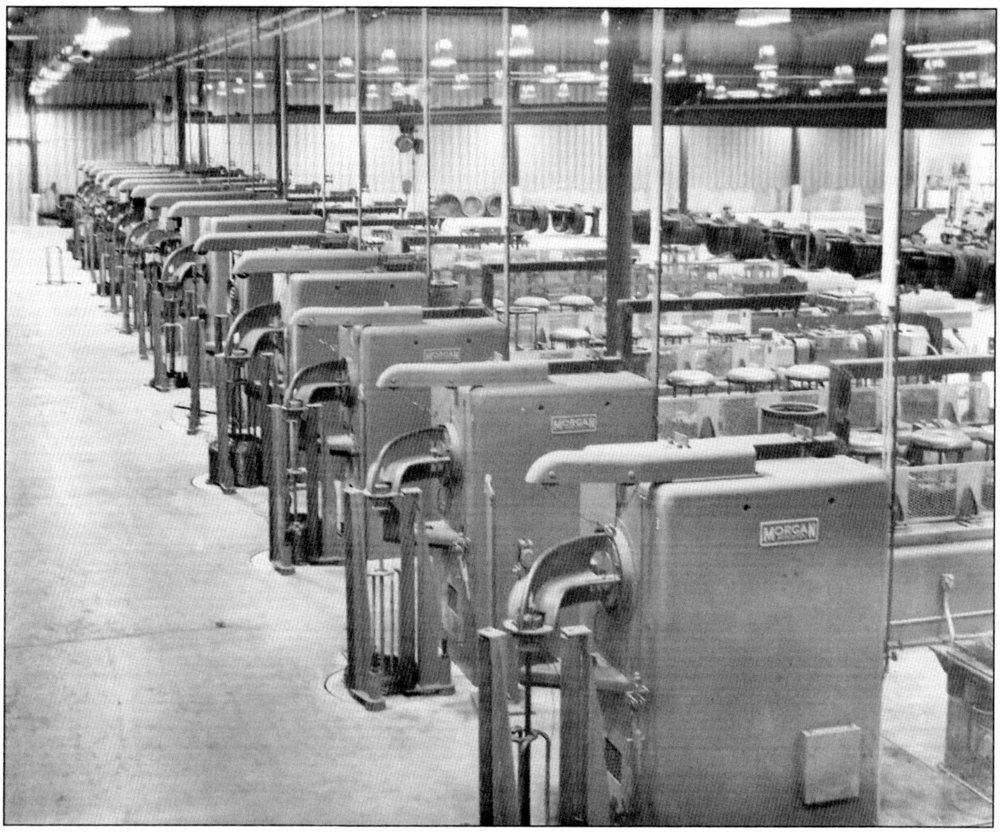

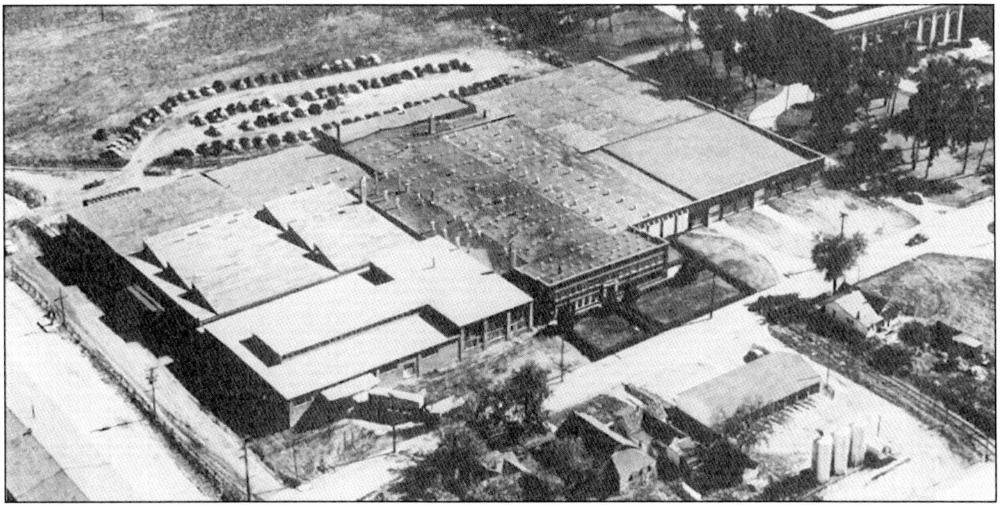

Steadley Company, 200 River Street. Kent Steadley became manager of Carthage Superior Bed Spring Company in 1926 and, two years later, acquired the company, changing its name and moving into one of Juvenile Shoe Company's former plants. The firm manufactured springs and components for furniture and bedding industries. This 1955 aerial view shows the many plant expansions that housed its 200 employees.

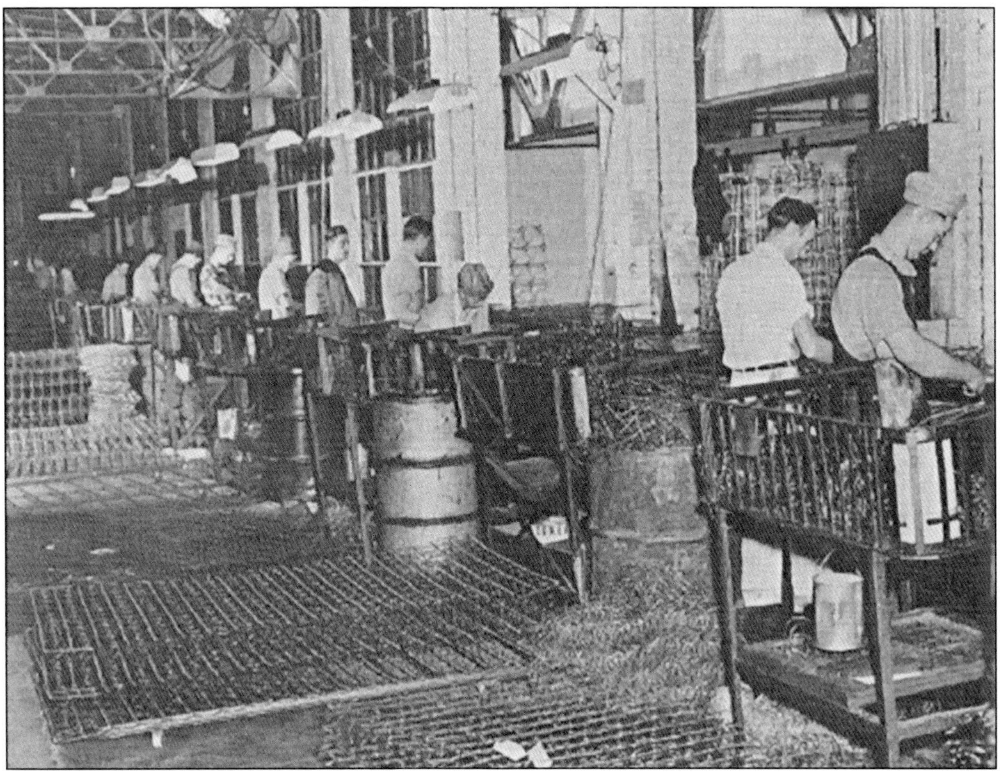

Steadley Company. Billed as "America's largest producer of springs devoted exclusively to the bedding industry" in 1955, Steadley consumed tons of steel each month to manufacture its product lines. Also in 1955, the company boasted that its production equipment was worth $1 million. In 1996, Leggett & Platt acquired Steadley.

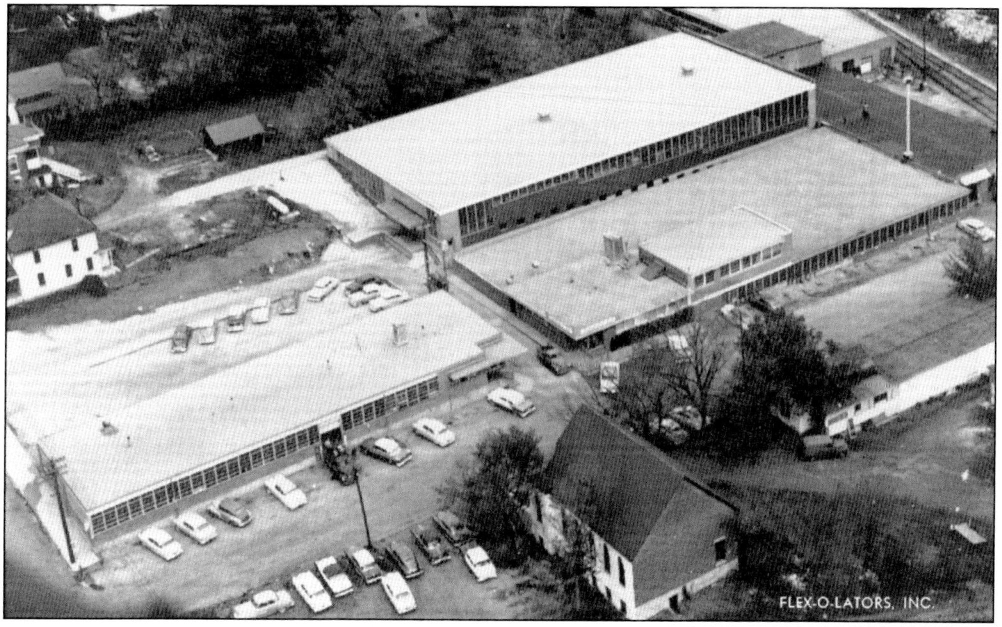

FLEX-O-LATORS, INC., 131 LOCUST STREET. C.E. "Jack" Platt, son of Leggett & Platt founder C.B. Platt, started his own company in 1942. It, too, manufactured springs and eventually specialized in automotive seating and other related components. In 1988, this company merged with Leggett & Platt and became its furniture component unit.

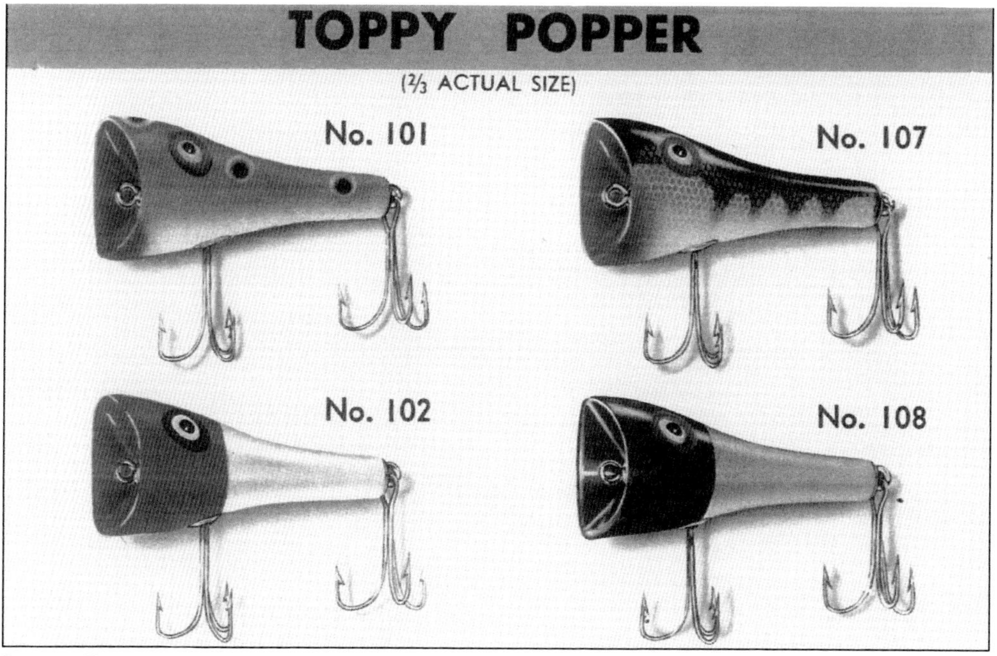

SIX AND BIDDLECOME LURES. Among Carthage's smaller manufacturing markets was the production of fishing lures. Illustrated are lures made by Calvin Biddlecome and Charles Six in 1948. The partnership split by 1950, and both Six and Biddlecome continued making lures. Six and his wife, Frankie, also ran Six's Sport Shop at 509 South Grant Street from 1946 until 1981, with lure production ceasing in 1978.

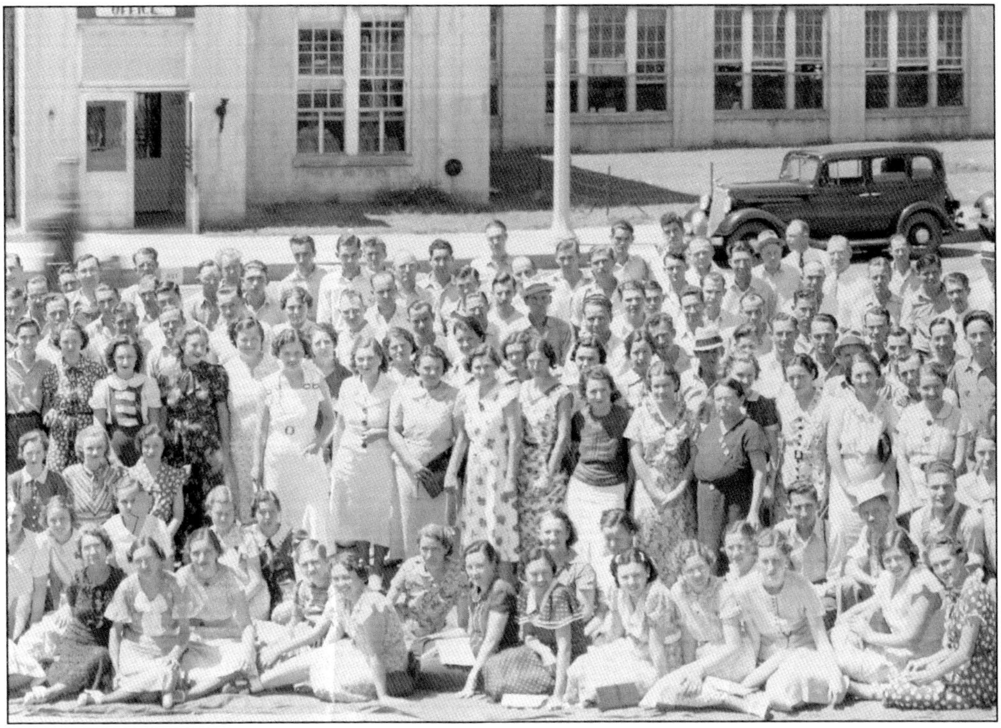

Carmo Shoe Company, 321 South Garrison Avenue. Shoe workers are posed opposite their factory about 1935, before it closed a few years later. In the early 1940s, Wolff-Tober Shoe Company moved in and then Sanders Grain and Commission Company along with furniture-maker Livon Industries in the late 1940s. For several years, the property was vacant before being torn down in 1961.

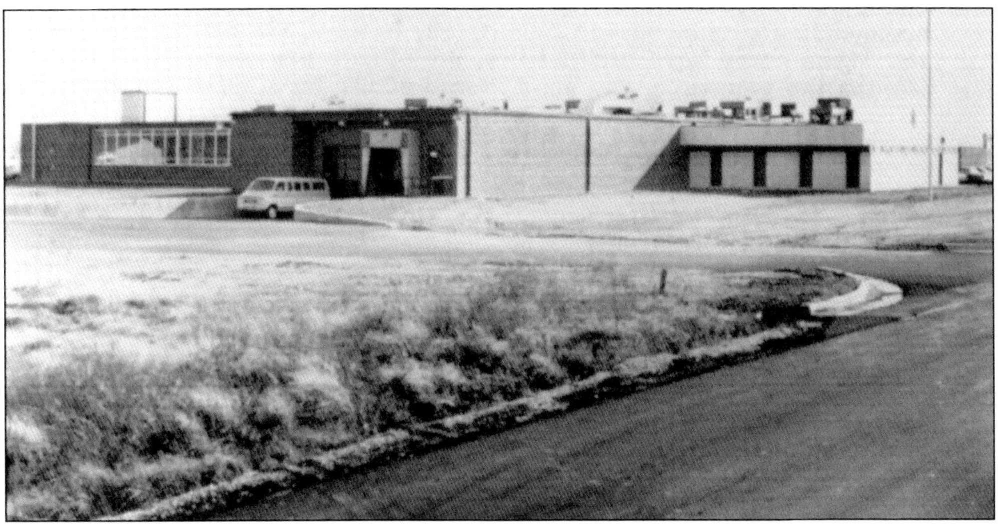

Juvenile Shoe Corporation, 2236 South Missouri Avenue. Juvenile returned to Carthage in 1971 and erected a new factory for the production of "Lazy-Bones" shoes for children and women along with golf and nurses' shoes. Gale Pate Sr. was president of Juvenile Shoe at this time. The facility, designed by A.C. Esterly, was expanded in 1989 when the Aurora, Missouri, plant closed. Justin Boot purchased the facility in 1990 and continues making work boots today.

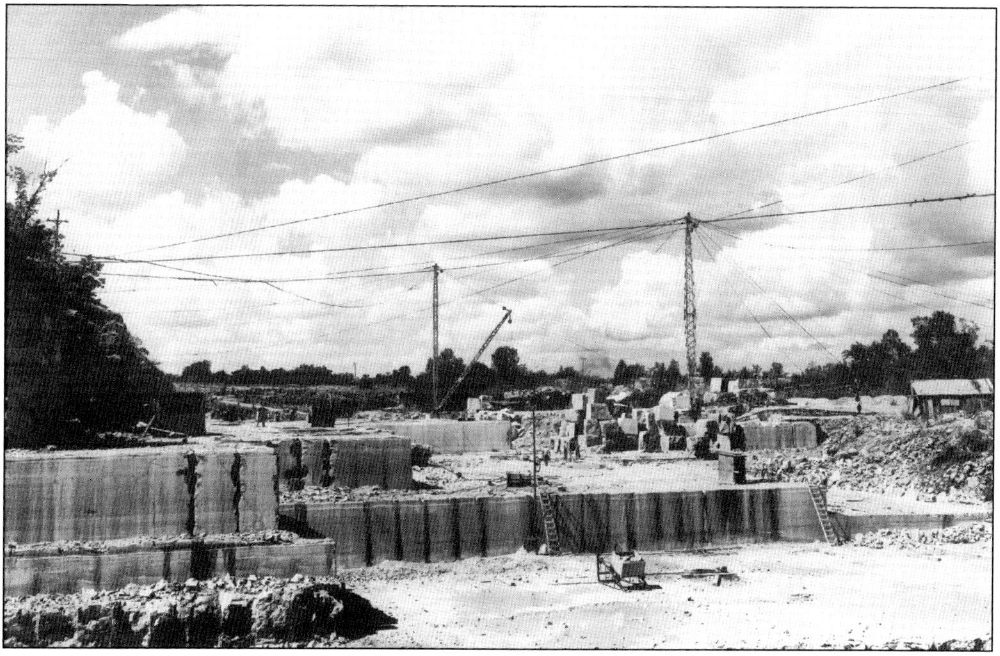

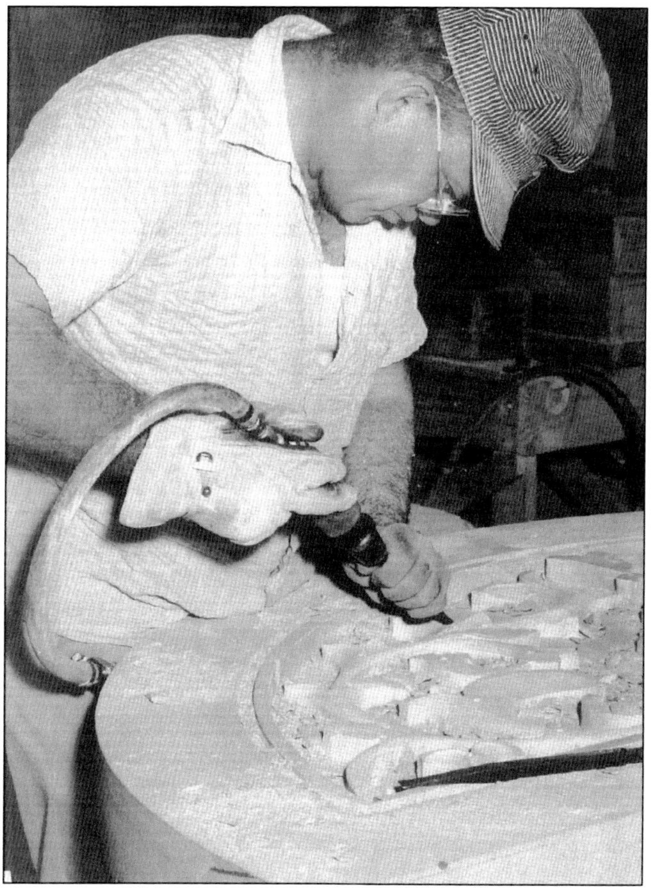

Carthage Marble Corporation, Northwest of Carthage. Following a trend in the industry, several of Carthage's independent stone quarries consolidated into one corporation in 1927. With this action, Carthage Marble became the world's largest marble quarrying and finishing concern west of the Mississippi River. This image, from a corporate promotional booklet, is from the late 1950s.

Carthage Marble Corporation. Stone-carver Oscar Grauberger works with a pneumatic chisel to cut decorative details into limestone. Buildings with Carthage Marble products can be found across the country.

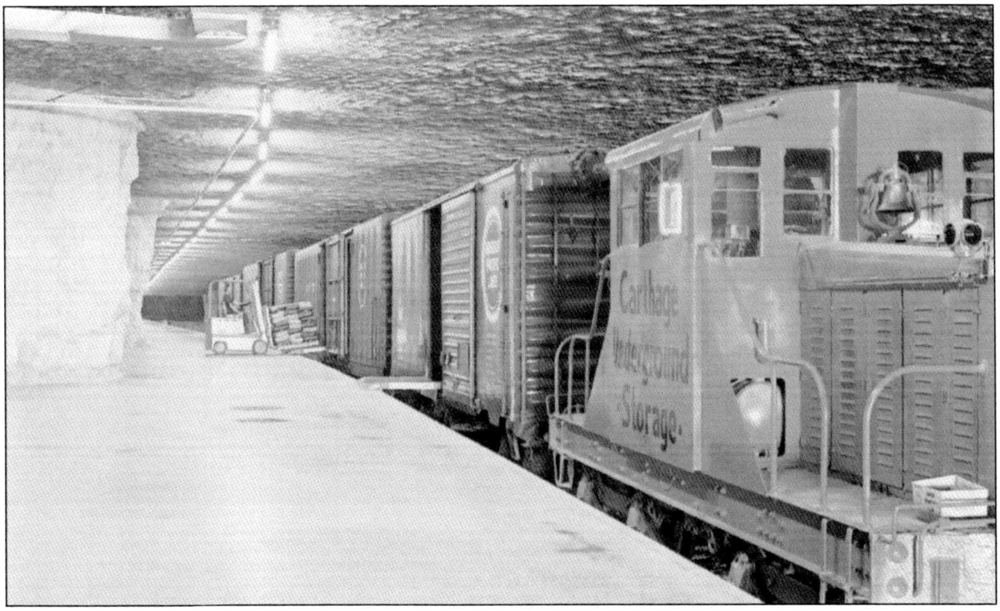

Carthage Underground Storage. As demand for limestone for construction started to drop in the late 1930s and the following decades, Carthage Marble began to diversify into other markets, such as flagging stone, crushed products, and interior finish work. In 1971, the corporation opened a new division, converting its underground quarries into over 1.2 million square feet of space for warehousing and distribution services. Today, it is part of Americold, Inc.

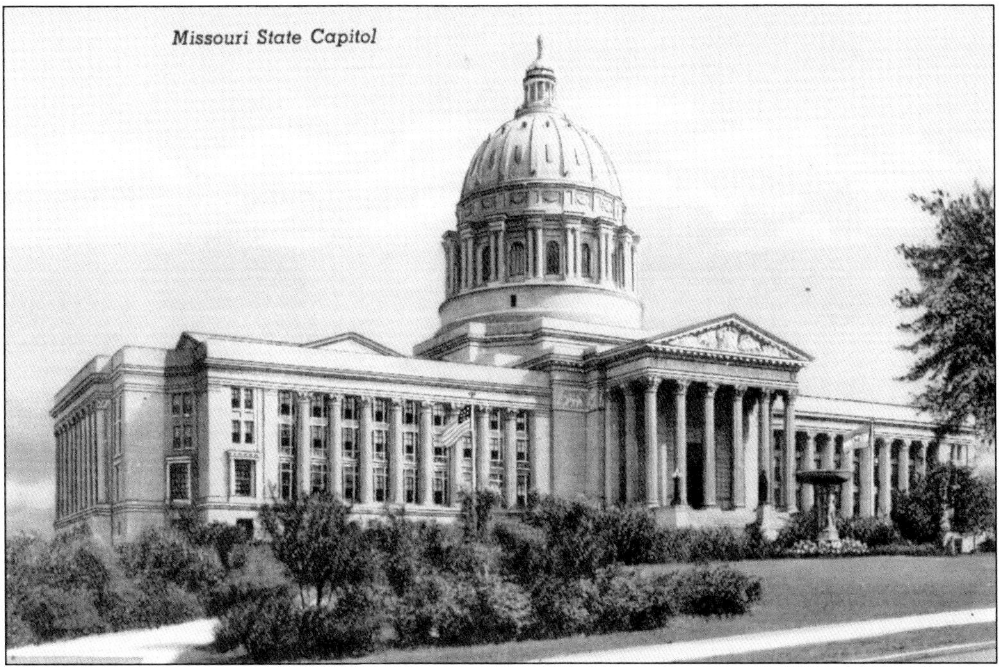

Missouri State Capitol, Jefferson City, Missouri. Considered one of the finest examples of the use of Carthage limestone is the Missouri Capitol. Completed in 1917, Carthage stone was supplied by the John Gill and Son Company, who later established Lautz-Missouri Marble, one of the companies that merged to form Carthage Marble Corporation.

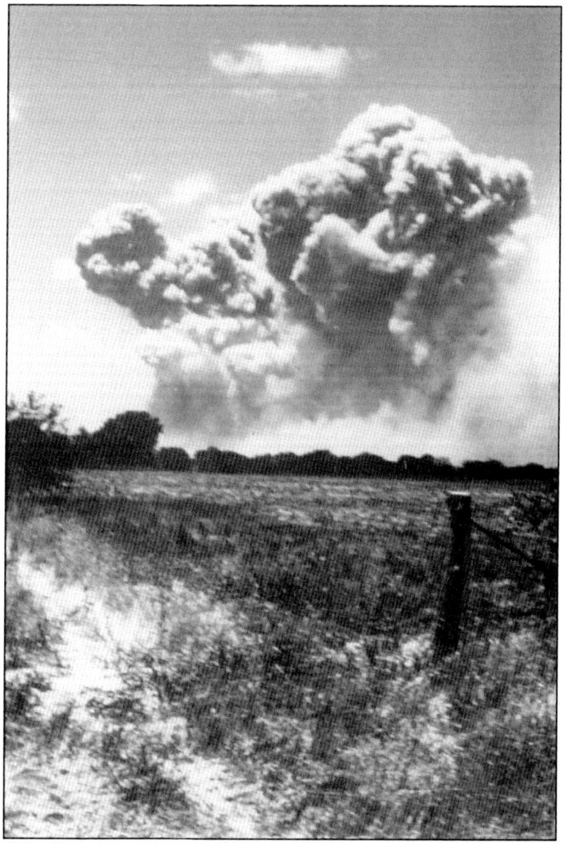

Hercules Powder Company, Southwest of Carthage. One of the most remembered events during Carthage's recent history was the explosion at Hercules on July 14, 1966. One employee, Maurice Crowell, was killed, and the southern portion of the plant area was destroyed. This view shows the smoke that rose 1,000 feet above the explosive manufacturer's site. (Courtesy of Lee Haggard.)

Hercules Explosion, 1966. The intensity of the blast was so great that buildings in Carthage and other towns several miles away were damaged; there was extensive damage to store windows in downtown Carthage. This view features the destroyed Vibronite-S can house. The plant was established in 1913, and explosions had occurred before, but none this destructive. (Courtesy of Lee Haggard.)

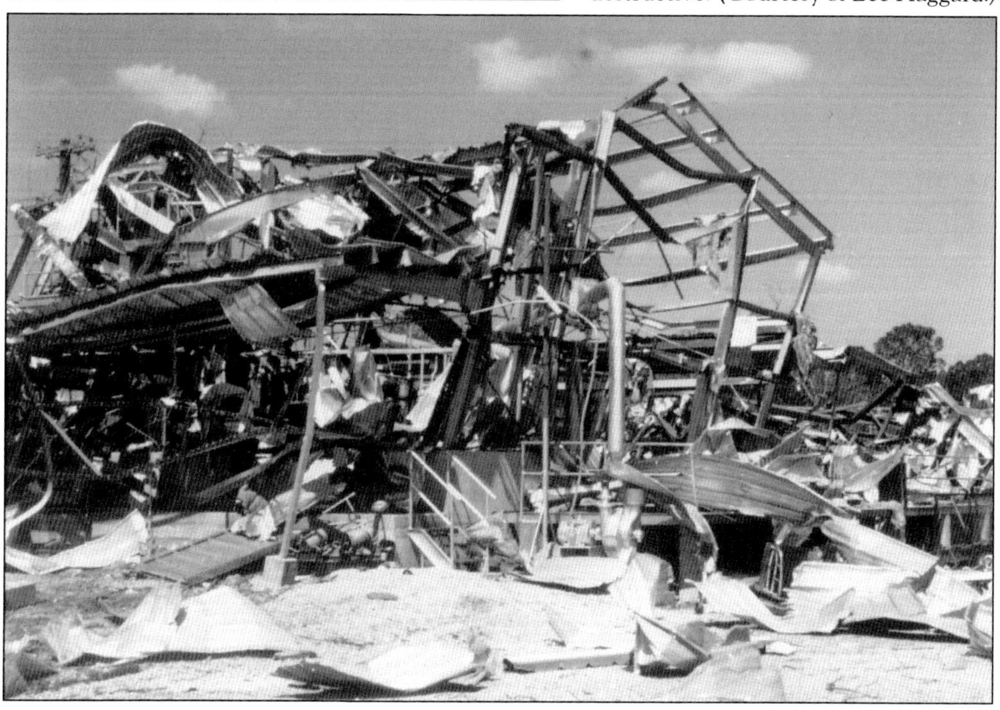

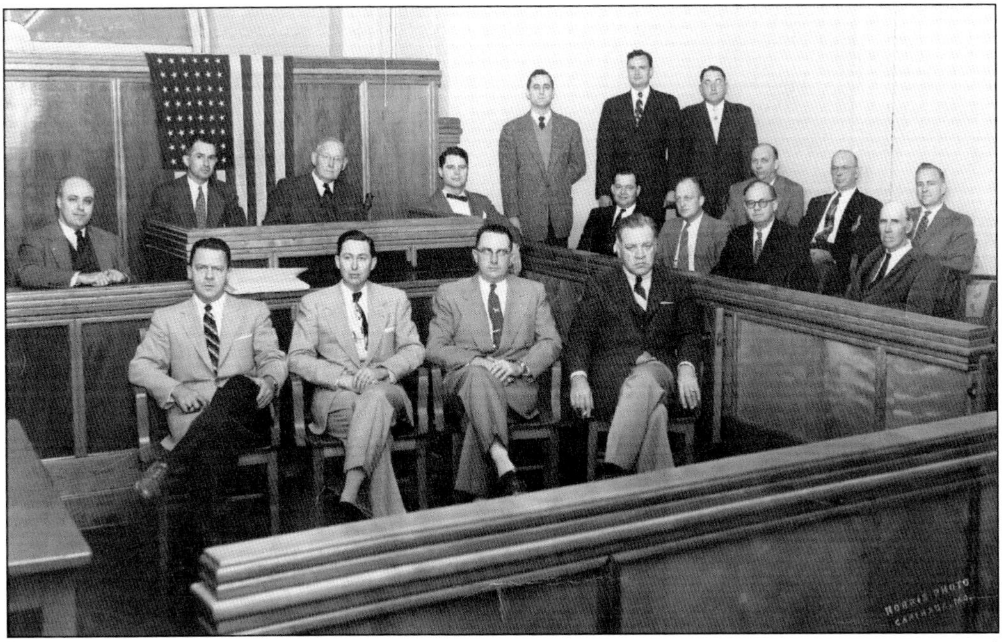

CARTHAGE LAWYERS. These men are gathered in a Jasper County Courthouse courtroom around 1955–1960. Sitting in front are Vernie Crandall, Max Glover, Robert Esterly, and John H. Flanigan Jr. At the judge's bench are an unidentified clerk, Herbert Casteel, Eli Scott, and George Flanigan. Standing are Laurence Flanigan, Richard Webster, and George Phelps. The jury box contains (first row) William Myers, Charles Tudor, Frank Birkhead, and Si Barton; (second row) Arkley Frieze, unidentified, and Charles Cook.

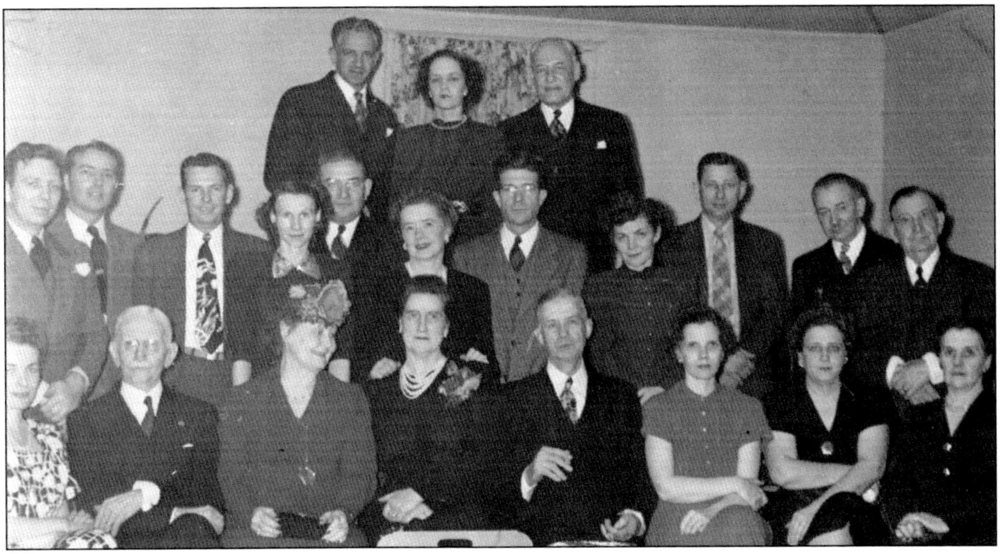

CARTHAGE PHYSICIANS. On the occasion of Dr. Webster's 1948 farewell party, the following people gathered: (first row) Ermina Clinton, Dr. Everett and Marian Powers, Ruth and Dr. Roger Webster, Geraldine Byrd, Ruth Wood, and Edna McIntire; (second row) Dr. William McNew, Dr. Russell Smith, Dr. C.H. and Allene Isbell, Dr. George Wood, Susan VanUrk, Dr. M. Foster and Rosa Whitten, Dr. Homer Byrd, Dr. Lloyd Clinton, and Dr. Karl Baker; (third row) Dr. Jules VanUrk, Betty Smith, and Dr. Emery McIntire.

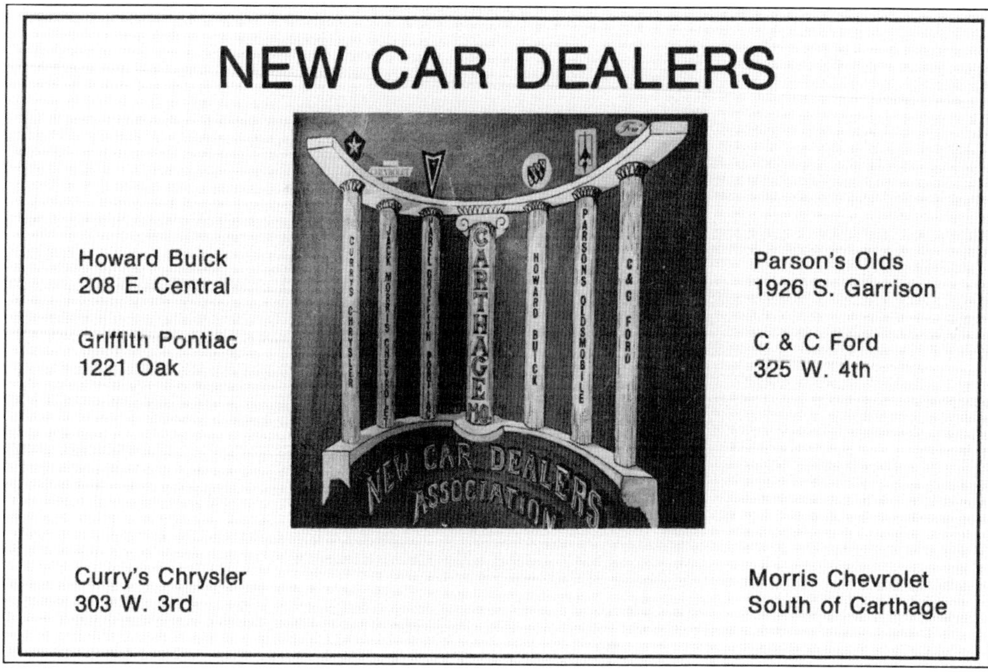

CARTHAGE CAR DEALERS, 1975 ADVERTISEMENT. Among older automobile dealers were Blackwood Dodge, Burtrum-Woolston Mercury, R&S Chevrolet, McGaughey-Wall Plymouth & Chrysler, Baird Oldsmobile, Jon Jones Mercury, Porter Brothers Studebaker, and Joy Plymouth & DeSoto. Joy's sign is still visible at 500 Oak Street and is often photographed by Route 66 tourists.

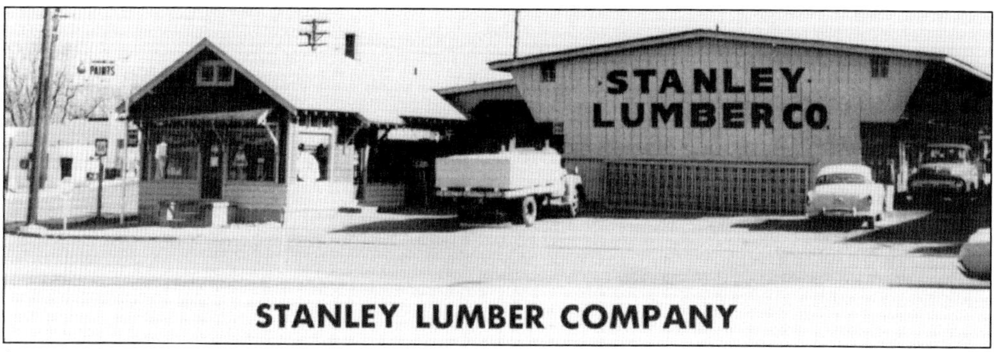

STANLEY LUMBER, 100 GRANT STREET. This location has been operated as a lumberyard since 1890 when Ben Thomas was the owner. Homer Stanley acquired part interest in the 1920s and owned the operations outright by 1947. Krtek Lumber took over in 1972, and today the property is the only building supply company (Henson Metal Building Supply) doing business downtown. This image is from the 1960s.

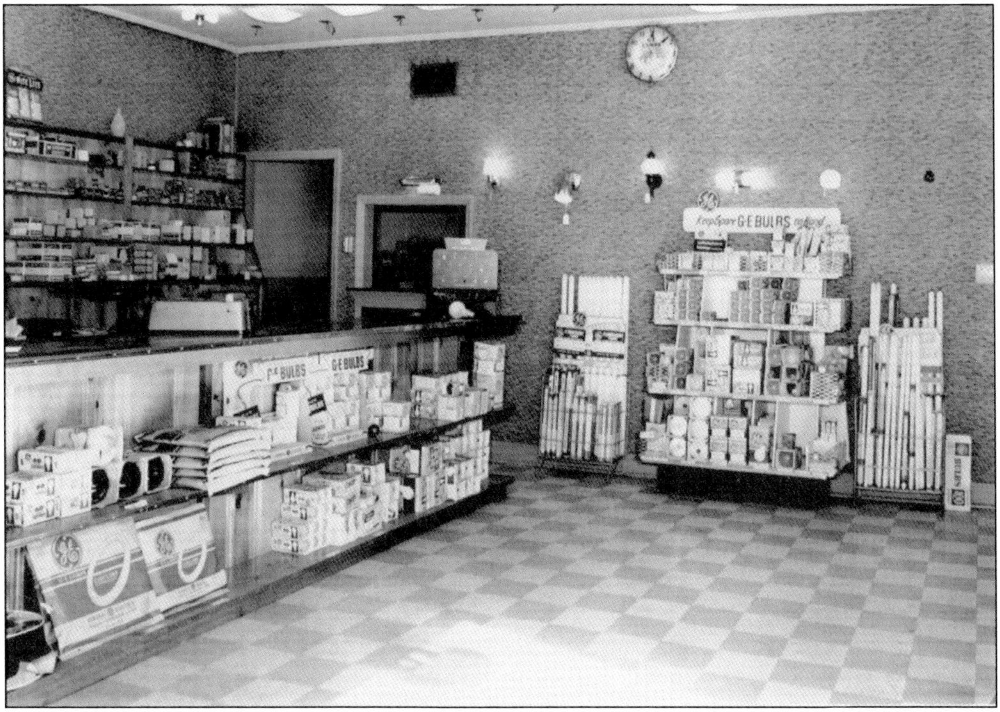

AAA Electric Company, 206 Grant Street. The downtown business district also was the location of many building-related businesses providing electrical, plumbing, and other construction supplies and services. One of the longest operating was AAA Electric. The store interior view is from the 1950s.

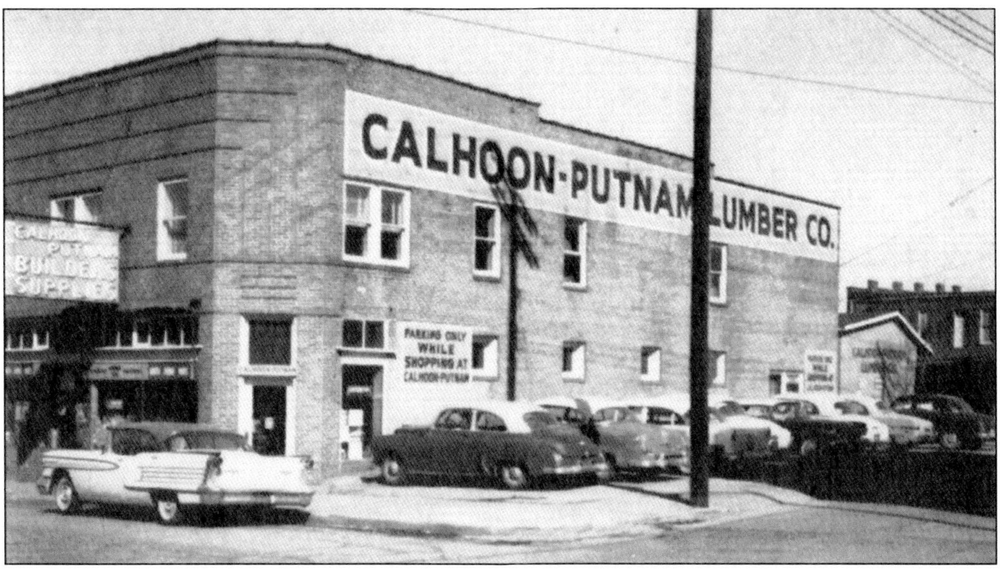

Calhoon-Putnam Lumber, 138 South Main Street. In the late 1940s, downtown had five lumberyards, and Calhoon-Putnam (later just Calhoon Lumber, owned by George and Myrtle Calhoon) operated at this location from the 1930s to the late 1970s. Today, the Calhoon-Putnam building, pictured in the 1960s, is part of the Carthage Crisis Center.

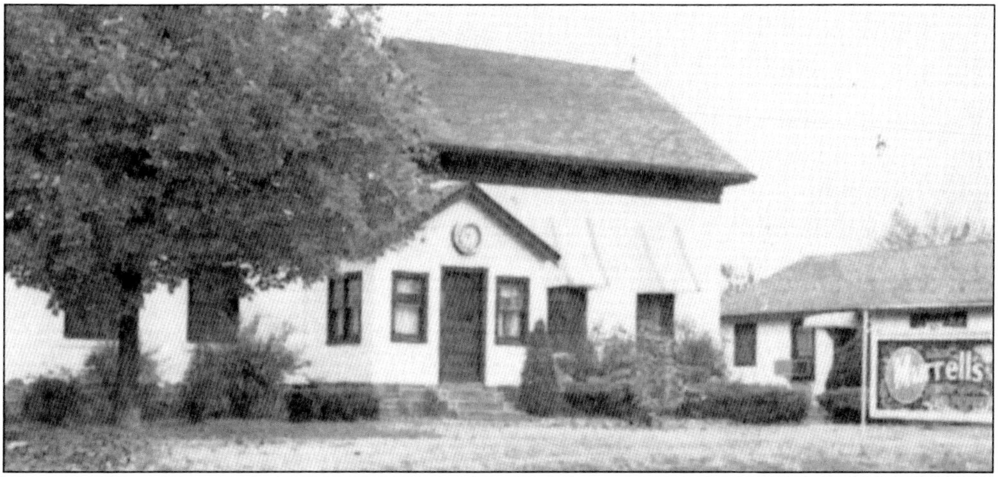

MURRELL'S POTATO CHIP, 525 NORTH GARRISON AVENUE. Murrell's Potato Chip, for most of its existence, operated inside the former Lincoln School building constructed in 1881. The potato chip business was first known as Murrell & Son and was owned by Hugh and Donald Murrell. Various businesses have occupied the site until 1990, when it became the office of architect Elliott Hunter.

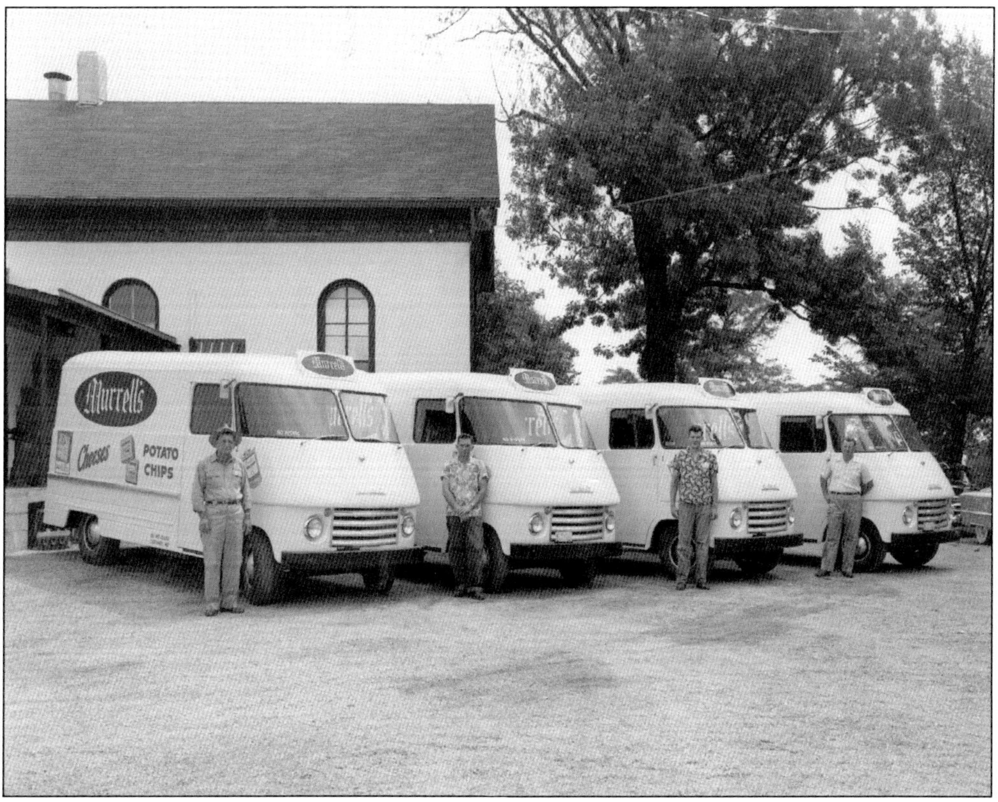

MURRELL'S FACTORY. Not only did the company make chips but it also roasted peanuts and distributed other snack products to groceries and food establishments, including Goettle's Drive-in, throughout the tri-state area via these trucks. Originally started in the late 1930s at another location, Murrell's was owned later by John and Betty Lovette when it closed in the 1960s.

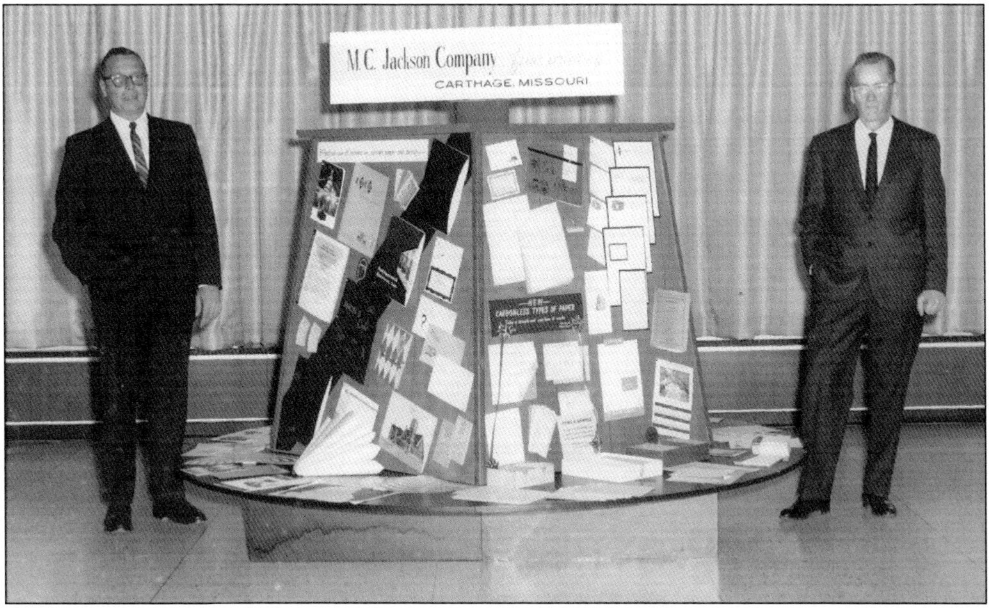

M.C. Jackson Company, 112 East Fourth Street. This company specialized in printing and office products. The printing plant was located at 509 South Main Street while the Fourth Street location sold business supplies and gift items. In this view, Parker Rogers (left) and Milo Jackson (right) show off the company's work in a display at the Bank of Carthage around 1968.

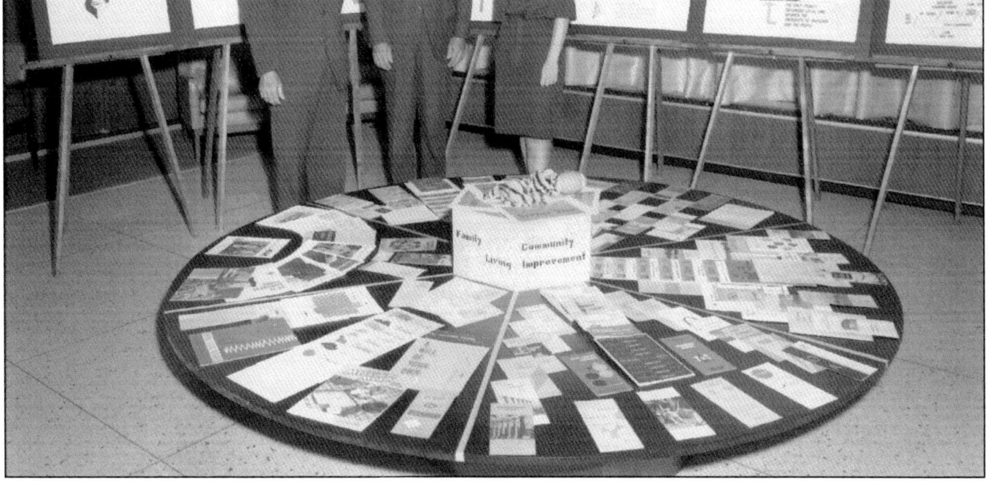

Jasper County Extension Council, Jasper County Courthouse. Also seen with a 1960s display at the Bank of Carthage are Hartford Patrick, Warren Jaynes, and an unidentified staffer of the University of Missouri, Jasper County Extension Council. Residents of southwest Missouri continue to receive a wide array of educational and business services from the council.

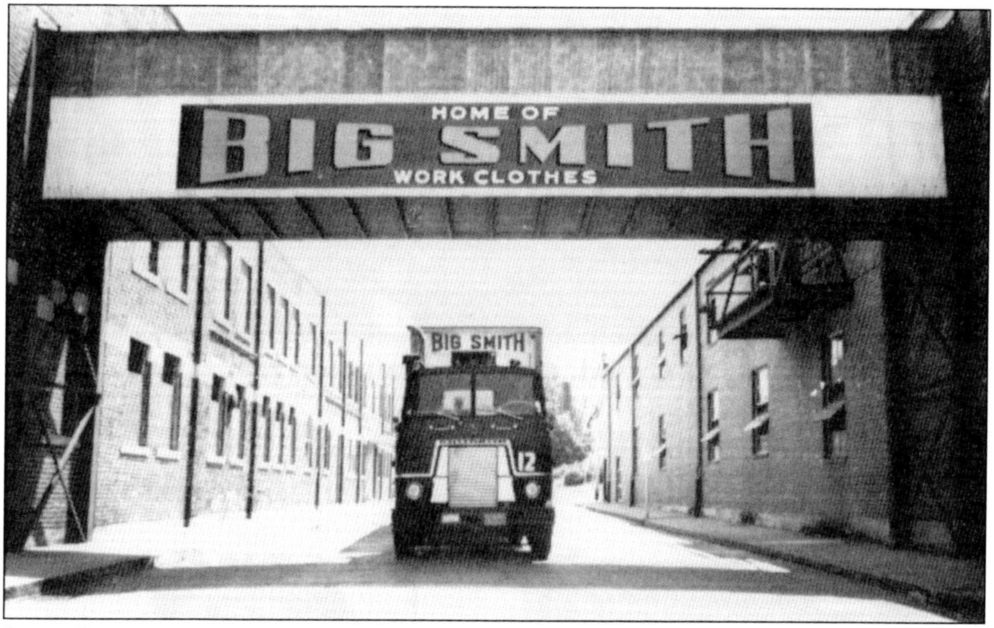

Smith Brothers Manufacturing Company, 526 Howard Street. Locally known as "Big Smith," this company began production in Carthage in 1916. During World War II, just as the workers did during World War I, the factory produced military clothing. After the war, production lines returned to manufacturing denim work wear, overalls, and casual clothing for all ages.

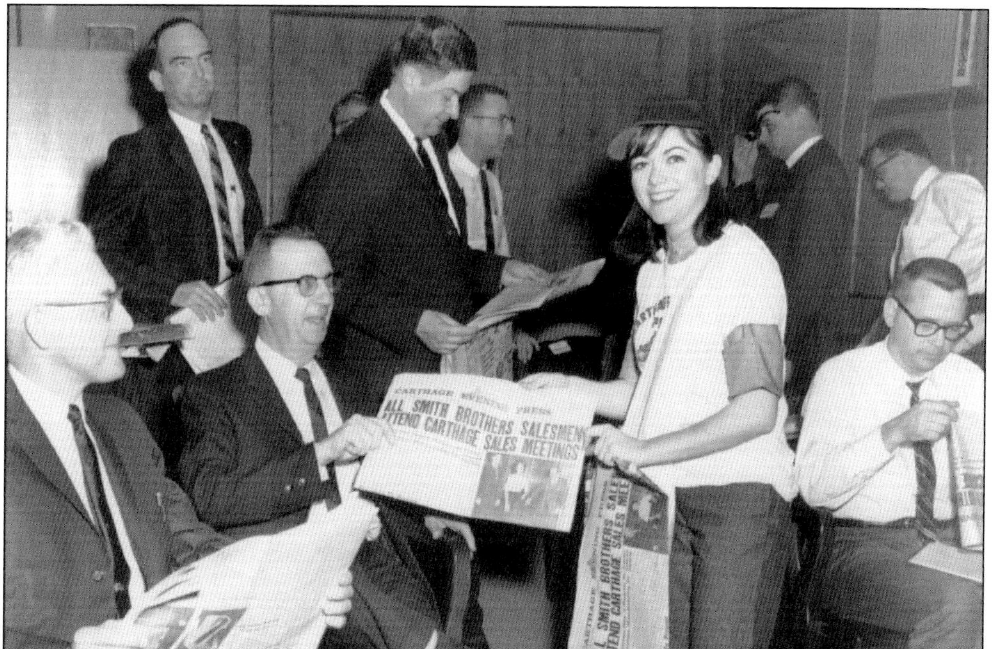

Smith Brothers. Headquartered in Carthage, regional salesmen would come to town annually for a conference at the nearby Drake Hotel. This 1965 photograph shows some of those unidentified salesmen with a *Carthage Press* newsgirl (also unidentified) passing out the newspaper featuring their meeting on the front page.

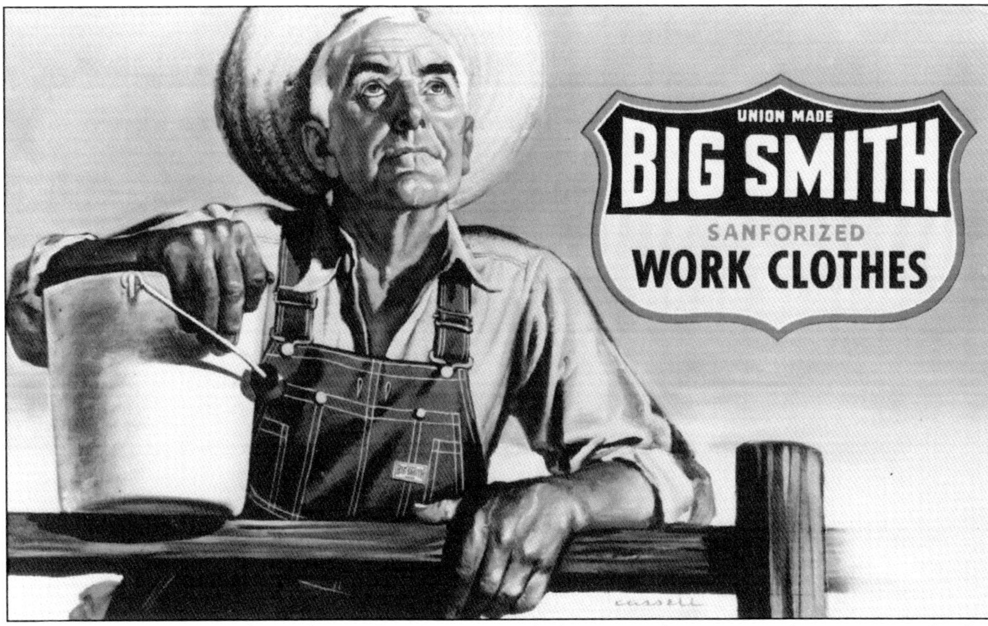

SMITH BROTHERS. In the 1950s and 1960s, artwork featuring farmers, outdoorsmen, and other industrial trades were featured in company advertising like this one, created by Robert Cassell of St. Louis, Missouri, for Smith Brothers. The advertising prints were sent to over 8,000 stores and dealers selling the Big Smith lines.

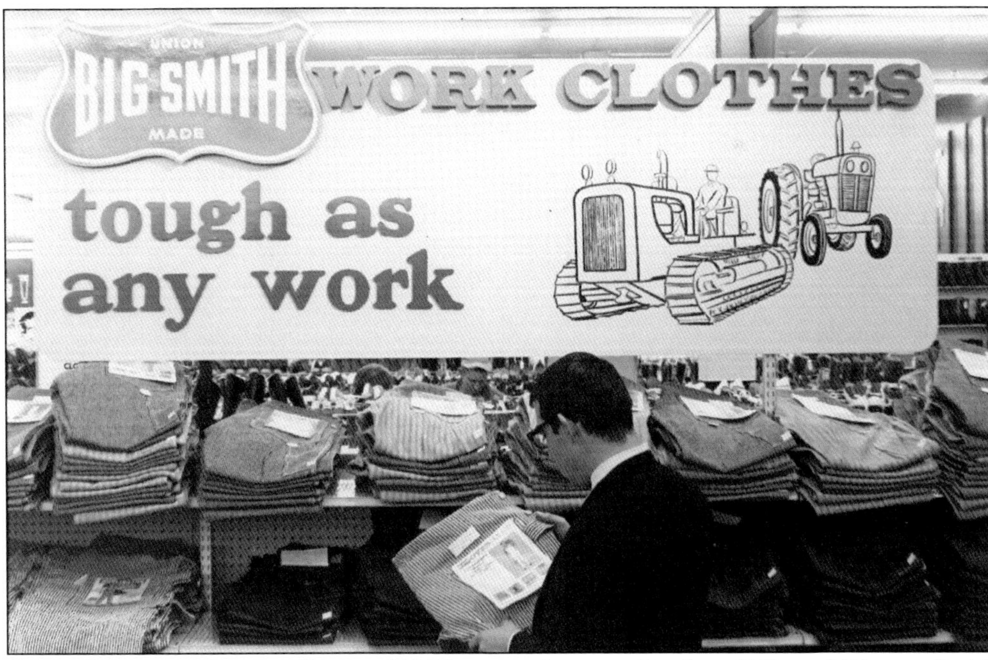

SMITH BROTHERS OUTLET STORE, 526 HOWARD AVENUE. Brothers E.O. and Clayton Smith guided Smith Brothers Manufacturing for many years. Plants were located in Carthage, St. Joseph, Neosho, Webb City, and Lamar, Missouri, as well as a plant in Bonham, Texas. Clayton Smith Jr. took over the company in 1959, and over 1,200 workers were employed by the 1960s. Production ceased in 2000 after a series of nonlocal owners.

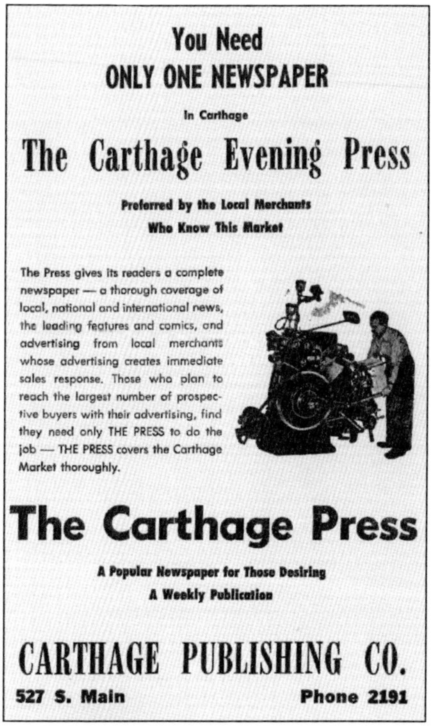

CARTHAGE *EVENING PRESS*, 527 SOUTH MAIN STREET. In 1950, the *Press* moved from the Sewall Building at 119 West Fourth Street, where it had been located since 1918, to the former Platt-Porter Wholesale Grocery Building, constructed in 1926. Here, father and son Elliel L. Dale and Robert Dale guided the newspaper operations for almost four decades.

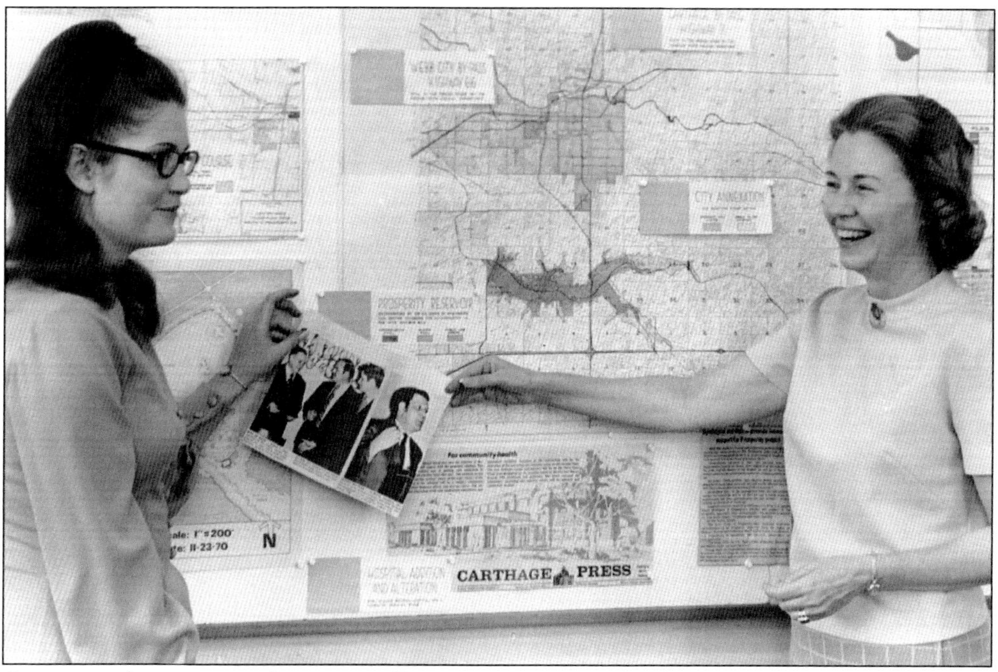

CARTHAGE CHAMBER OF COMMERCE. From 1940 to 1990, the chamber of commerce has been an active partner cultivating Carthage's development and economic diversity. Rachel Thornton (right), chamber executive secretary through most of the 1970s and 1980s, had a "profound and everlasting" impact on Carthage, as declared by Mayor Harry Rogers in 1987 at her retirement. Here, she is with assistant Maryland Rice in their Memorial Hall office in 1971.

Four

EDUCATION

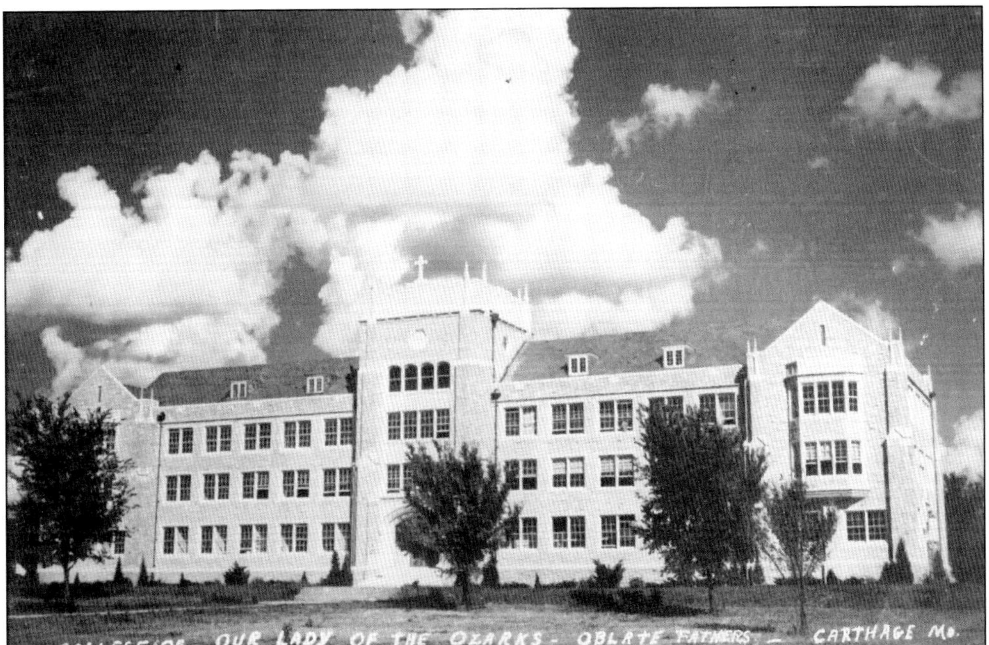

OUR LADY OF THE OZARKS (OLO), 1900 GRAND AVENUE. Established in 1944 in the former Ozark Wesleyan College Building (erected in 1926), this Catholic boarding school for young men was started by the Missionary Oblates of Mary Immaculate. Three bishops presided over the dedication, and OLO's first principal was Rev. Valentine Goetz. The school operated until 1971. At its peak, 170 students attended and a faculty of 10 was employed.

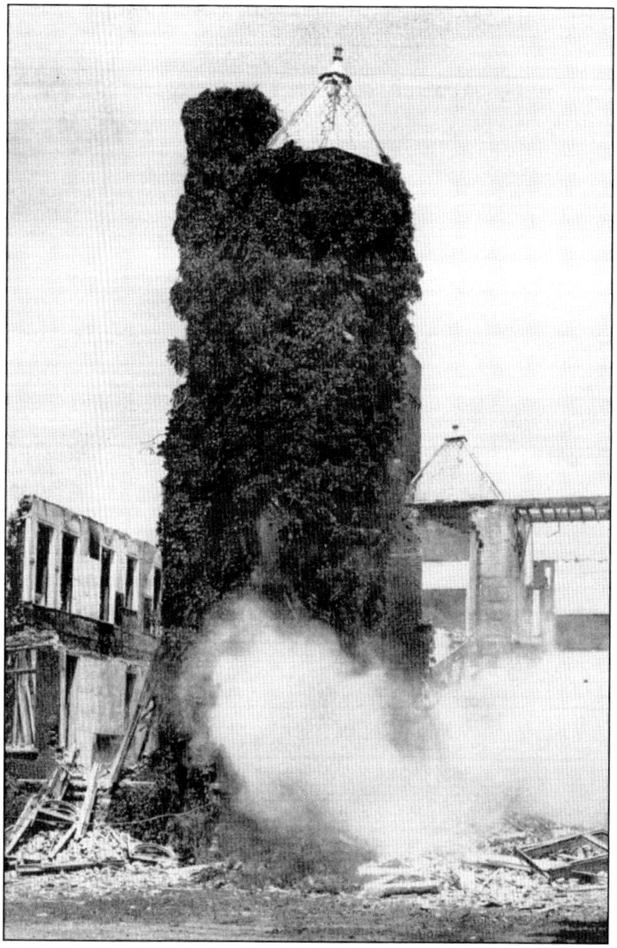

Carthage High School, 714 South Main Street. In the 1940s, it became apparent that additions to the high school building (now used as Carthage Junior High School) would have to be made. Once World War II was over, the community began campaigning for the additions. The changes would mean the destruction of the 1892 Manual Arts Building in 1950.

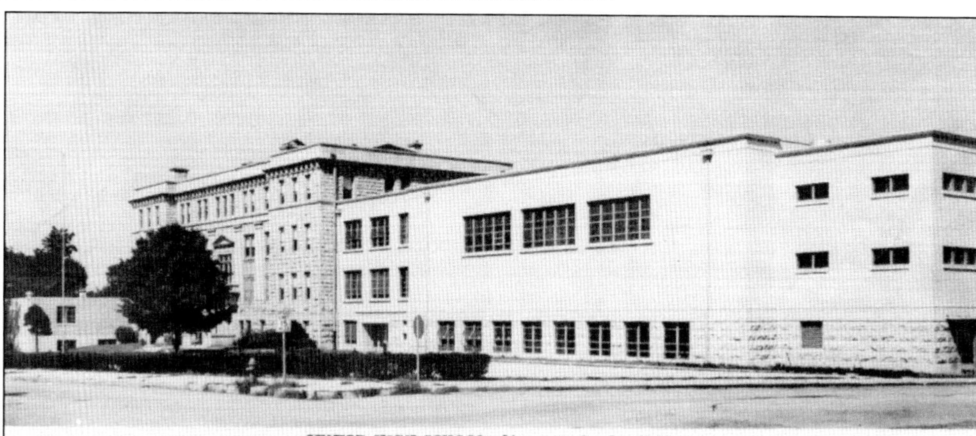

SENIOR HIGH SCHOOL—34 rooms, Grades 10-12

Carthage High School. Using talking points such as fire safety and overcrowding, voters passed an increase in property tax (24¢ on $100 valuation) to build a new addition and gymnasium completed in 1951. The high school principal was John Harp Jr., and the school system's superintendent was J.L. Campbell. Other additions, including a new auditorium in 1988, would follow; the auditorium used in its construction the last building stone available from Carthage Marble Corporation.

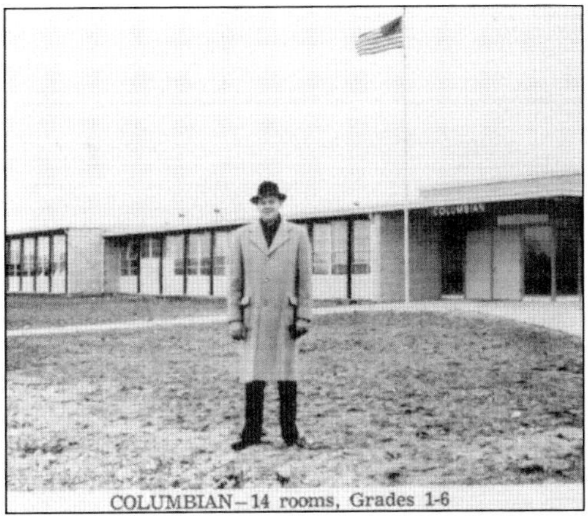

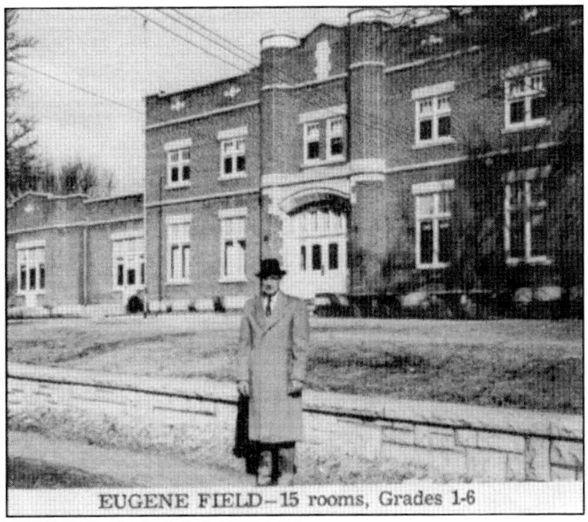

COLUMBIAN AND EUGENE FIELD ELEMENTARY SCHOOLS. Eugene Field School (613 East Chestnut Street) opened in 1917. Columbian School (1015 West Macon Street) opened the fall of 1956, and third-grader Dickie Gerard Jr. was the first pupil to enter the new school. Glen Jarmin was its first principal. Pictured are 1958–1959 school board president H. Lang Rogers at Columbian and vice president Hugh McWilliams at Eugene Field.

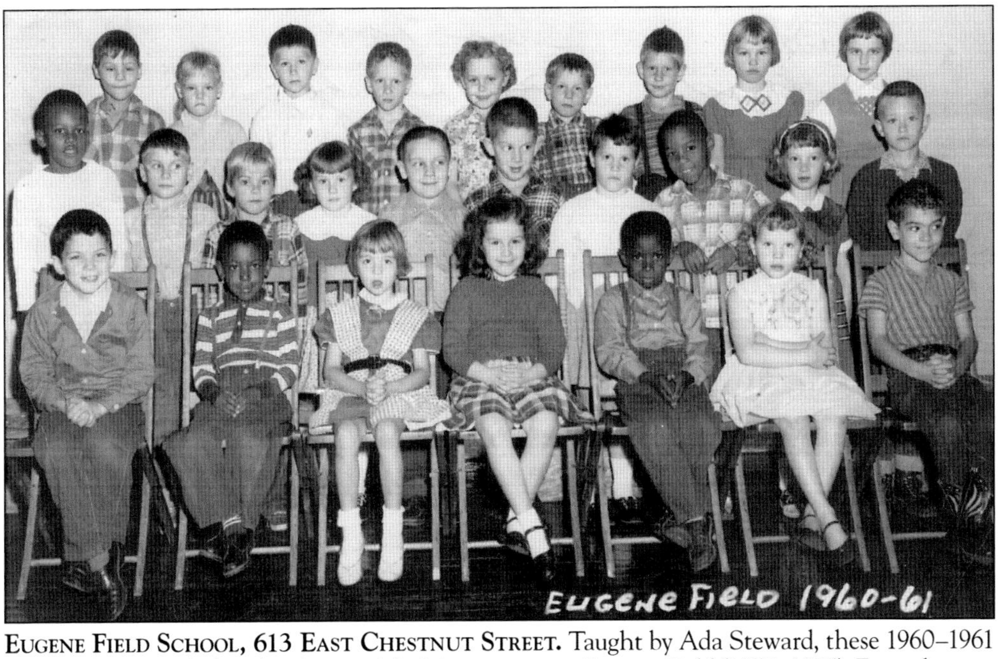

EUGENE FIELD SCHOOL, 613 EAST CHESTNUT STREET. Taught by Ada Steward, these 1960–1961 first graders attended a school named for Missouri writer Eugene Field (1850–1895). From the year it opened in 1917 until 1950, Lula Stanley was the school's principal. Other long-serving principals were Robert Duvall (1970–1984) and Tom Bewick (1984–1997). The school closed in May 1997, and Steadley Elementary opened in August 1997. (Courtesy of Teresa Babcock Henry.)

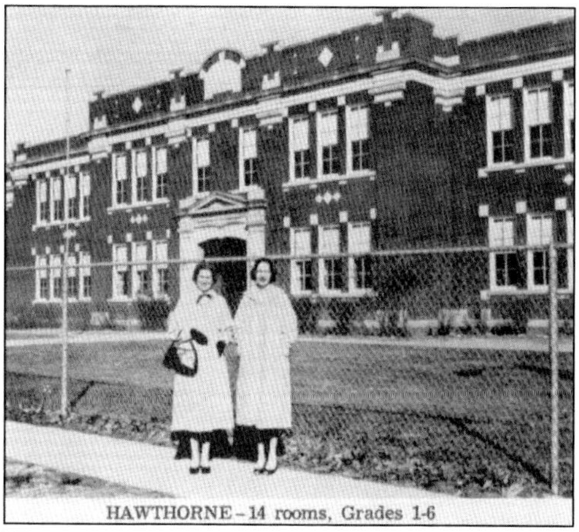

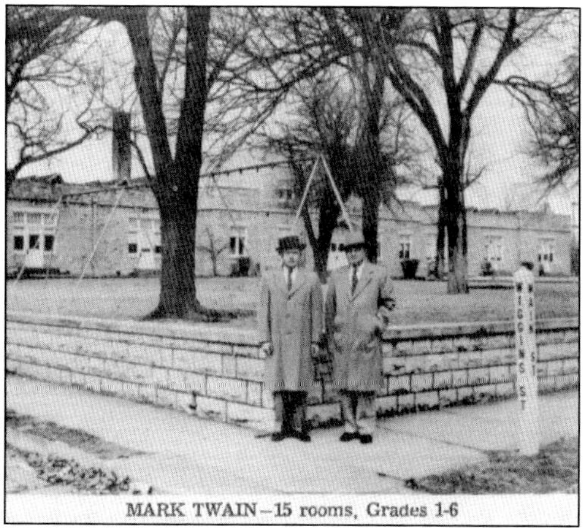

HAWTHORNE AND MARK TWAIN ELEMENTARY SCHOOLS. Hawthorne School (811 West Central Avenue) opened in 1922, and Mark Twain School (1435 South Main Street) opened in 1917. Pictured are 1958–1959 school board members Alice Hiatt and Dorothy Bader in front of Hawthorne School, and Clayton Metcalf Jr. and Elza Johnson in front of Mark Twain School.

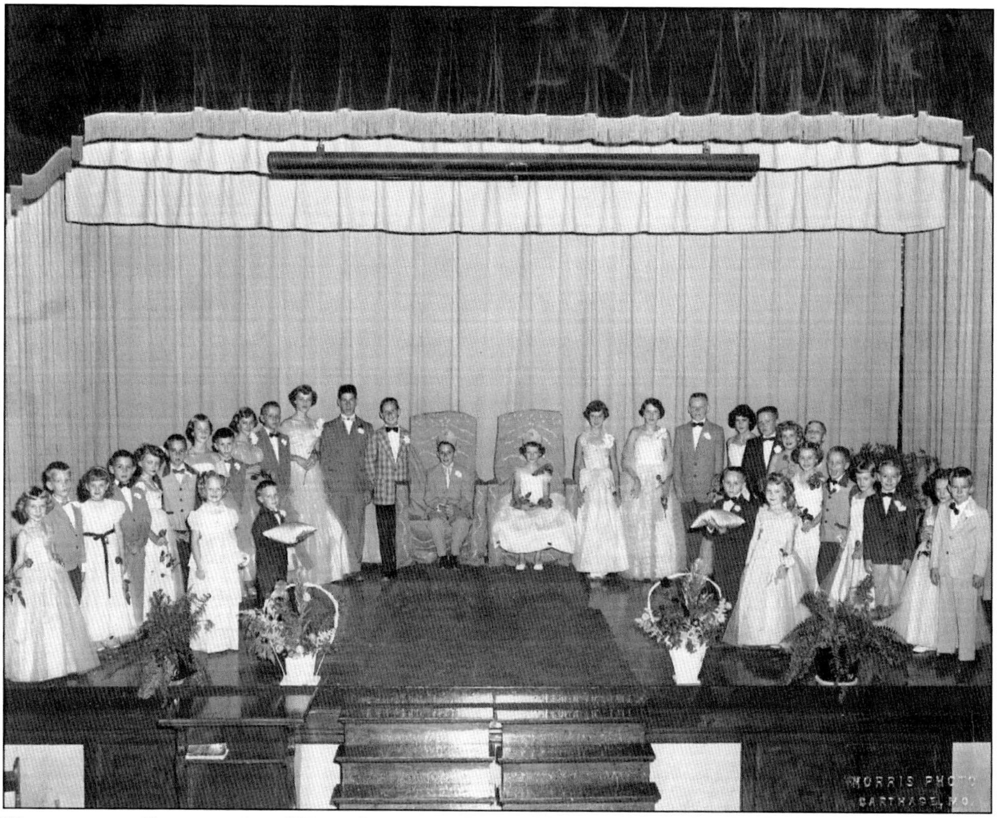

HAWTHORNE SCHOOL, 811 WEST CENTRAL AVENUE. Many of the schools held fundraisers and special public events in conjunction with their Parent-Teacher Associations, and such an event is pictured here from the 1954–1955 school year at Hawthorne. The students are unidentified in this Moyne Norris photograph. Hawthorne continued to serve the community until May 1997.

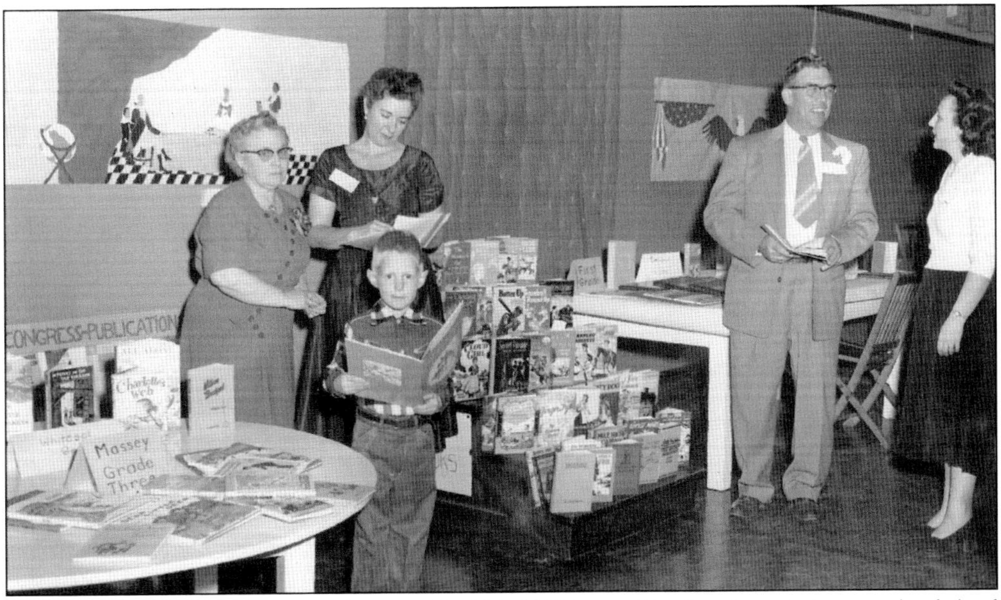

HAWTHORNE SCHOOL. Also from the school's 1954–1955 Parent-Teacher Association scrapbook (and unidentified) is this image featuring a book fair at the school. Hawthorne's long-term principals were Eleanor Henley, who arrived after Benton School was closed and served to the early 1950s, and Basil Hill, who served from 1956 to 1974.

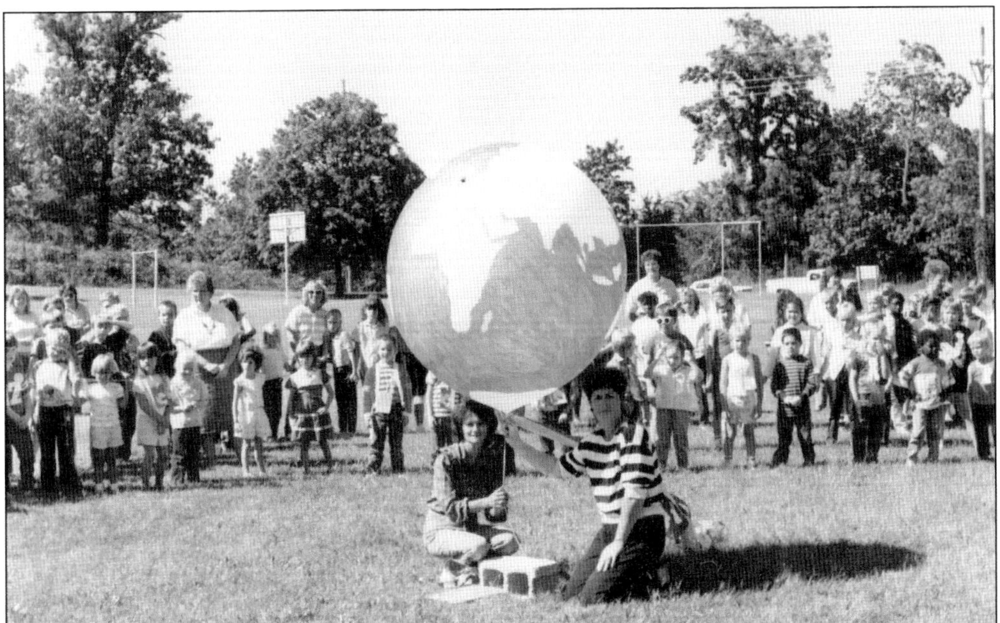

HAWTHORNE SCHOOL. Students and teachers are in the yard of the school for an Earth Day celebration in the 1980s. The building was demolished in 1999, but many school records, scrapbooks, and photographs were donated to the Powers Museum in 1998. Select items can be consulted in the museum's reference library or online.

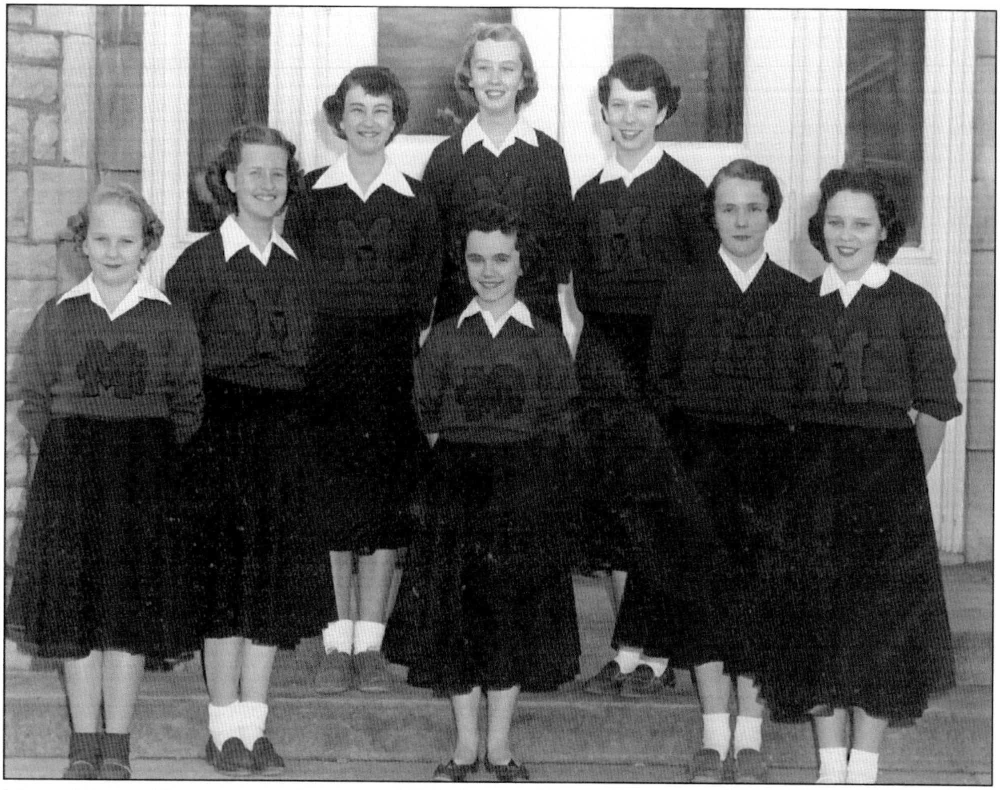

Mark Twain Elementary School, 1435 South Main Street. School cheerleaders (above) in 1955 came from the seventh and eighth grades and included, from left to right, Marcia Selby, Linda Swarens, Elaine Noah, Kay Fitzgerald, Kathleen McDonald, Carolyn McCurry, Deloris Johnson, and, in the center, Nancy Key. The image below shows part of the school's first-grade rhythm band in 1947. (Both courtesy of Kathleen MacDonald Chick.)

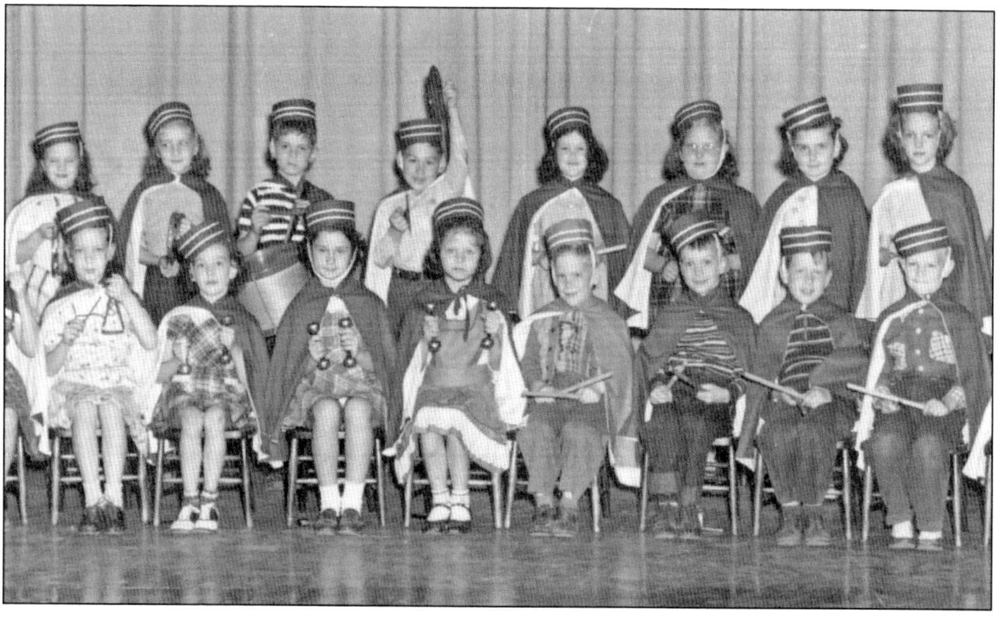

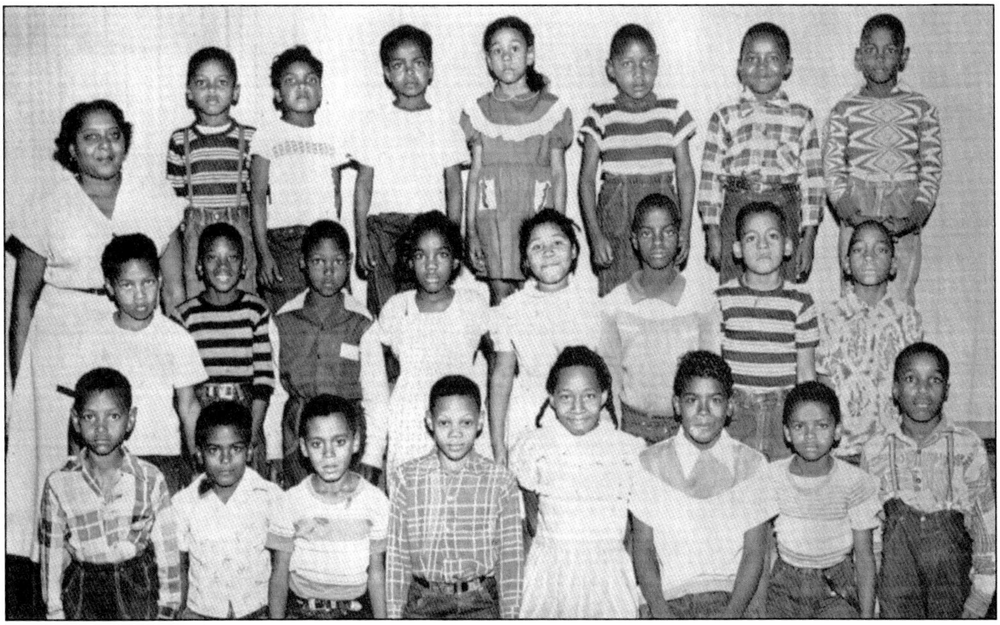

LINCOLN SCHOOL, 820 SOUTH WATER STREET. Carthage public schools were segregated from the 1880s until the mid-1950s. Among the 1953–1954 elementary students at Lincoln were (first row) Bruce Cortez, Elimo Lounis, Mike Davis, Art Cortez, Theresa Strickland, Mondo Lounis, Willie Triplett, and Bob Williams; (second row) Dave Wofford, Richard Hill, unidentified, Tally Ann Williams, Beverly Strickland, Larry Rice, James Burns, and Billy Mitchell; (third row) Mrs. Gidder (teacher), unidentified, George Triplett, Steve Triplett, unidentified, Winston Strickland, Tommy Brown, and Tink Cheney.

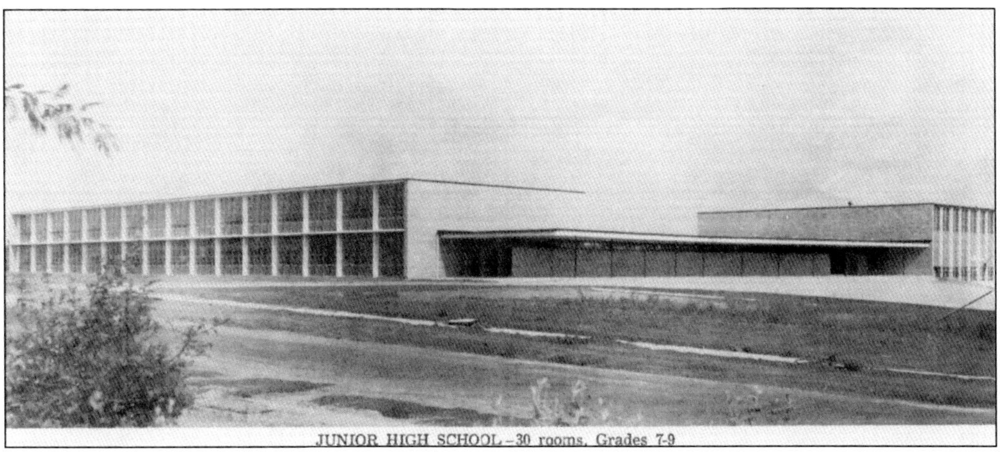

CARTHAGE JUNIOR HIGH SCHOOL, 827 EAST CENTENNIAL AVENUE. Built in 1957–1958 at a cost of $680,000, the original school was constructed to hold 750 students. The school's first principal was Dwight Sergent. Several additions have been built over the decades, and the building now serves as the Carthage Middle School.

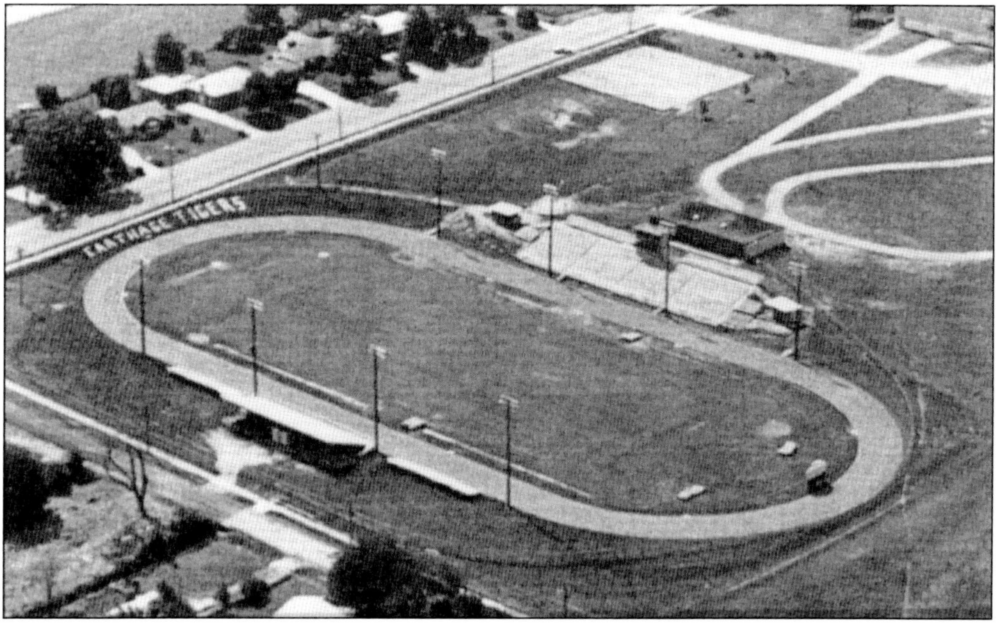

K.E. Baker Stadium, Thirteenth and River Streets. Named for longtime athletic director Karl E. Baker Jr., the stadium was built in 1958 and expanded in 1962. Many more improvements have occurred through the decades, and some of those changes have been made courtesy the Kent D. and Mary L. Steadley Memorial Trust.

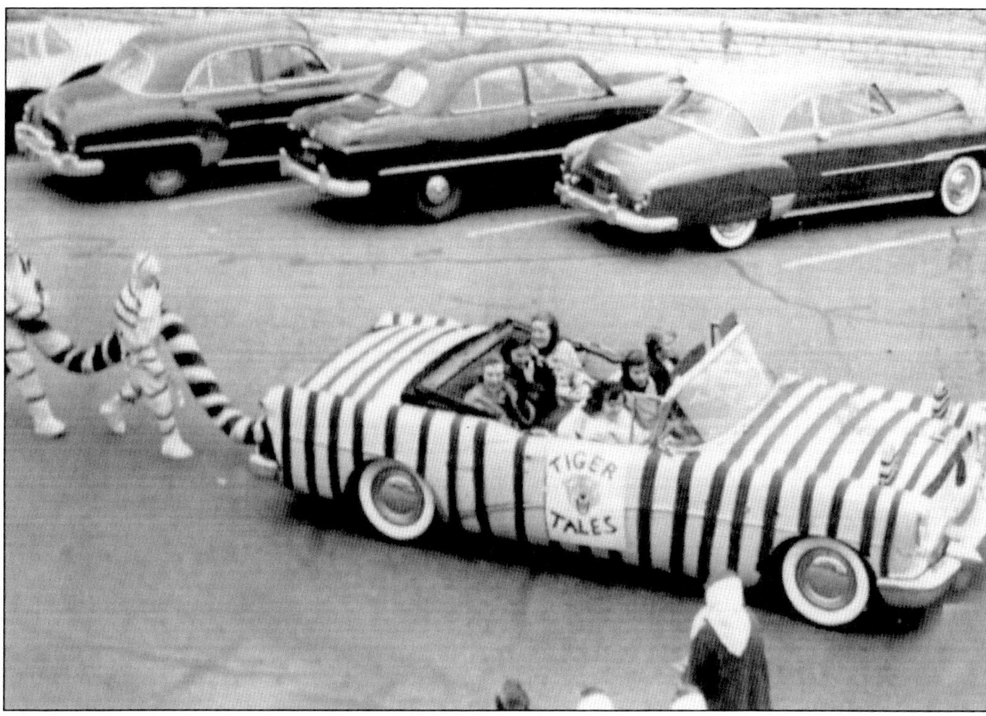

Homecoming Parade Car. Decorated for the high school's homecoming in 1955, this decorated "tiger" car probably holds some of the newspaper staff of *Tiger Tales* and is moving in line for the parade to the K.E. Baker Jr. Stadium. *Tiger Tales* was established in 1935.

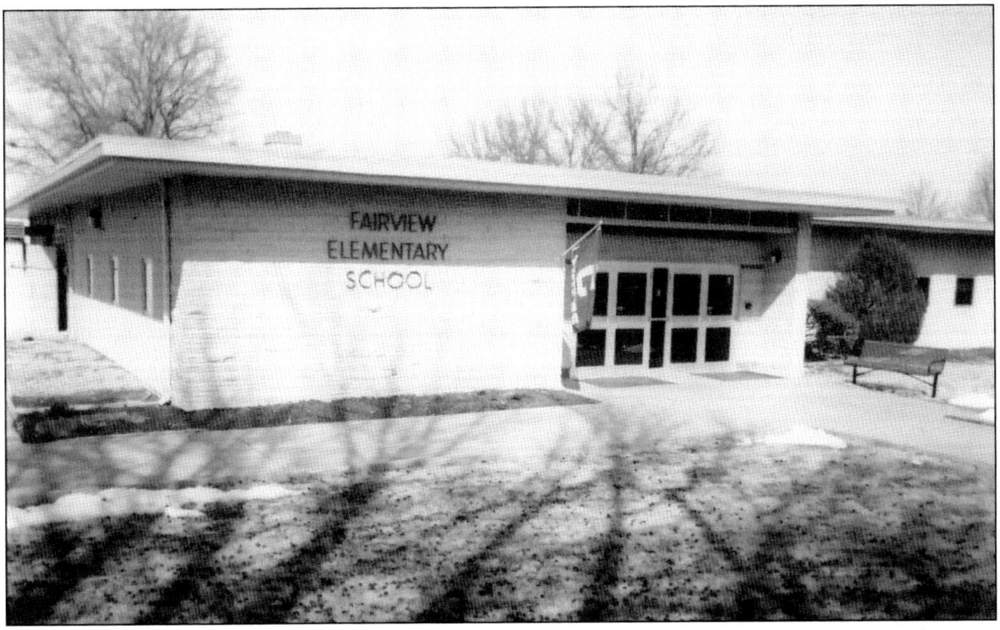

Fairview Elementary School, 1201 East Fairview Avenue. Built in 1967–1968 by M-P Construction with Central Woodworking providing the millwork, Fairview served the growing population of the southern part of town with guidance from principal Ralph Whitten. When opened in March 1968, the entire school system had an operating budget of almost $2 million with 160 administrators and teachers, along with 91 support staff.

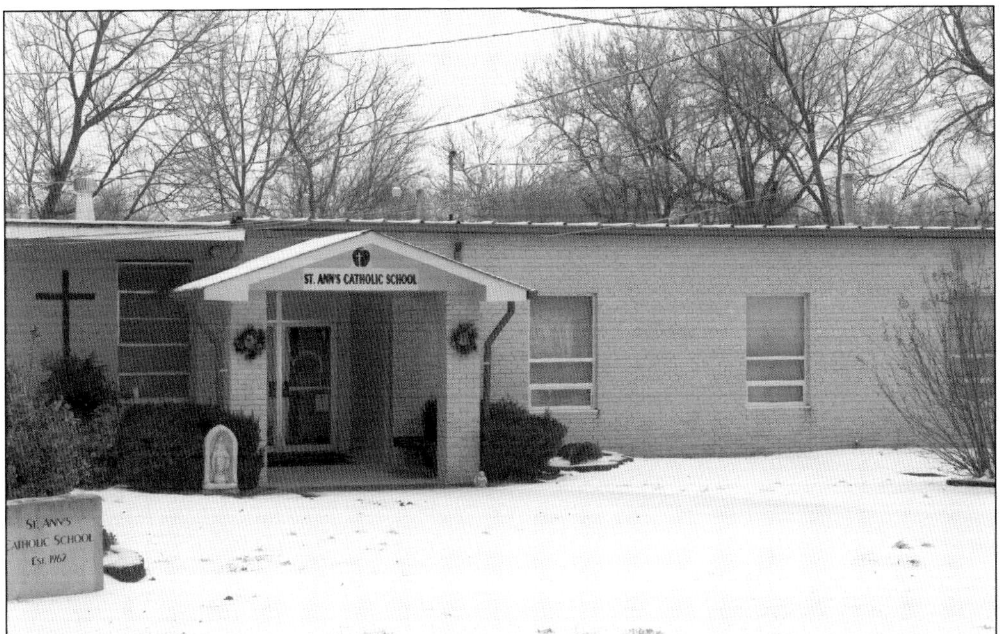

St. Ann's Catholic School, 314 East Budlong Street. St. Ann's Catholic School opened in 1962 after being designed by Robert Braeckel of Joplin, Missouri, and constructed by Lee Hodkin of Carthage. Until 1971, Sisters of the Most Precious Blood of O'Fallon, Missouri, served as teachers. (Photograph by Koral Martin.)

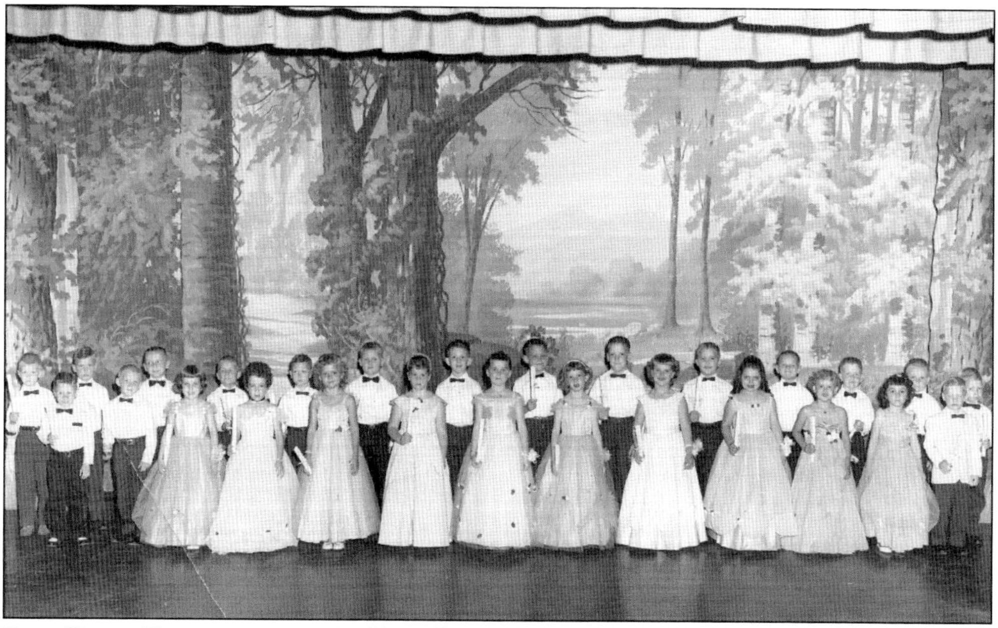

Rosa-Paula Kindergarten, 129 East Third Street. Several kindergartens not associated with the local school system operated in Carthage from the 1940s to mid-1960s, including one operated by sisters Rosine and Pauline Stanley. Those attending in 1959–1960 are presented at their graduation ceremony held at Eugene Field School in this photograph by Carl Taylor. (Courtesy of Teresa Babcock Henry.)

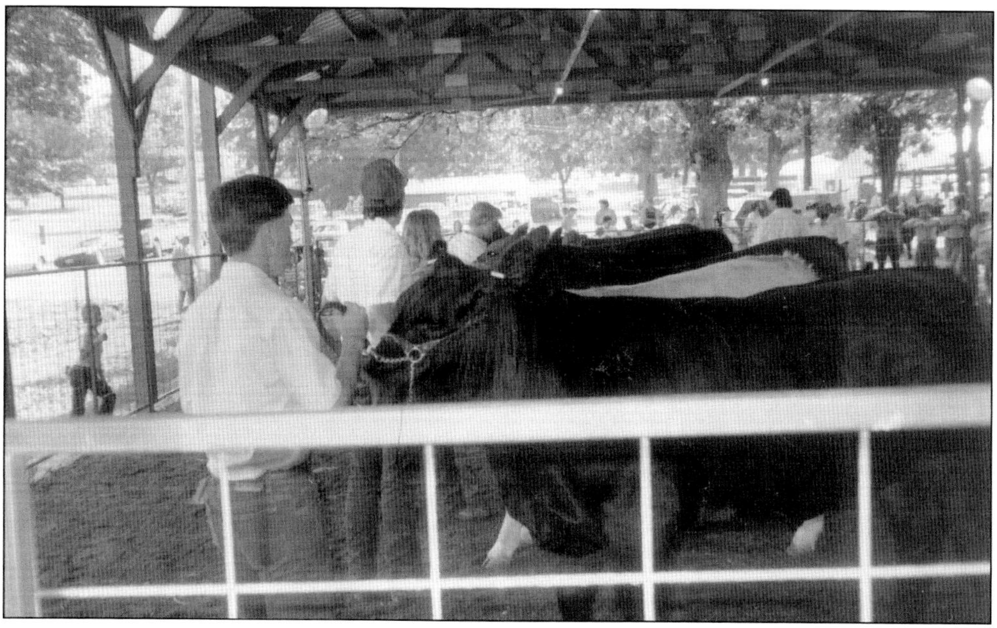

Jasper County 4-H Youth Fairgrounds, Municipal Park. Working with the Jasper County Extension, 4-H clubs throughout the area have provided wonderful educational opportunities for many years. Chief among those events is the Youth Fair held in July. Stock exhibits, as seen in this late-1980s photograph, are among the most popular features of the fair. (Courtesy of Lora Honey Phelps.)

4-H AND FUTURE FARMERS OF AMERICA ANNUAL DINNER. In the 1960s, Future Farmers of America (FFA) and 4-H honored several former residents who had gone onto careers of note away from Carthage. Dr. Harlow Shapley (1885–1972) was one such honoree for his work as an astronomer and author. He attended Carthage Collegiate Institute in 1905 and 1906 to shore up his education before attending the University of Missouri.

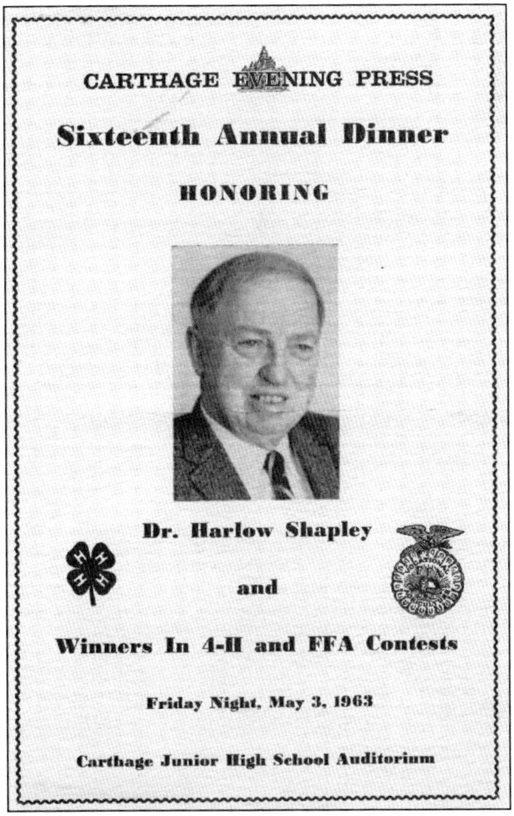
CARTHAGE EVENING PRESS

Sixteenth Annual Dinner

HONORING

Dr. Harlow Shapley

and

Winners In 4-H and FFA Contests

Friday Night, May 3, 1963

Carthage Junior High School Auditorium

FFA BARNWARMING DANCE. The Future Farmers of America hold an annual dance, a tradition since the 1940s, at Carthage High School. Pictured is a dance from the late 1980s. The dance helps to raise money for educational projects. The two members of Future Farmers of America who sell the most tickets become King and Queen of the Barnwarming Dance. (Courtesy of Lora Honey Phelps.)

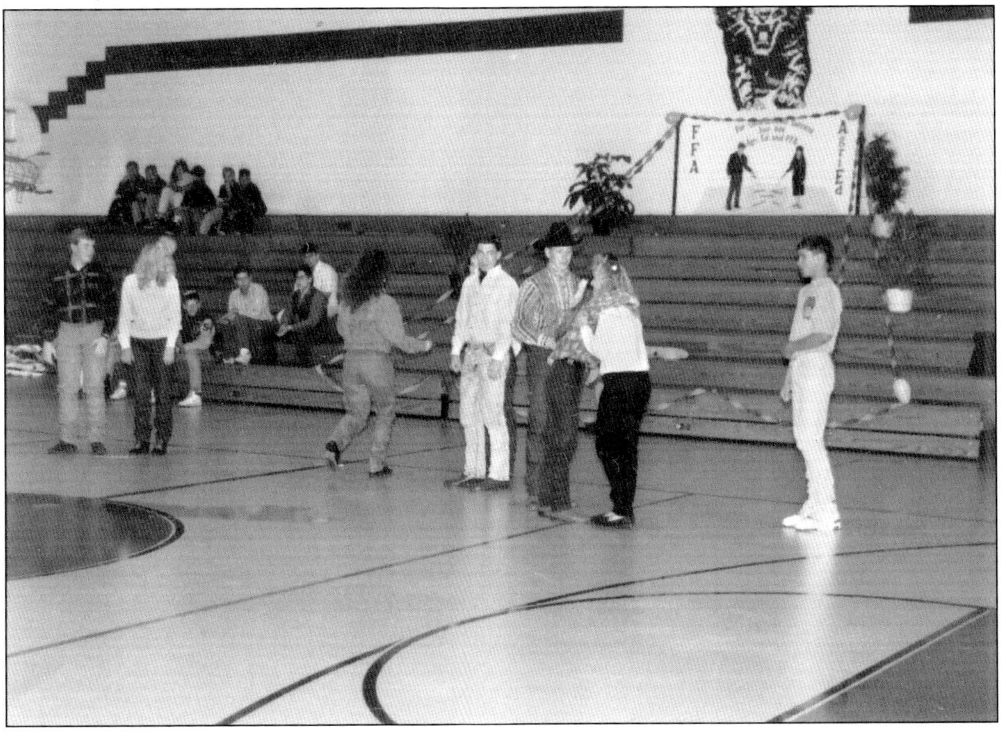

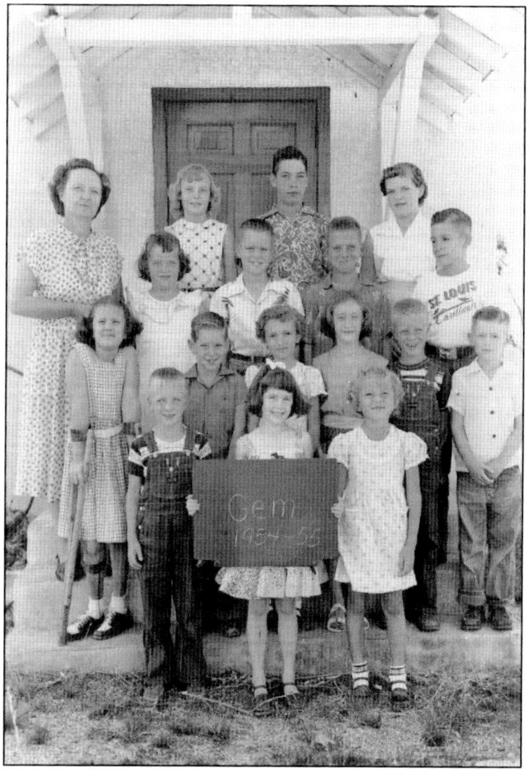

GEM SCHOOL, SOUTHEAST OF CARTHAGE. This rural school included the following students in 1954: (first row) Walter Wicklund, Linda Moss, and Alice Filarski; (second row) Alyce Moss, Eugene Aubry, Linda Filarski, Bobby Brown, Grieb Wicklund, and Gale Turner; (third row) Gayme Hopkins, Richard Moss, Ronnie Boswell, and Larry Turner; (fourth row) teacher Twyla Arnett, Janice Boswell, Billy Bowman, and Shirley Block.

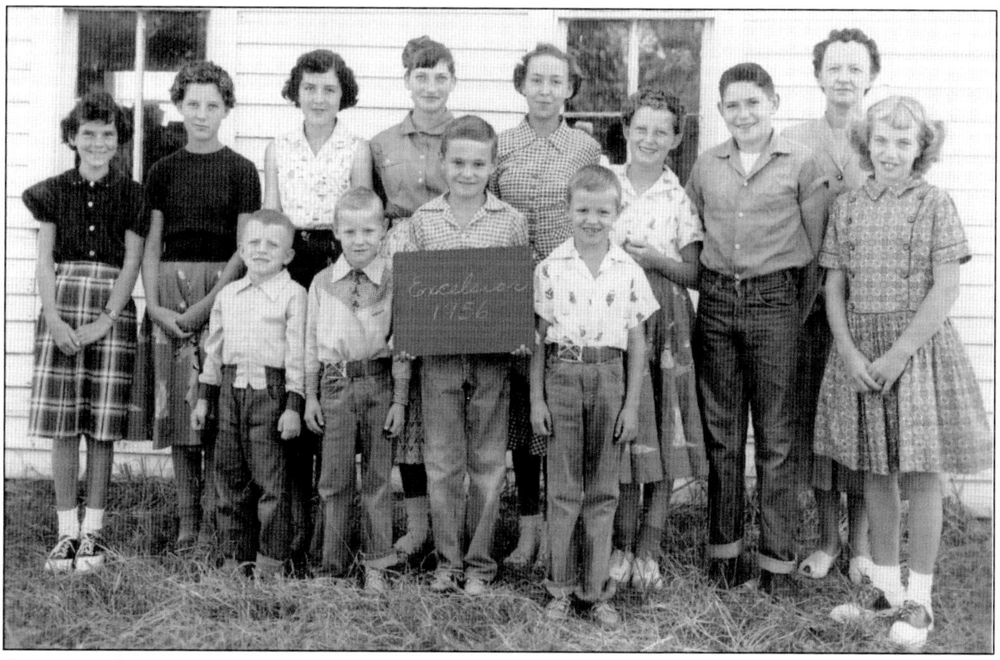

EXCELSIOR SCHOOL, SOUTHEAST OF CARTHAGE. The following students attended Excelsior School in 1956: (first row) Bruce Vantrease (visitor), Perry Smith, Mike Smith, and Steven Smith; (second row) Charlotte Howard, Linda Meyer, Barbara Howard, Della Southard, Judy Ann Long, Brenda Fay Meyer, Carl Goodnight, teacher Twyla Arnett, and Linda Sue Spoor.

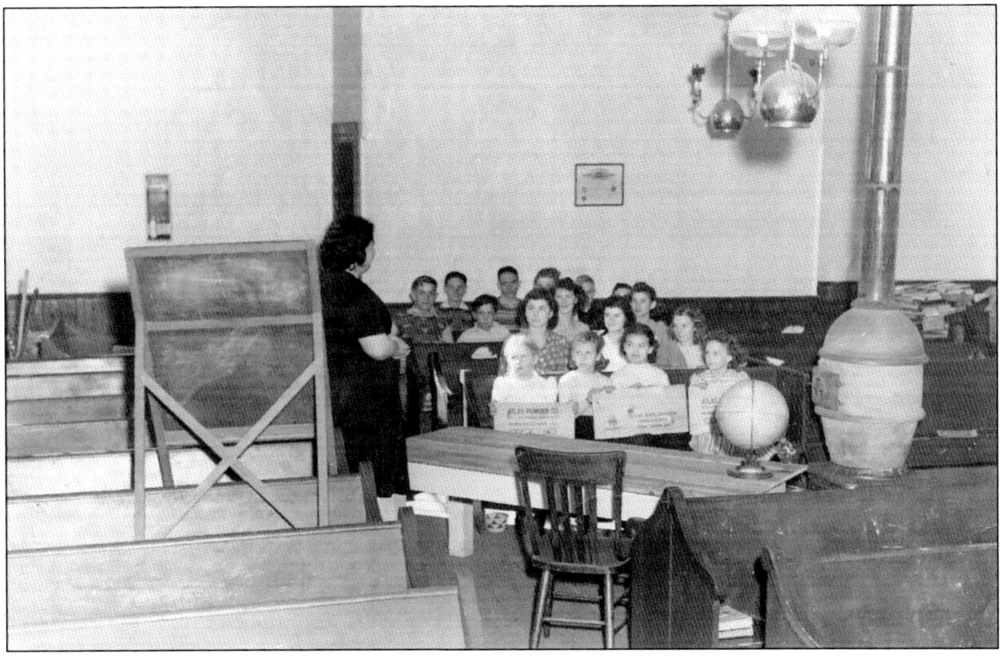

CHARTER OAK SCHOOL AT MADISON CHURCH, NORTHEAST OF CARTHAGE. An unidentified teacher is pictured with her students in 1943. They are in a nearby church, since fire had damaged their school. Note the Atlas Powder crate panels being used by the girls in the front pew; the crates were probably used as a writing surface. (Courtesy of Lena Swoveland.)

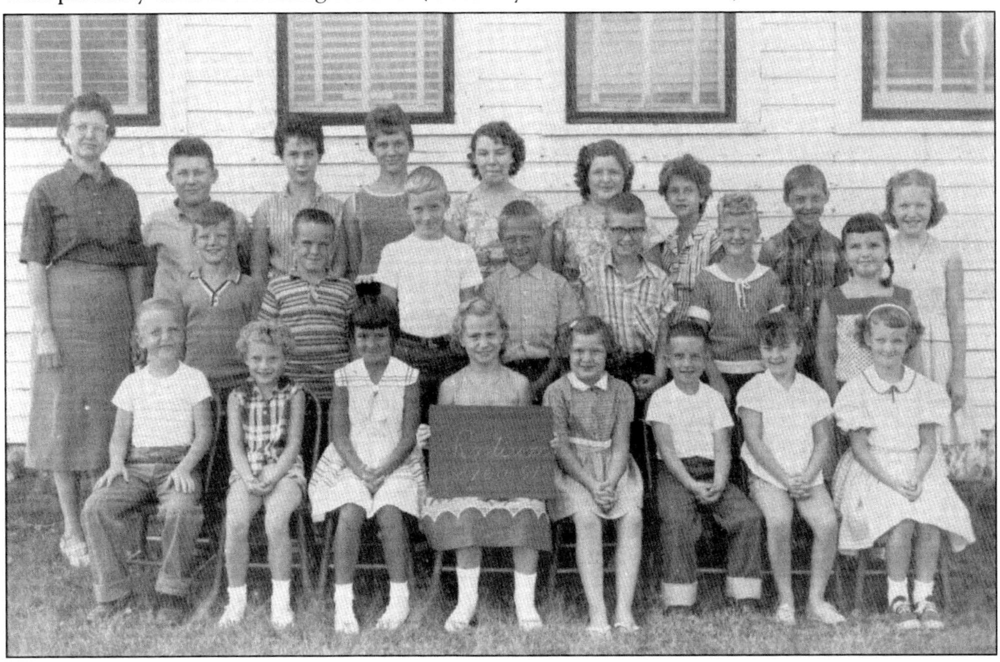

RADIUM SCHOOL, US HIGHWAY 66 EAST. Pictured are Miss Luellen and her 23 enrolled students, including four eighth-grade graduates in 1961. The old schoolhouse is still visible (near County Lane 118) but has been altered. This school, as well as other rural schools surrounding Carthage, was consolidated into the school system in the 1960s. (Courtesy of Wade Utter.)

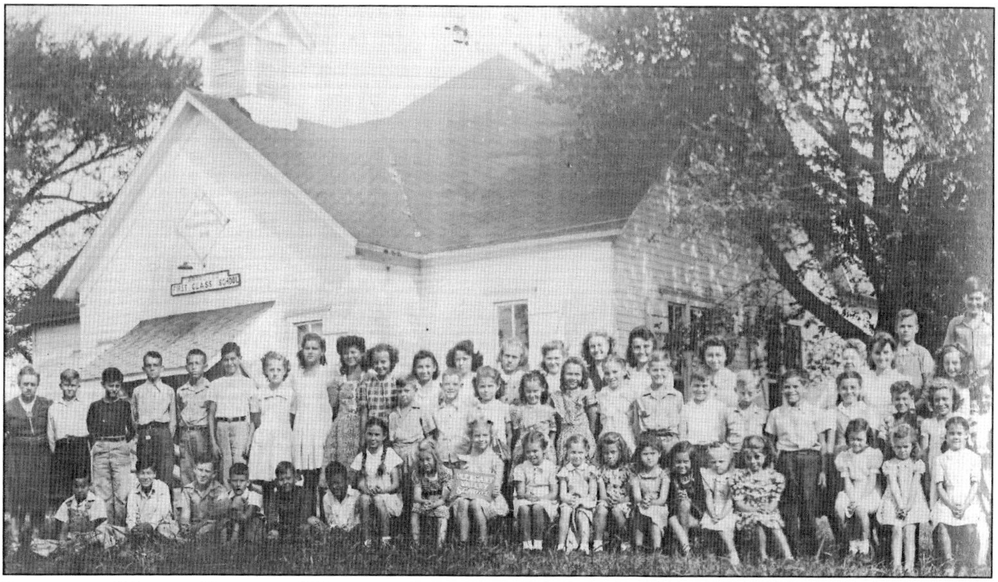

Pleasant Valley School, West of Carthage. Pleasant Valley was one of the largest rural schools in the area. A third of its pupils is visible in this detail from a larger 1945 photograph. Principal Inez Rogers is on the left. Pleasant Valley and High Point Schools were consolidated into a new building in 1958 that is still used today in the Brooklyn Heights area. (Courtesy of Lee Haggard.)

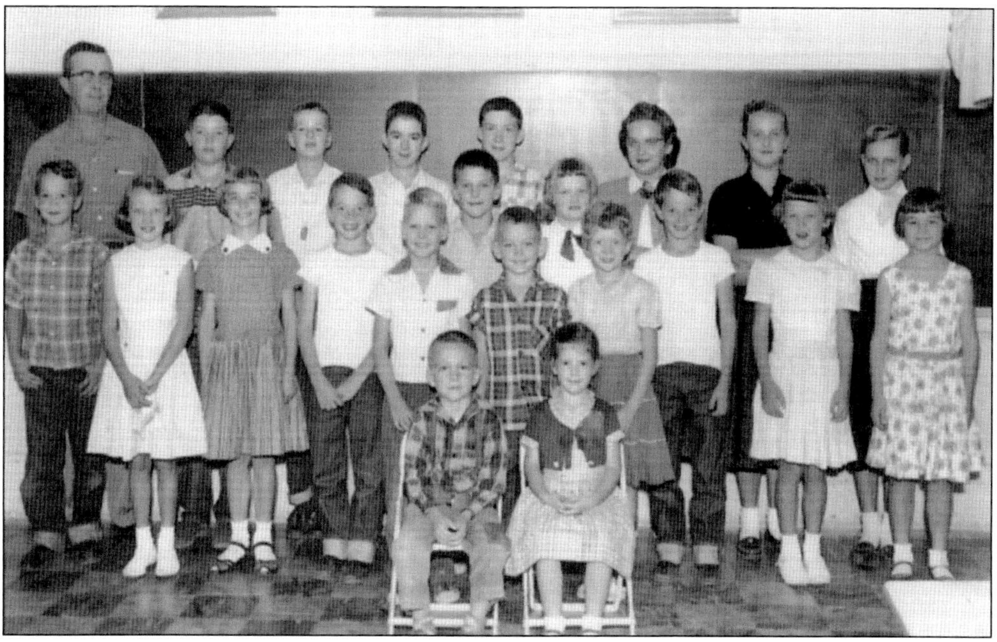

Berean School, US Highway 71, South of Carthage. In 1959–1960, Dwight Harris taught at Berean, one of four rural schools due south of Carthage. His students, pictured, were (first row) Ray Shull and Linda White; (second row) David Smith, Dixie Anderson, Emily Jones, Bruce Jacobs, Charles Krummel, Tom Krummel, Koy Ackerman, Sheryl Anderson, Mary Shull, Brian Jacobs, Sue Anderson, and Mary Jane Jones; (third row) Ted Jacobs, Allen Fisher, Don Davis, Lavanis Spry, Sue Jacobs, Sally Ukena, and Sharon Ukena. (Courtesy of Dixie Anderson Vacca.)

Five

WORSHIP

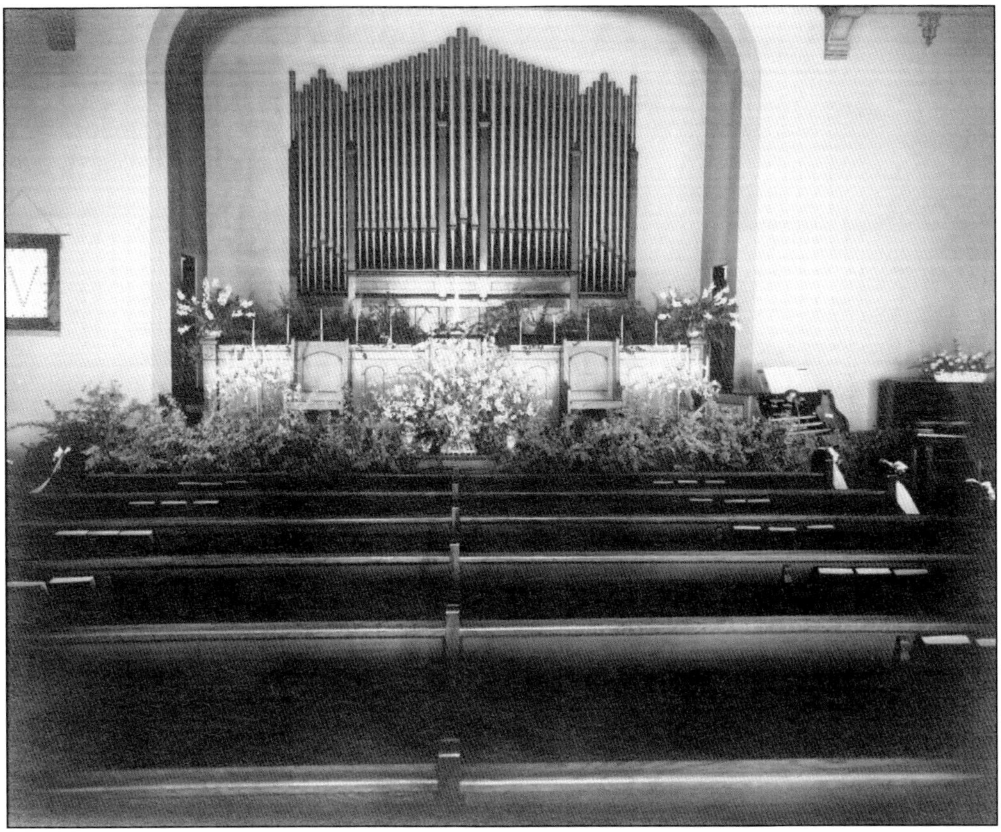

FIRST PRESBYTERIAN CHURCH, 115 WEST CHESTNUT STREET. The sanctuary of this church, built 1916–1917, is decorated for the 1943 wedding of Marian Louisa Powers. Note the "V for Victory" banner on the left side. These banners hung in homes, stores, and churches across town during World War II. In 1924, the pipe organ was installed by the Women's Society at the cost of $10,000.

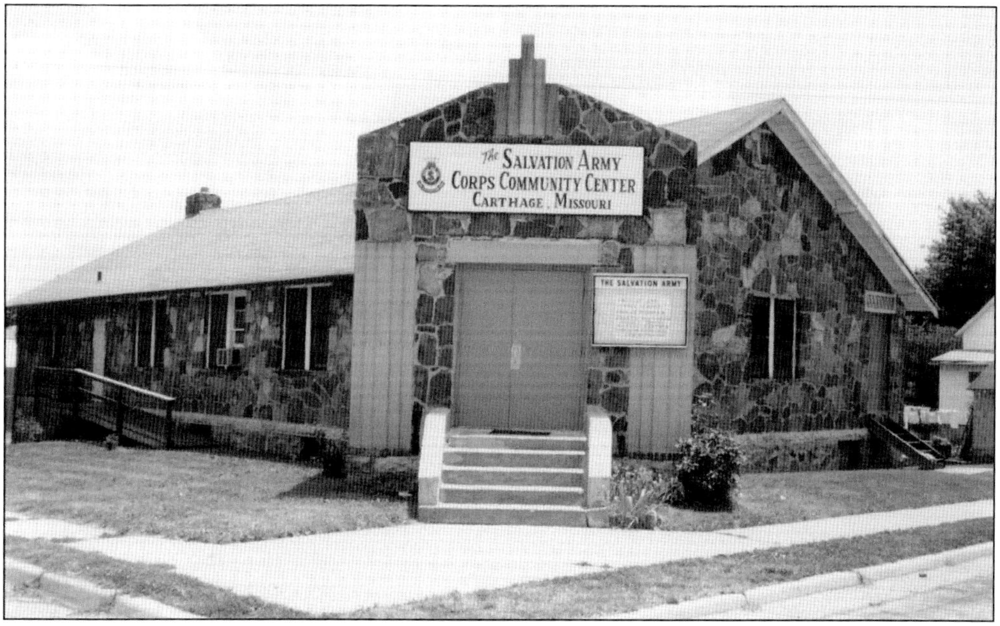

SALVATION ARMY CITADEL, 502 FULTON STREET. The Salvation Army has been serving the community for many years. Constructed of fieldstone, this building served as headquarters for the Salvation Army until 2000, when the organization moved to the former Fairview Christian Church building. Today, this structure houses the Iglesia Cristiana Hispano-Americana.

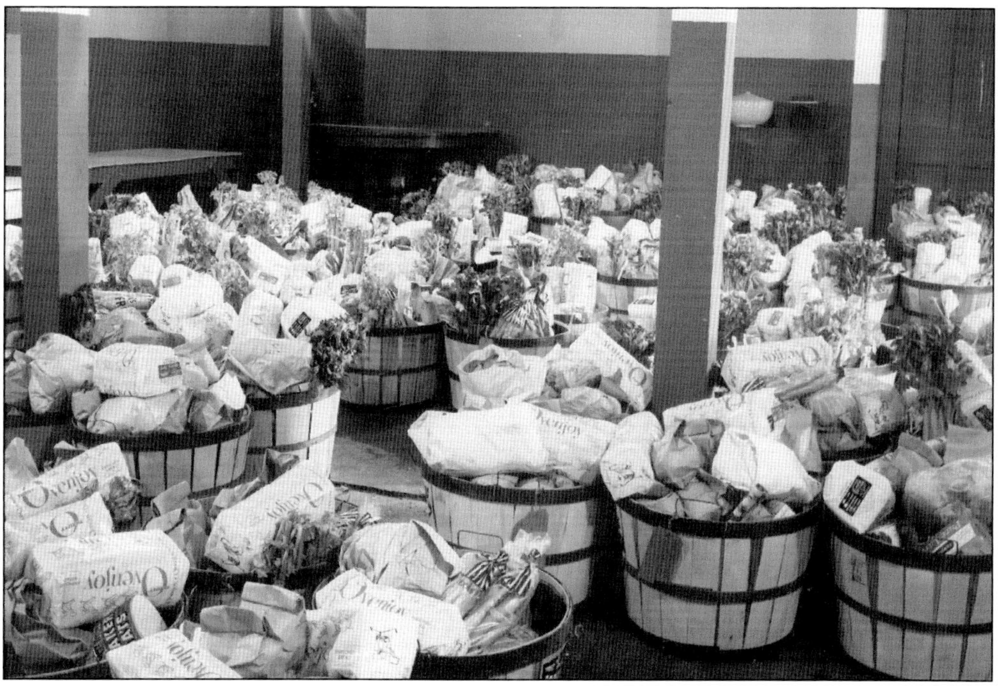

SALVATION ARMY CHRISTMAS BASKETS. Carthage Soroptimists, Rotarians, and Jaycees made the 1956 Salvation Army's annual children's Christmas party possible. Carl Taylor photographed the 200 baskets of foodstuffs that were packed by Soroptimists and stored in the basement of the citadel; these baskets were given to local families at Christmastime.

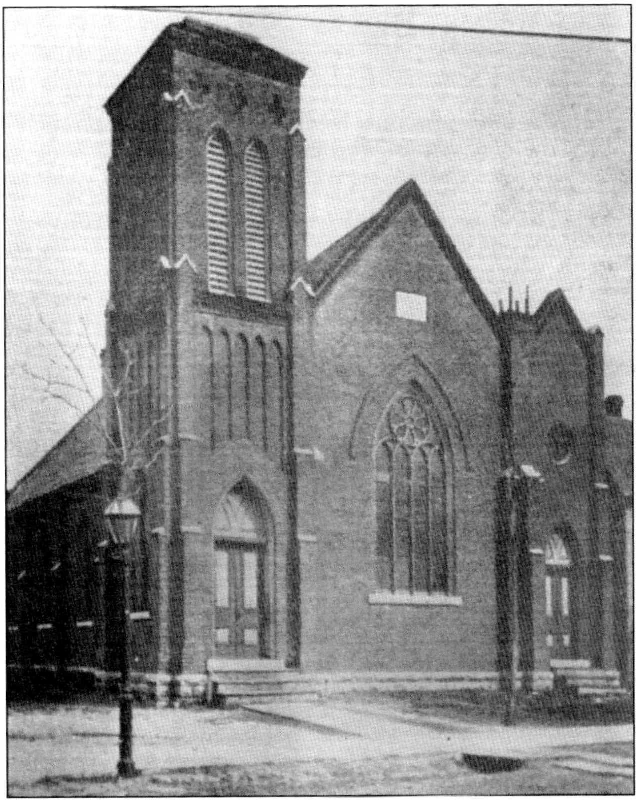

FAITH LUTHERAN CHURCH, 800 HOWARD AVENUE. Moving into the former Methodist Church (South) building in the early 1940s, Carthage's Lutheran congregation worshiped in this 1881 structure until the mid-1960s, when they began to construct a new church home (see below). Once Faith Lutheran Church moved, Grace Episcopal Church acquired the property and expanded its facilities.

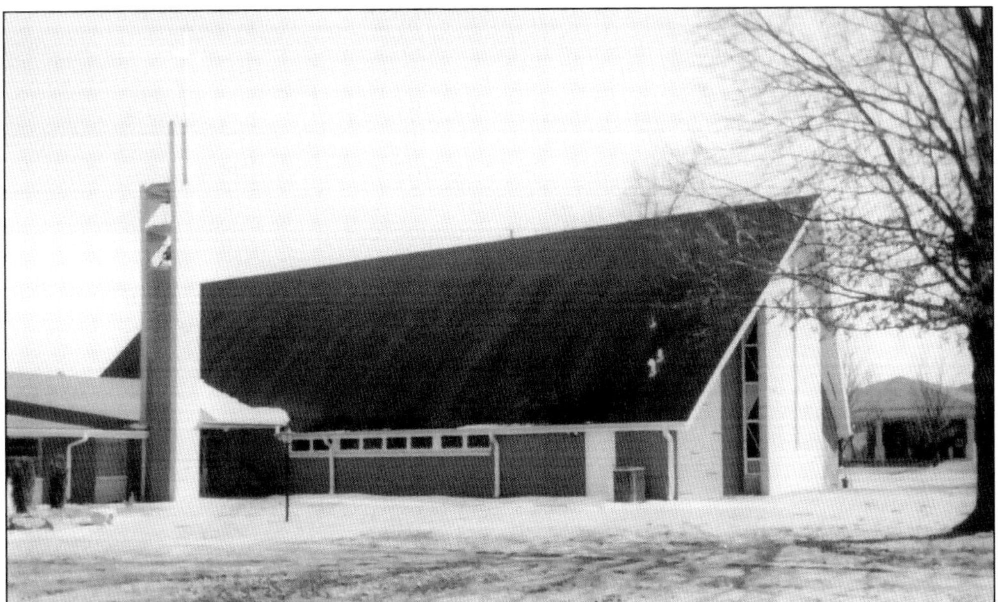

FAITH LUTHERAN CHURCH, 2134 GRAND AVENUE. In the fall of 1966, Rev. August Jarus broke ground for a new church built south of town by Homer Carr Construction Company. The church cost $122,000 and was completed a year later. During construction, the ladies aid society's collected trading stamps for kitchen equipment to be used in the new fellowship hall.

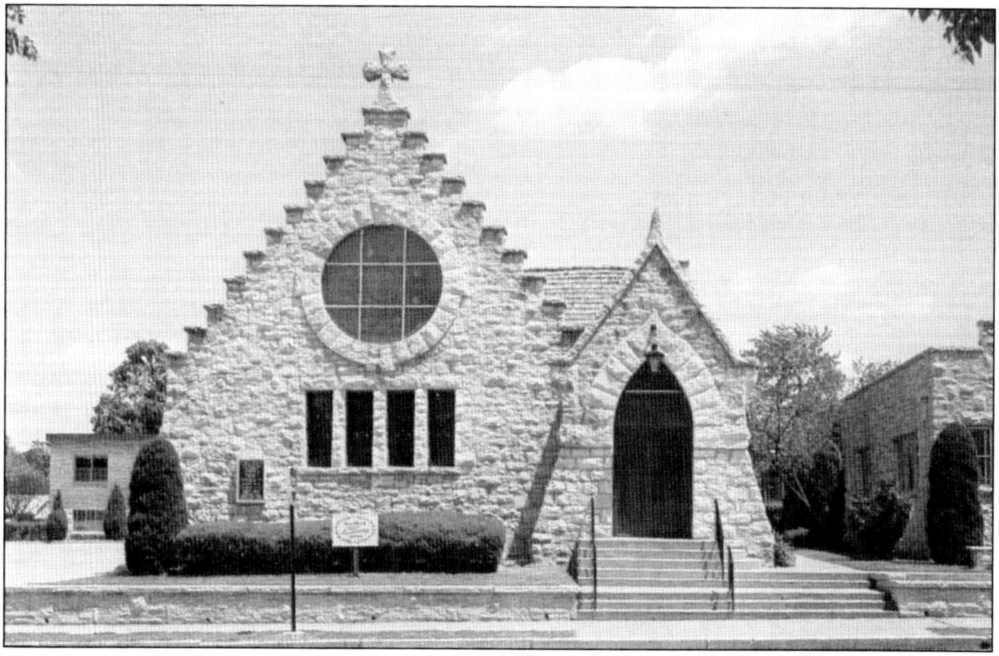

GRACE EPISCOPAL CHURCH, 820 HOWARD AVENUE. Located in one of the first buildings constructed entirely of Carthage limestone, the church, erected in 1889, is the oldest such structure in town still being used for worship. Additions to the parish house, sanctuary, and educational wing have taken place every decade from 1940 to 1990. Grace celebrated its centennial in 1969 when this postcard was made. The rector was Rev. Canon Vincent C. Root.

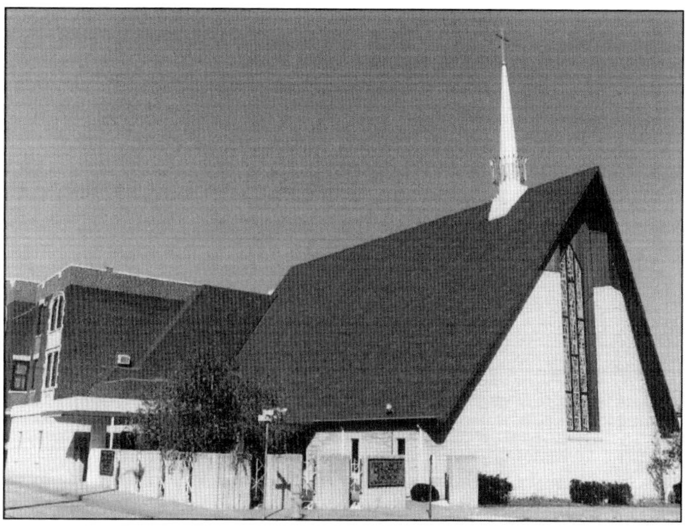

FIRST UNITED METHODIST CHURCH, 617 SOUTH MAIN STREET. The historic sanctuary of this church (built in 1888–1889) was destroyed by fire in 1973. It was replaced with this modern edifice designed by Paul Rich of Springfield, Missouri, and built by M-P Construction Company of Carthage. The exterior features Carthage limestone, and the dedication of the new sanctuary in 1974 was led by Rev. H.L. Thompson.

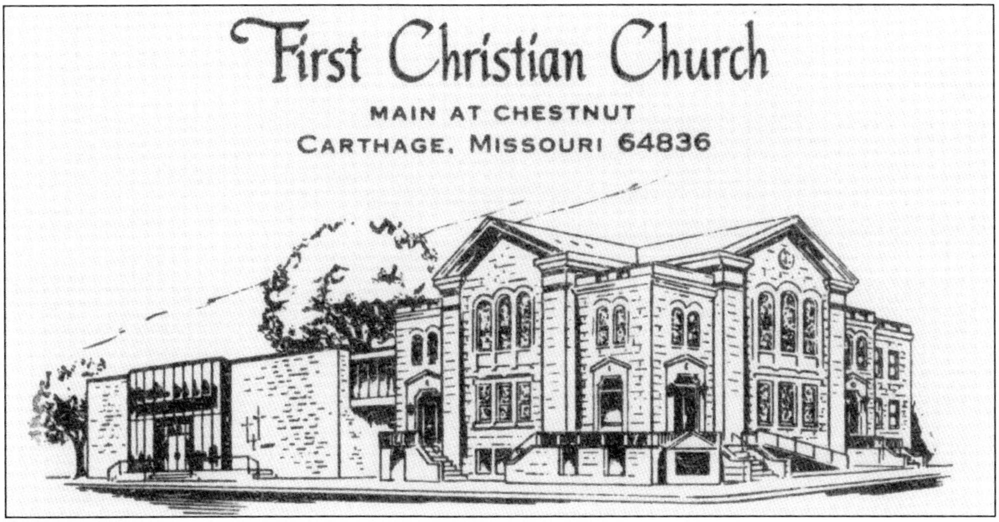

FIRST CHRISTIAN CHURCH AND EDUCATIONAL BUILDING, 800 SOUTH MAIN STREET. In the late 1950s and 1960s, congregations in older churches near downtown began to outgrow their buildings. First Christian Church, originally built in 1909–1910, expanded to the east with their educational building in 1975 under the leadership of Pastor Robert A. Lyttle.

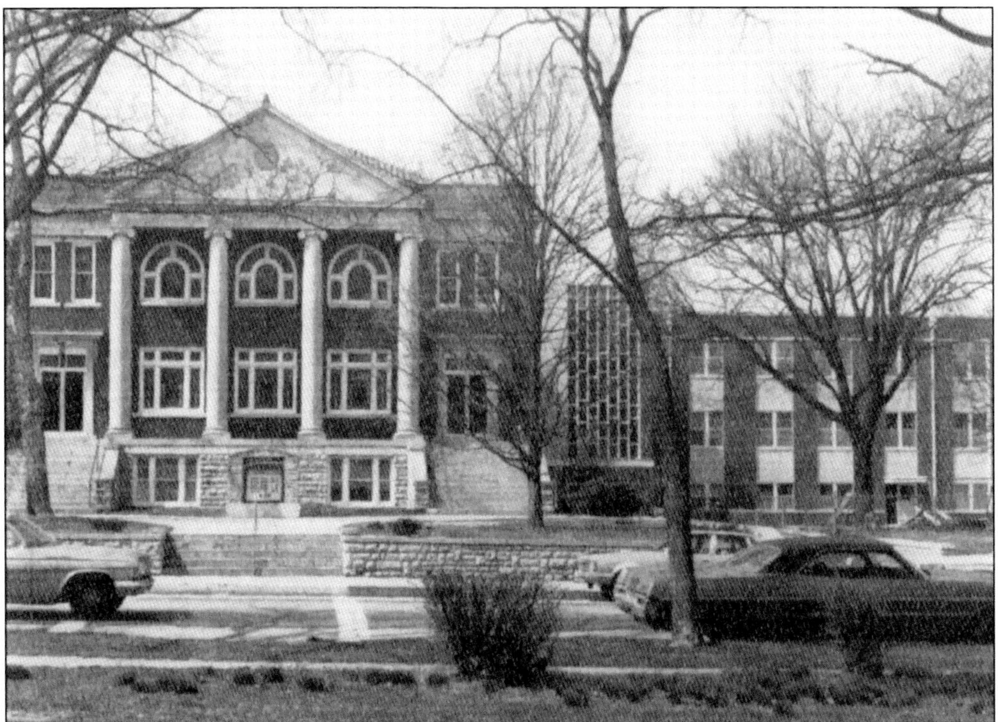

FIRST BAPTIST CHURCH AND EDUCATIONAL BUILDING, 631 SOUTH GARRISON AVENUE. Ralph Howard and the church building committee planned for eight years to construct an educational wing. Among the contractors and suppliers were Homer Carr Construction, Nelson Roofing, Hesser Electric, Steward Sheet Metal, Calhoon Lumber, and Ward & Phillips Furniture. Dr. Merle Mitchell presided over the dedication in 1960. (Courtesy of First Baptist Church.)

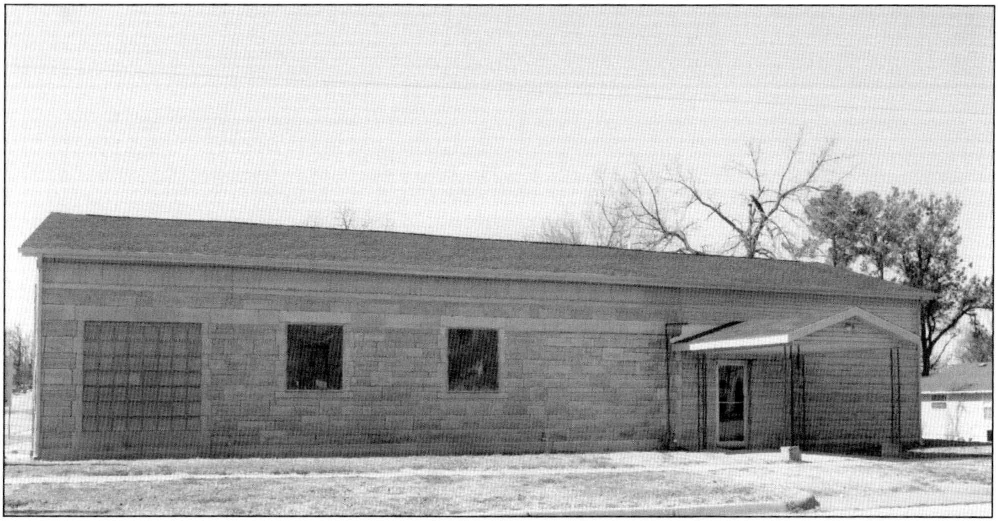

Former Kingdom Hall of Jehovah's Witnesses, 803 West Chestnut Street. Established in a building constructed to house the Grauberger Monument Company and built of Carthage limestone, this structure became home to Jehovah's Witnesses in 1956. The building was used until a new Kingdom Hall was built east of Carthage in 1984. Now the building serves the Landmark Missionary Baptist Church. (Courtesy of Nancy Brewer.)

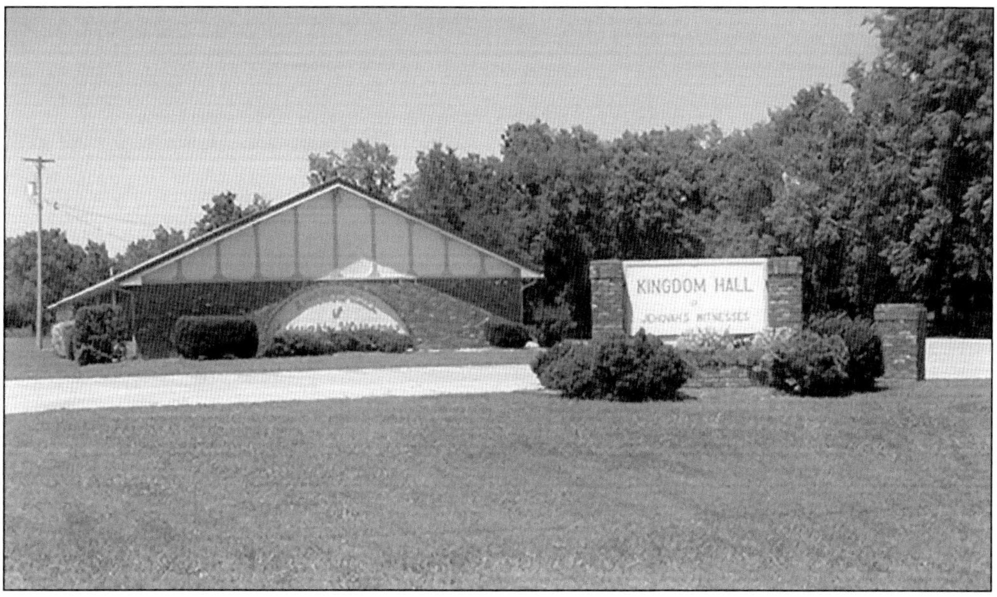

Former Kingdom Hall of Jehovah's Witnesses, Highway 96, East of Carthage. Constructed entirely by Jehovah's Witnesses craftsmen and helpers, this building was erected in three days, starting on a Thursday. It was completed in time for a Watchtower study and public talk held Sunday. Coy Garrison ordered all the building materials from the TAPJAC store. The Kingdom Hall was replaced by a new structure on 1608 Robert Ellis Young Drive in 2009. (Courtesy of Nancy Brewer.)

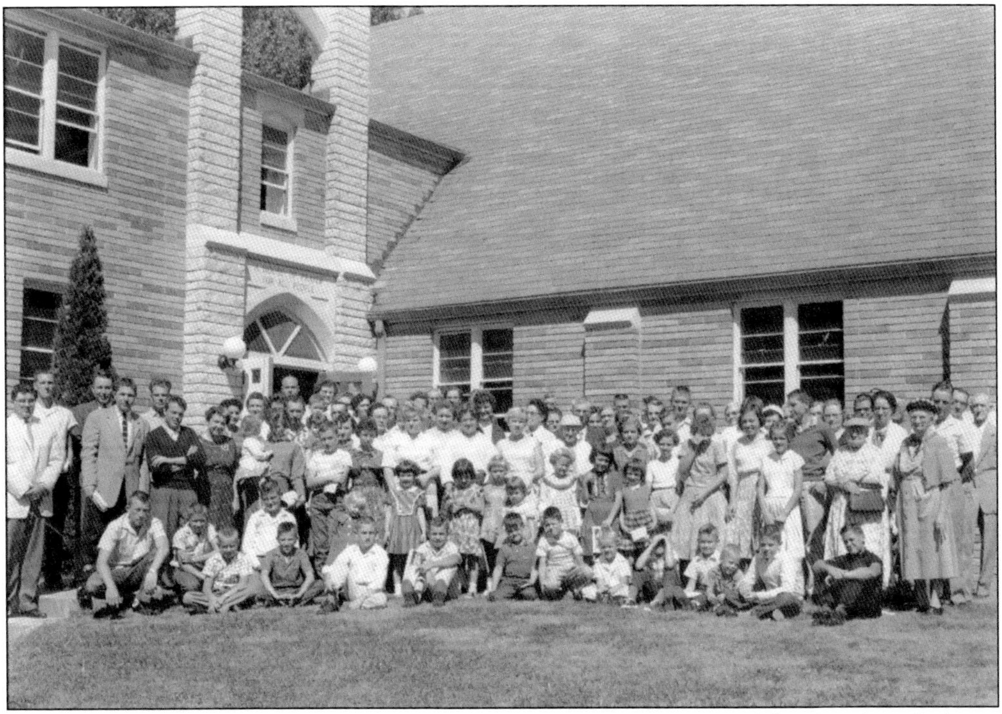

GRAND AVENUE CHURCH OF GOD, 1185 GRAND AVENUE. Construction of this church took almost two years (1952–1954). Much of the labor and material was donated, so the congregation paid only $32,500 for construction and furnishings. Rev. L.G. Hardesty was the first pastor and lived next door in the parsonage at 1175 Grand Avenue. (Courtesy of Grand Avenue Church of God.)

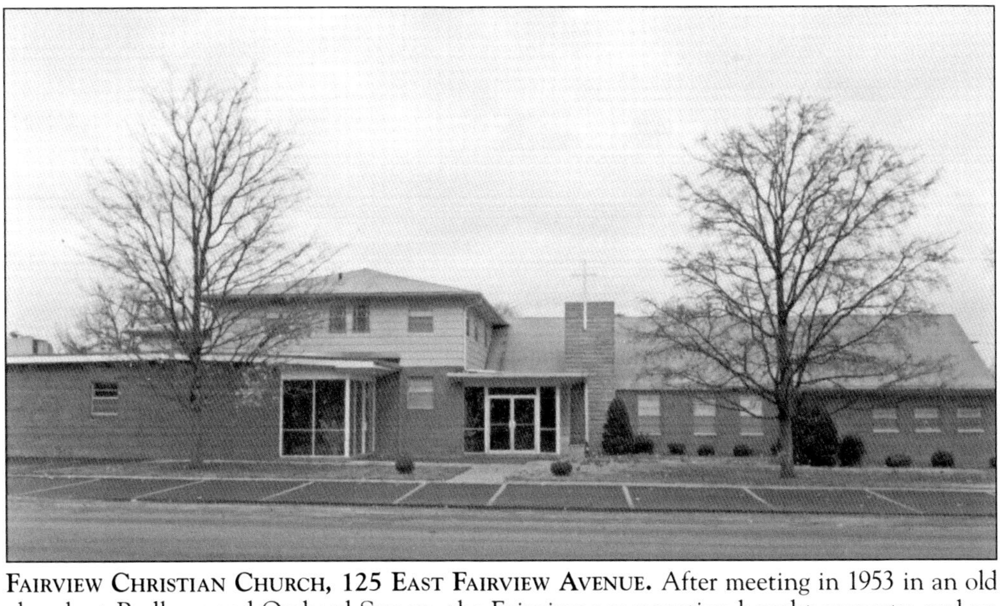

FAIRVIEW CHRISTIAN CHURCH, 125 EAST FAIRVIEW AVENUE. After meeting in 1953 in an old church at Budlong and Orchard Streets, the Fairview congregation bought property, and an educational building was built in 1957. An auditorium followed in 1959, and numerous additions were made through the years until the congregation remodeled the former Walmart building at Grand Avenue and Airport Drive in 2000. (Courtesy of Fairview Christian Church.)

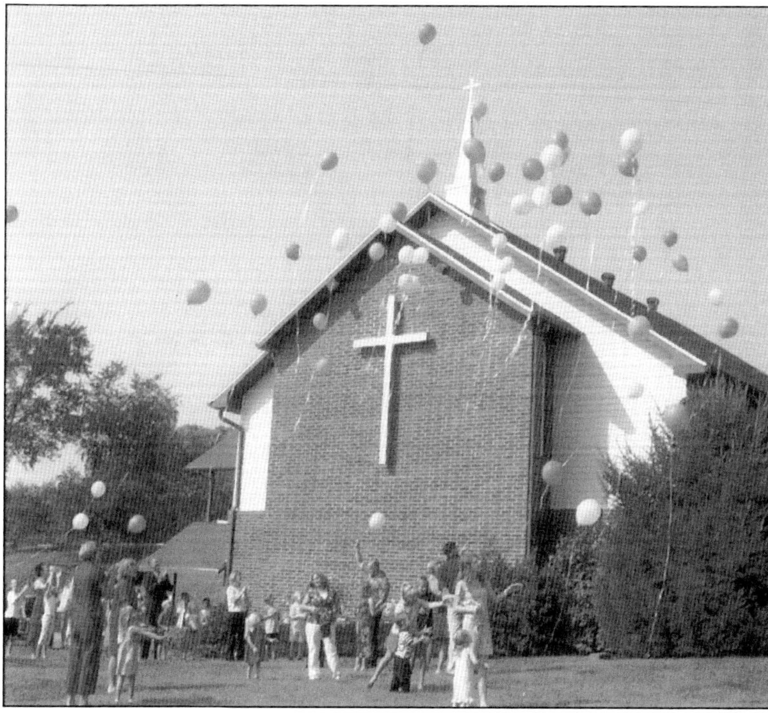

Good Shepherd Lutheran Church, Highway 96, West of Carthage. This congregation organized in 1987 and, for several years, held its services in a trailer on-site. A building was constructed by the Lutheran organization Laborers for Christ and was dedicated in early 1996. (Courtesy of Good Shepherd Lutheran Church.)

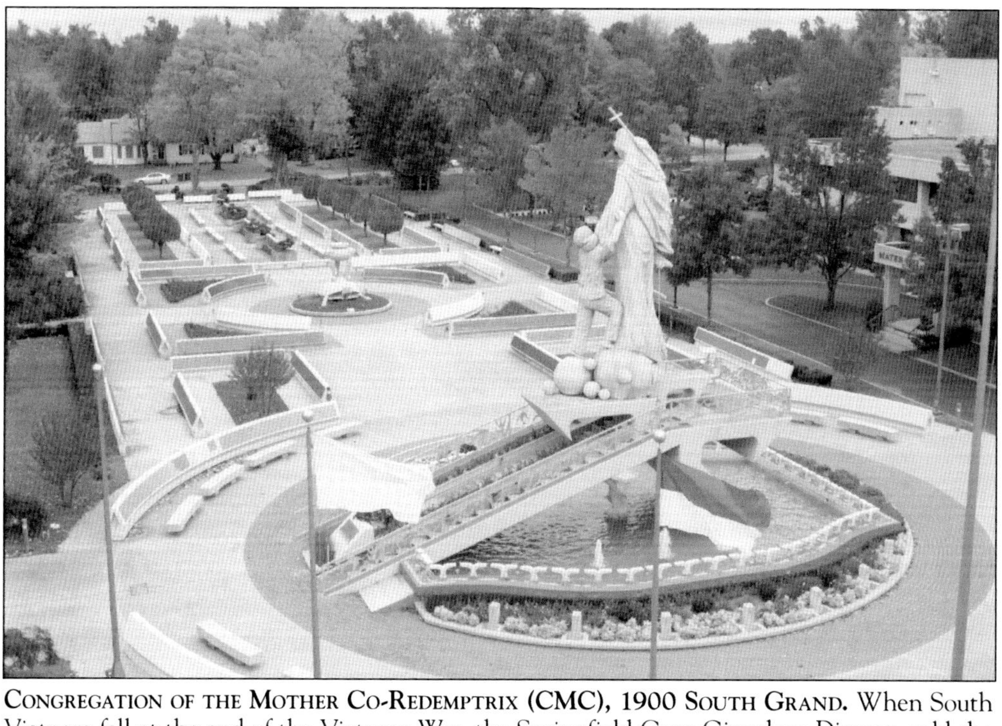

Congregation of the Mother Co-Redemptrix (CMC), 1900 South Grand. When South Vietnam fell at the end of the Vietnam War, the Springfield-Cape Girardeau Diocese, sold the former Our Lady of the Ozarks property to this Catholic order of priests and brothers. Looking west from the roof of the main administration building, this view includes the Immaculate Heart of Mary Shrine and the Holy Vietnamese Martyrs Pastoral Center and Auditorium.

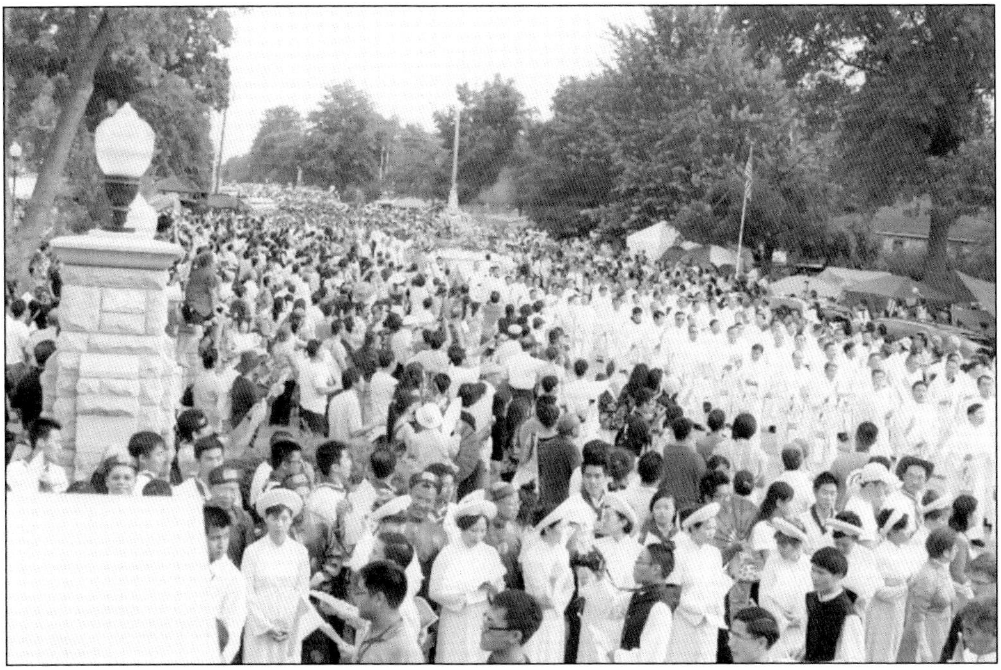

Marian Days at CMC. Beginning in 1978, CMC began sponsoring an annual pilgrimage to their campus that has turned into a spiritual celebration and reunion for tens of thousands of Vietnamese American Catholics who attend. The highlight of the event is the Saturday processional through the residential blocks adjacent to the campus prior to an open-air Mass in front of the main building.

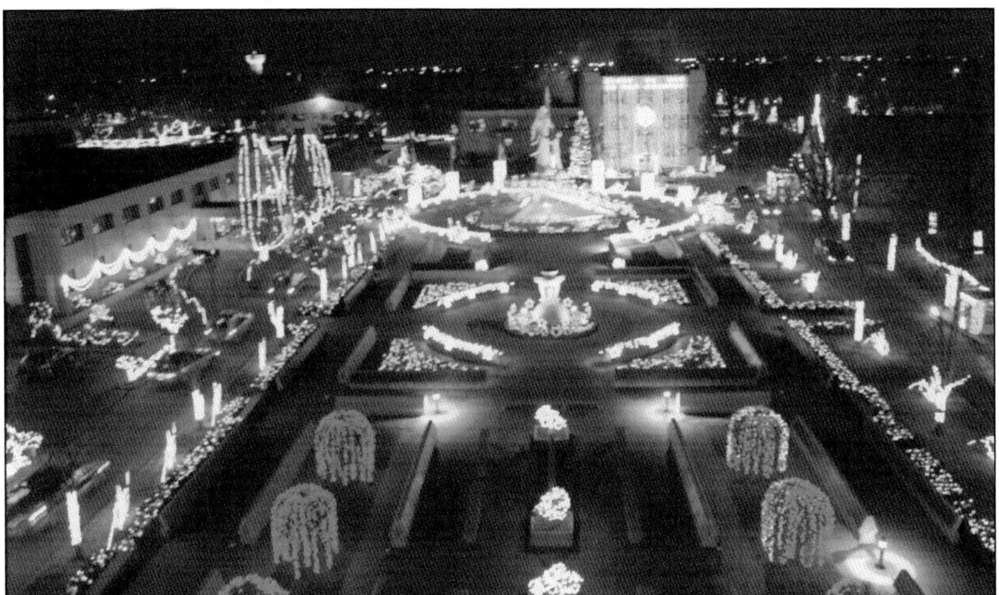

Way of Salvation Display at CMC. What started as a small light display in 1984 as a thank-you from CMC to the residents of Carthage grew into a larger collection of lighted scenes from the Bible in 1985 titled "Sins and Salvation." Renamed "Way of Salvation," this Christmas holiday tradition continues with the hard work of the CMC community and donations from display visitors.

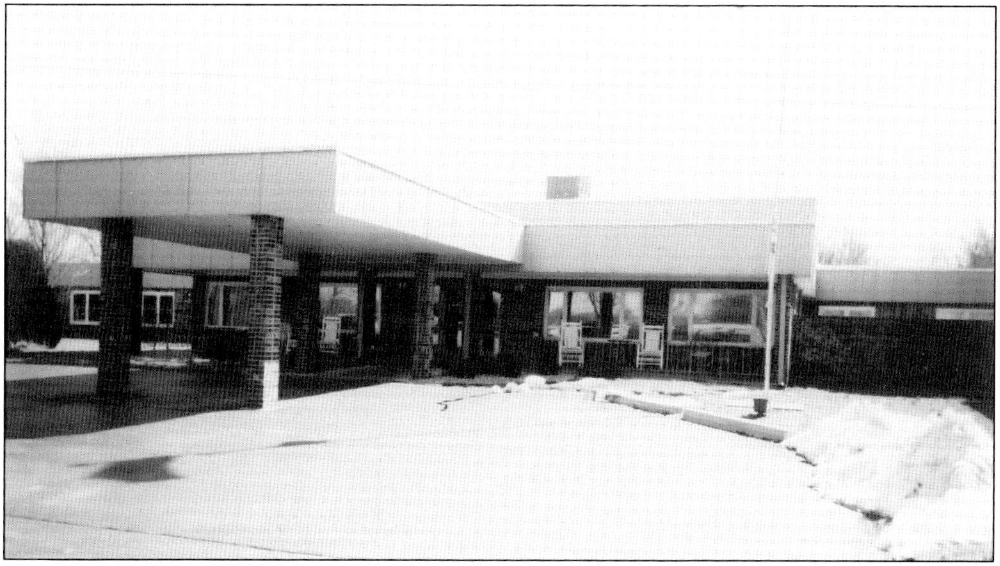

St. Luke's Nursing Center, 1220 West Fairview Avenue. Opened in 1972, the impetus for St. Luke's came from the Western Missouri Diocese of the Episcopal Church. It has expanded many times on the original property donated by Elizabeth Phelps. Among those on the original board were Lt. Col. Edward Buster, Dr. Foster Whitten, Laurence Flanigan, Robert Humber, Ted Evans, Kermit Cordonnier, and Clayton Smith.

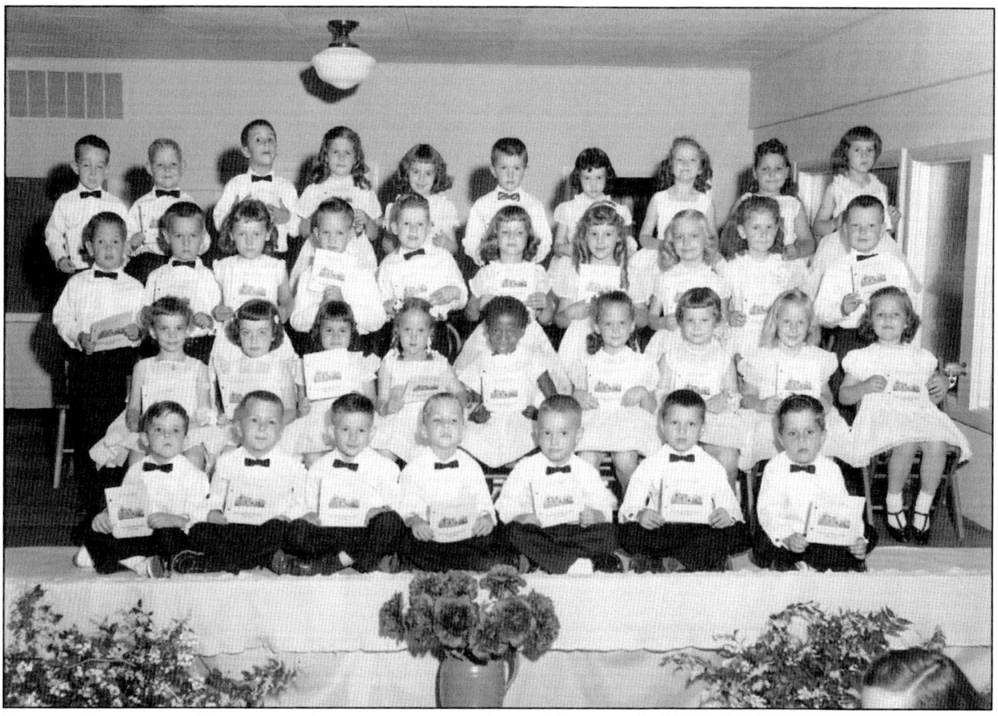

Grace Episcopal Church Kindergarten. Grace Episcopal Church also sponsored a parish day school for kindergarten pupils from the late 1950s to the 1960s. Talitha "Tillie" Wallace ran it. Pictured are the 1958–1959 morning and afternoon kindergarten classes at their graduation ceremony. (Courtesy of Donna Evans.)

Six

Leisure Time and Community Events

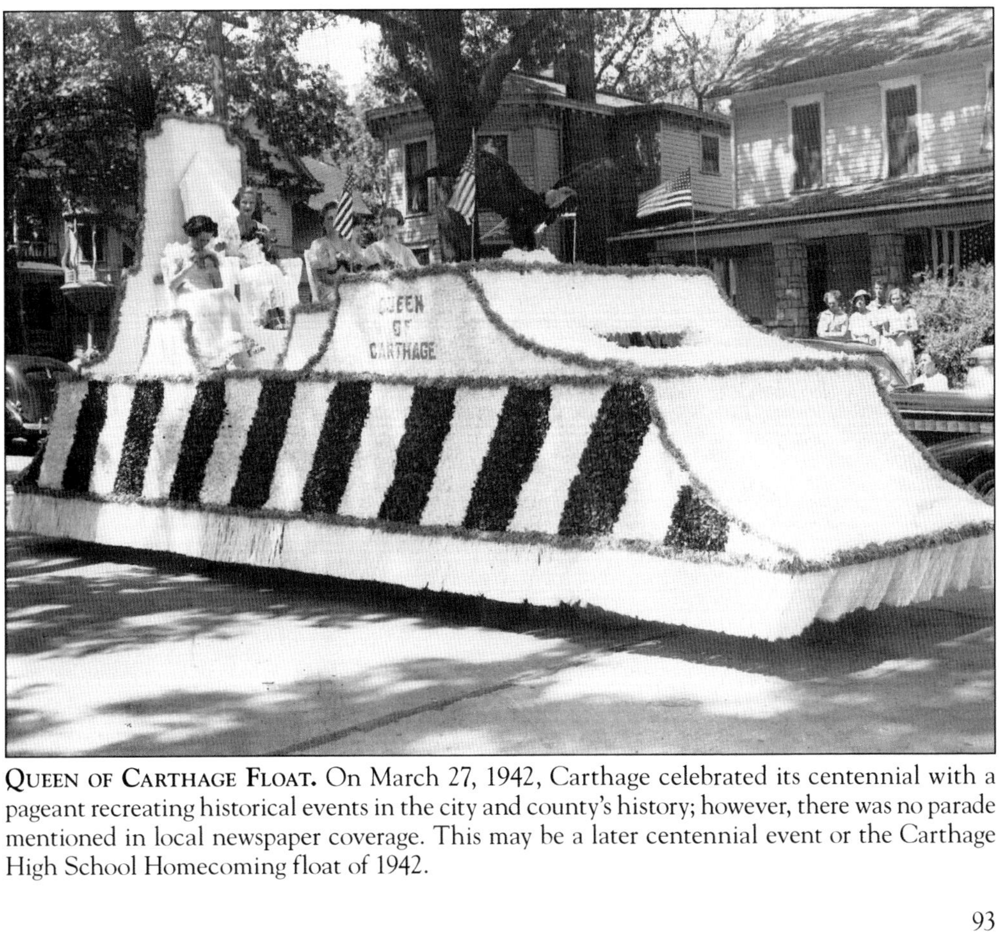

Queen of Carthage Float. On March 27, 1942, Carthage celebrated its centennial with a pageant recreating historical events in the city and county's history; however, there was no parade mentioned in local newspaper coverage. This may be a later centennial event or the Carthage High School Homecoming float of 1942.

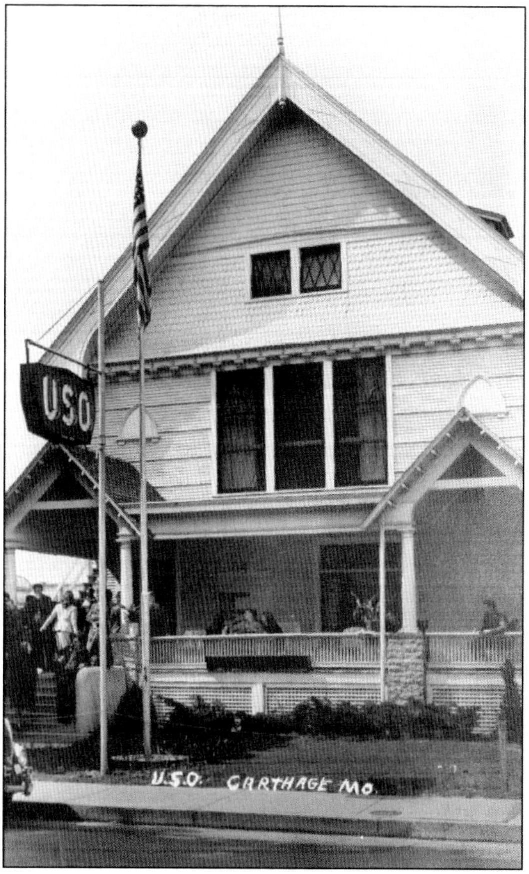

Carthage USO Club, 127 East Sixth Street. Located in the former Elk's clubhouse, which became Carthage's Recreation Center in the 1930s, the USO club operated from 1943 to 1946. Service and social clubs, churches, and other volunteers provided free activities for visiting soldiers, even offering free lodging in their homes. Many of the soldiers came from Camp Crowder, located south of Carthage in Newton County.

Camp Crowder, Neosho, Missouri. Constructed in 1941–1942, Camp Crowder impacted all of southwest Missouri. Ultimately, it contained over 66,000 acres and was a temporary home to 45,000 people. The US Army's Signal Corps members, as well as Women's Army Corps soldiers, were trained here. In 1943, the camp also became a prisoner of war installation housing primarily German soldiers.

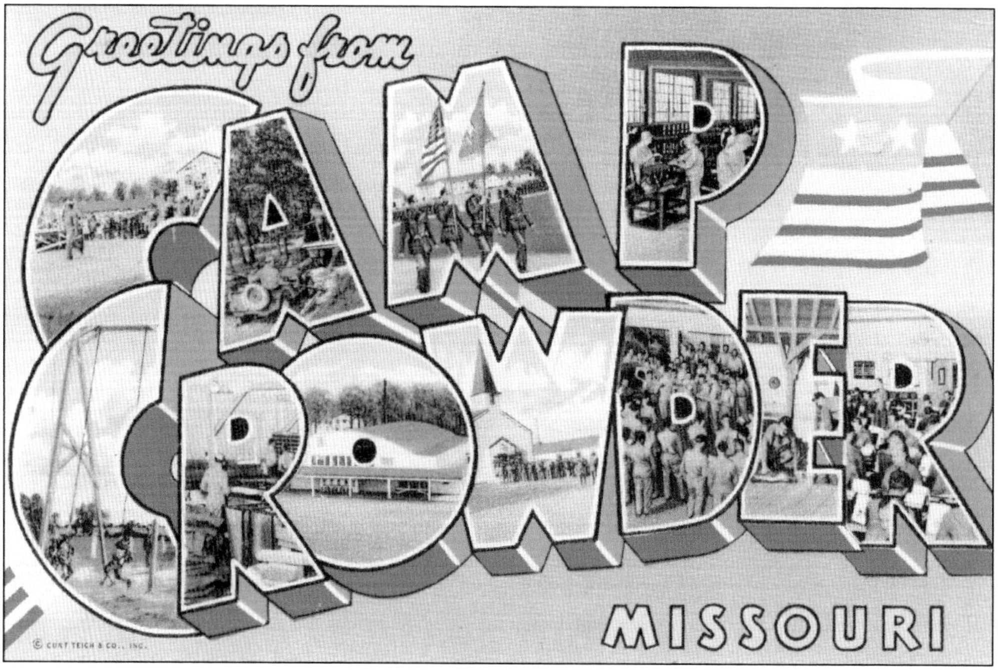

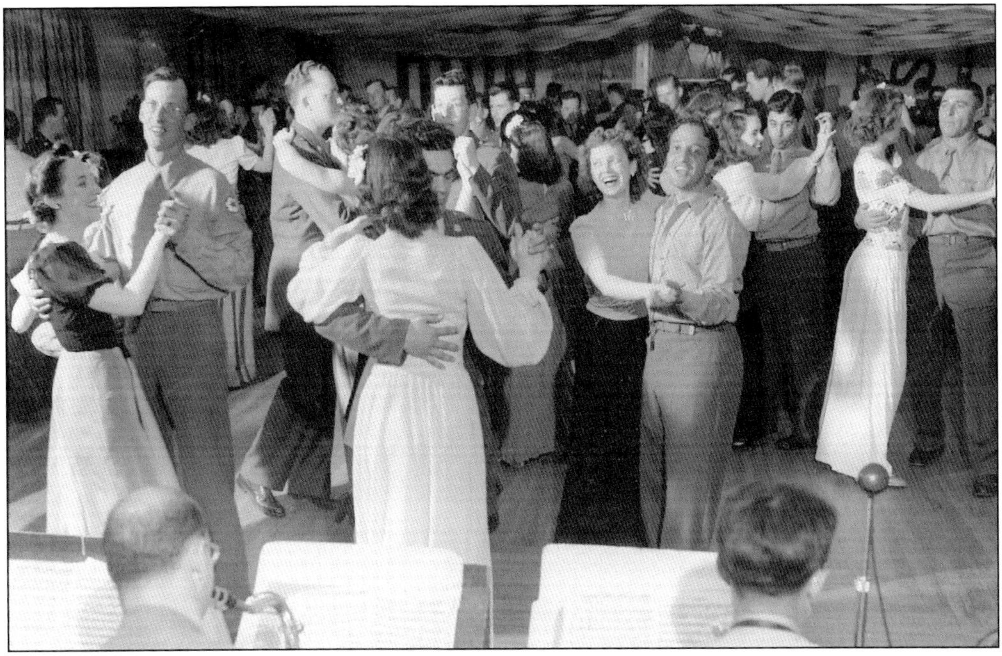

Carthage USO Club. Dances and social mixers were popular entertainments with both locals and soldiers. Businesses advertised in the *Camp Crowder Messenger* encouraging soldiers to visit. One advertisement placed by the Steadley Company said, "We want you to visit Carthage often and make this your Home Town . . . we would like to know you as a friend."

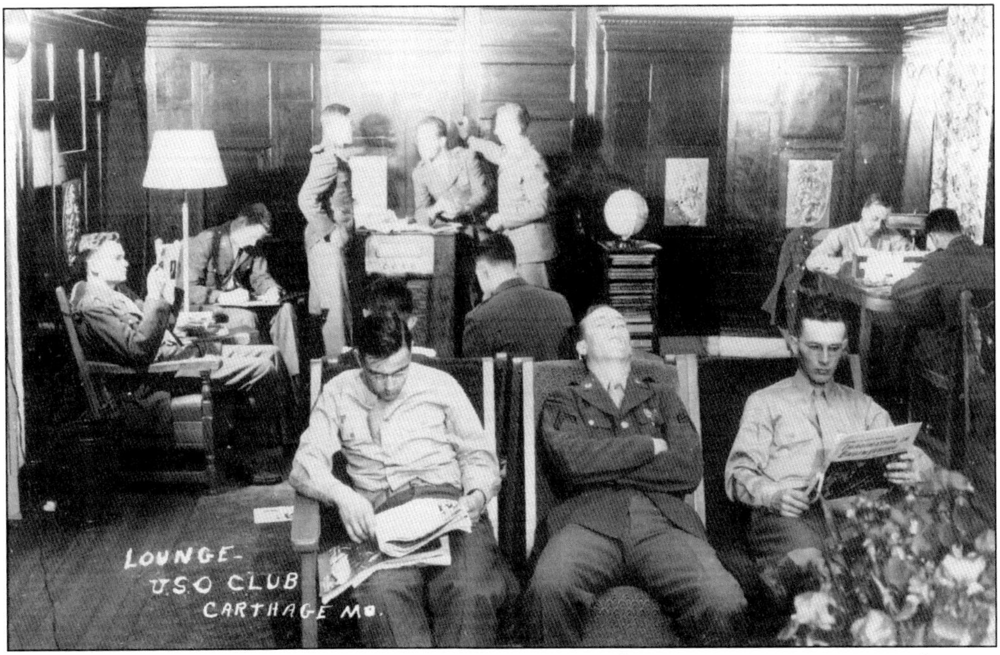

Carthage USO Club. The club also allowed for more relaxing entertainments in its lounge. As Pennsylvania soldier David Wallace reported home, "I am seated in this lounge at this very moment, listening to the Philharmonic. Am spending a restful weekend away from camp. Carthage a nice town—rooms in private homes."

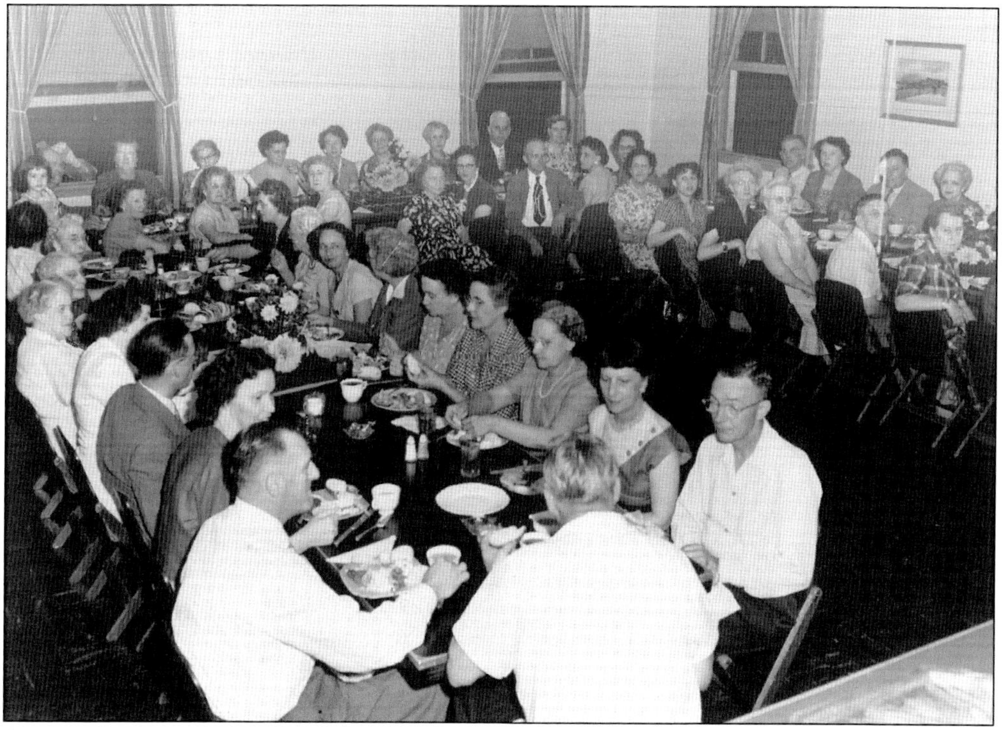

Civic Center, 127 East Sixth Street. Rained out from an outdoor dinner at Municipal Park in 1950, the Soroptimist members and their husbands moved to the Civic Center, the former USO club, for their event. This property became the Tiger Den, and although most of the house structure is gone, portions of the building are still used by the Carthage R-9 Schools.

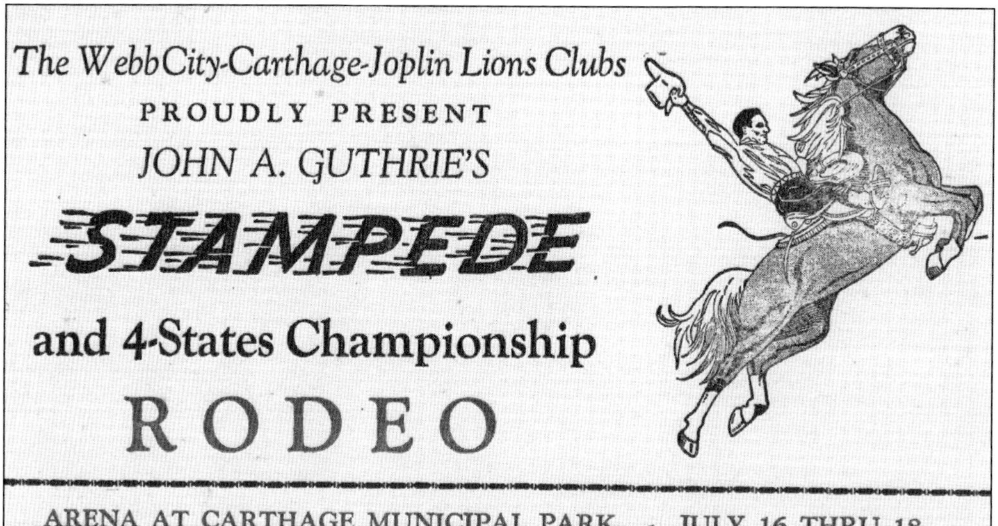

Rodeo in Municipal Park, Oak Street. This blotter advertises John Guthrie's Stampede and 4-States Championship Rodeo, sponsored in part by the Carthage Lions Club. In the 1940s, Guthrie performed numerous times in this area, including at the Ozark Empire District Fair in Springfield, Missouri. Frank Autry, cousin to radio, film, and television cowboy performer Gene Autry, was Guthrie's arena director.

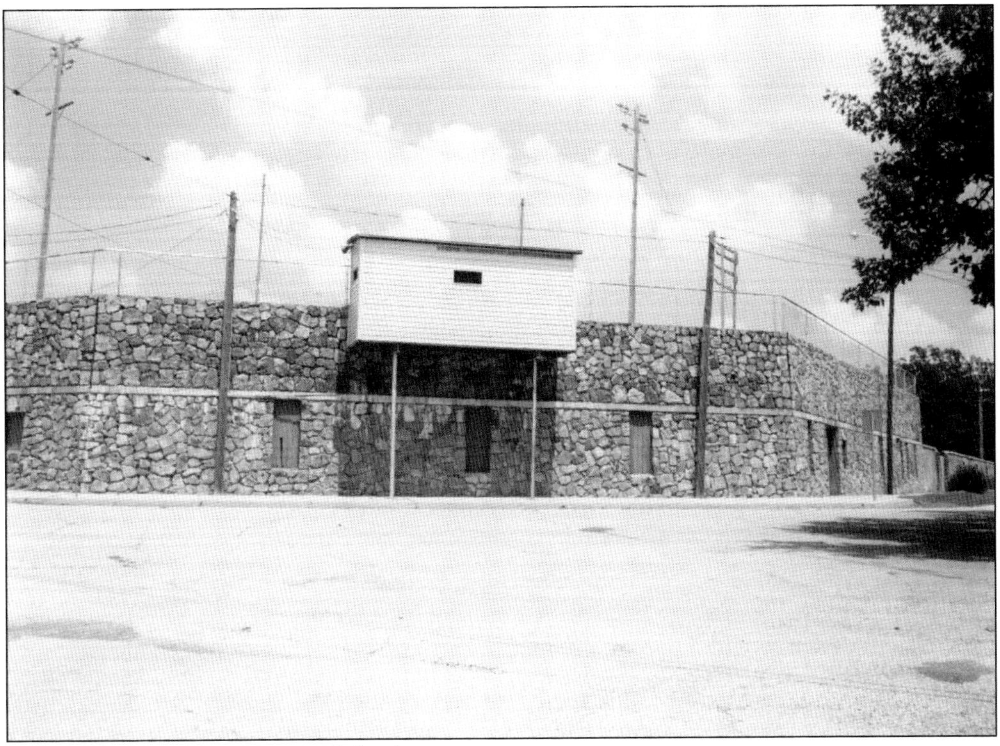

Municipal Park Stadium. Built by the Works Progress Administration (WPA) in 1937–1938 as an outdoor amphitheater costing $60,000, the structure was quickly converted to a ballpark located off US Highway 66. Its grandstand was built of fieldstone, and its bleachers could hold 3,000 spectators. Today, known as Carl Lewton Stadium, it honors a former teacher, principal, coach, and National Baseball Congress umpire Hall of Famer who died in 2009.

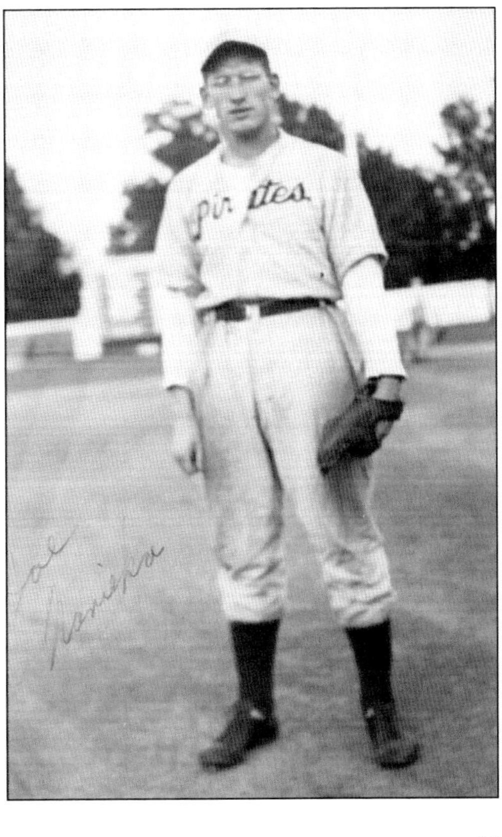

Carthage Pirates, Joe Narieka. A farm team for the Pittsburgh Pirates, the Carthage Pirates played Class D baseball in the Arkansas-Missouri Baseball League. Narieka, who hailed from Linfield, Pennsylvania, was part of the team from 1938 to 1940. In 1938, a total of 33,000 people attended 66 home games in the Carthage stadium.

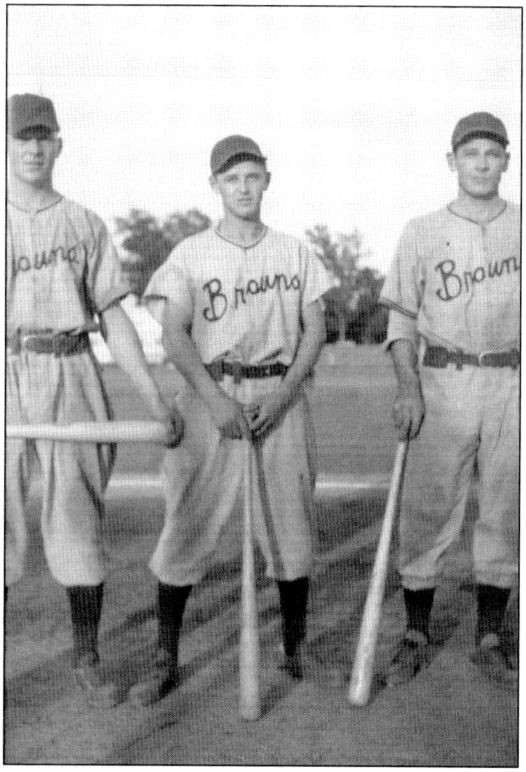

CARTHAGE BROWNS BASEBALL TEAM MEMBERS. From left to right are first baseman Roy Meyer, outfielder Joe Szuch, and catcher Frank Mancuso. After playing for Carthage in 1941, Mancuso joined the St. Louis Browns. The Carthage Browns, of the Western Association, lasted one year. Not a single full-team photograph is known to exist.

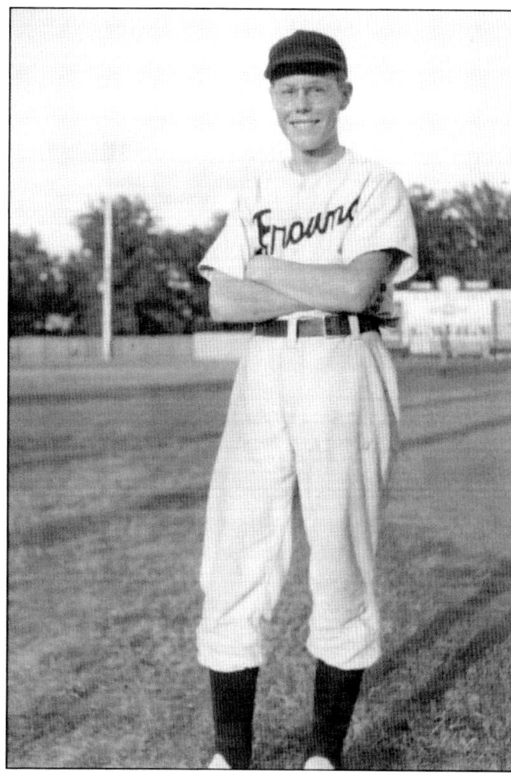

CARTHAGE BROWNS BATBOY RAYMOND BAIRD. The Baird family of Carthage boarded many of the baseball players from the various leagues. In 1941, their son Raymond Jr. became the Browns batboy when the St. Joseph Pony Express Riders of the Western Association moved their operation to Carthage and changed the team name.

CARTHAGE CARDINALS, WILLIAM BUCK. This team, which Carthage residents E.L. Dale and A.H. Moorman helped to found, was part of the Kansas-Oklahoma-Missouri League, otherwise known as the KOM League. This was a Class D farm team for the St. Louis Cardinals. Pitcher and first baseman William Buck played in the 1947 and 1948 seasons. In 1949, the team name changed to the Carthage Cubs.

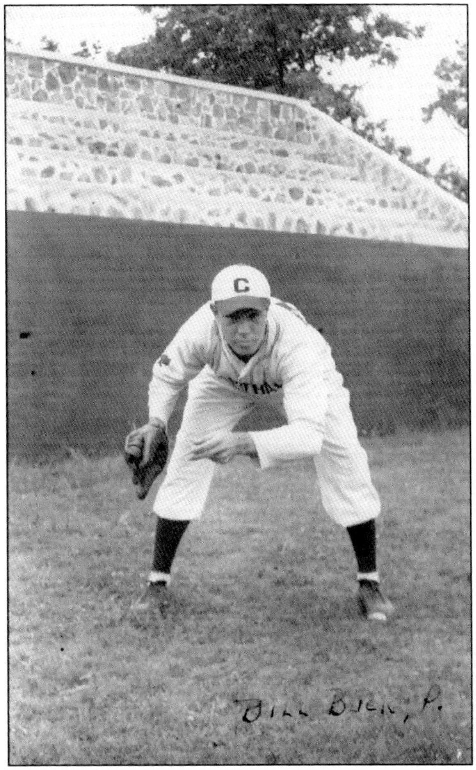

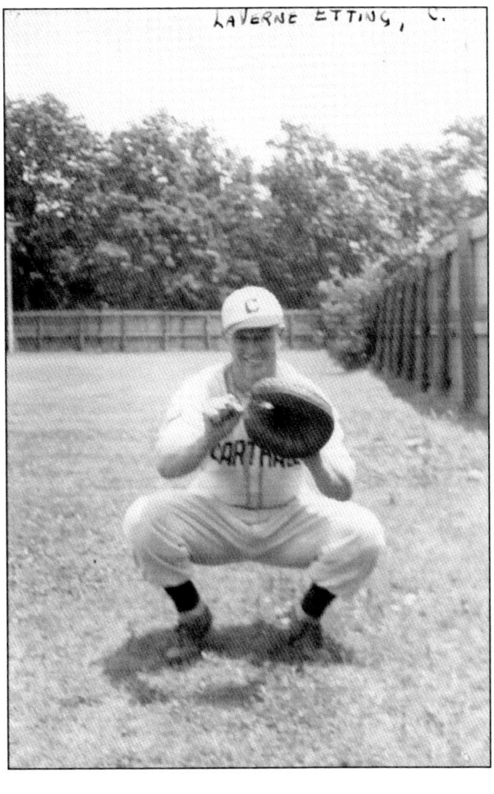

CARTHAGE CARDINALS, LAVERNE ETTING. Catcher Etting was part of the 1946 Cardinals team. He came from Bellvue, Iowa, and continued his career in Maryland and Wisconsin. The other towns in the KOM League in 1946 were Chanute, Iola, and Pittsburg, Kansas; and Miami and Bartlesville, Oklahoma. Carthage fielded a team until 1951. The KOM ceased after the 1952 season.

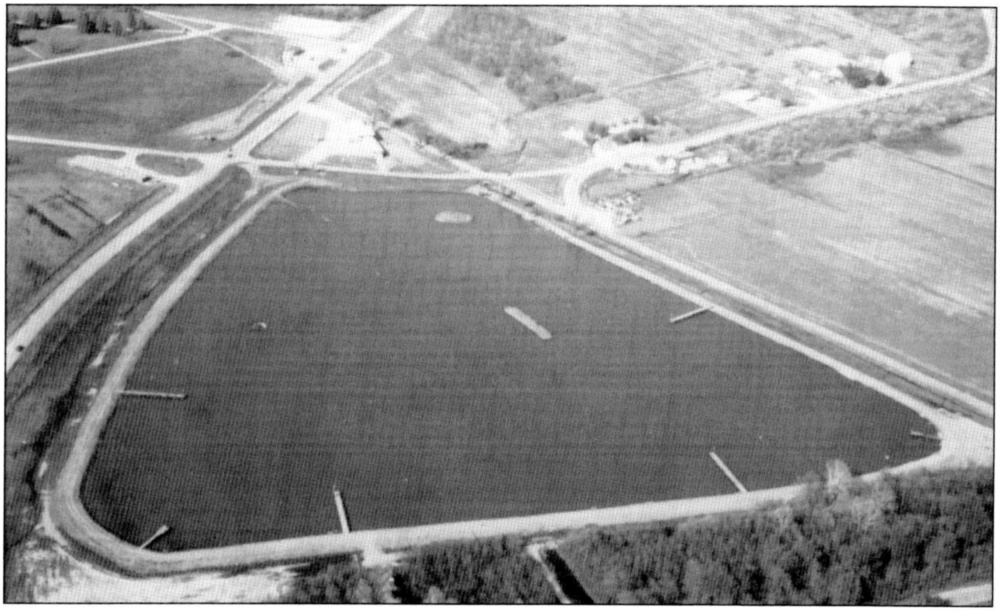

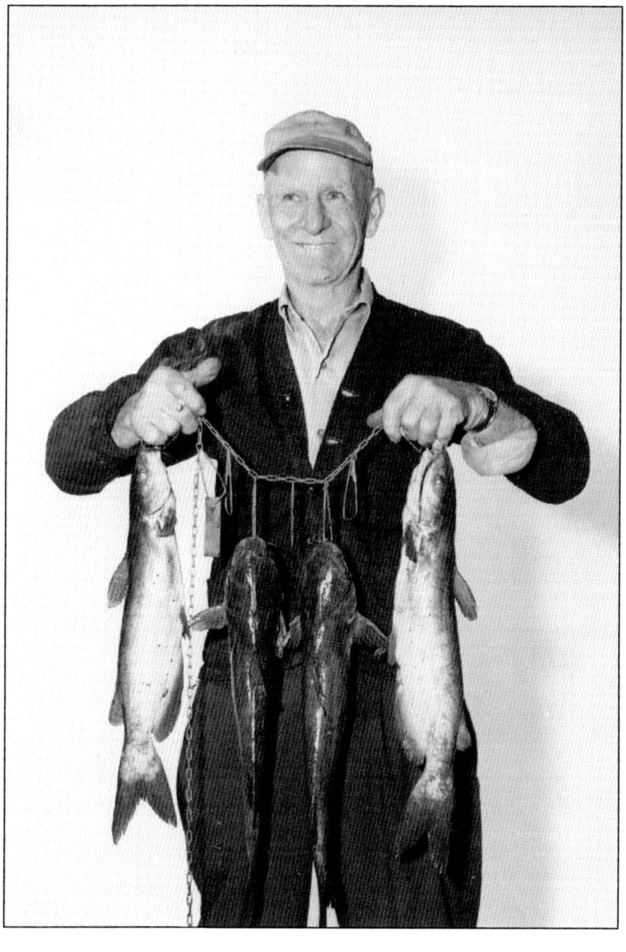

Kellogg Lake, US Highway 66 East. In 1953–1954, when a new alignment of the highway was constructed, members of the Carthage Sportsmen's Protective League (CSPL), founded in 1921, decided to create a 28-acre lake with additional park and picnic areas using Missouri Highway Department and private funds. It became a favorite fishing spot for residents, and in the winter, ice-skating took place here. The CSPL disbanded in the 1970s, and the group's records were donated to the Powers Museum in 1998. The postcard above, as well as this mid-1950s photograph of Earl Reed and his catch, both come from this collection.

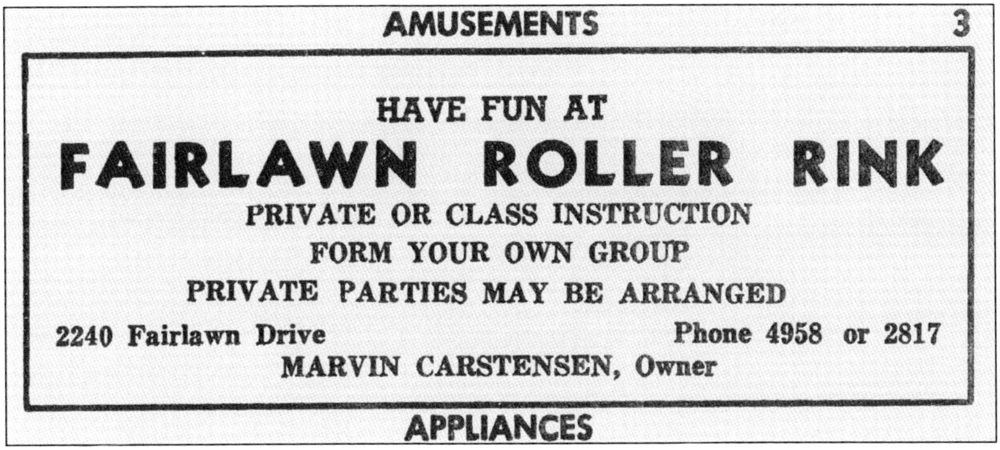

OTHER FORMS OF ENTERTAINMENT IN CARTHAGE. Prior to Municipal Park Dance Pavilion being used for roller-skating, Fairlawn Roller Rink, advertised above, was operating and was owned by Marvin Carstensen. Located at 510 Grant Street, Whisler Bowling Alleys, pictured below, was Carthage's second such facility in the 1940s. The first was located inside the Carthage YMCA at 526 South Main Street. Whisler was later known as Winford Alleys and then as Carthage Bowl. By 1960, Carthage gained another bowling alley, called Bell Lanes; it was at the end of Grand Avenue. Star Lanes, as seen on page 26, opened in 1961.

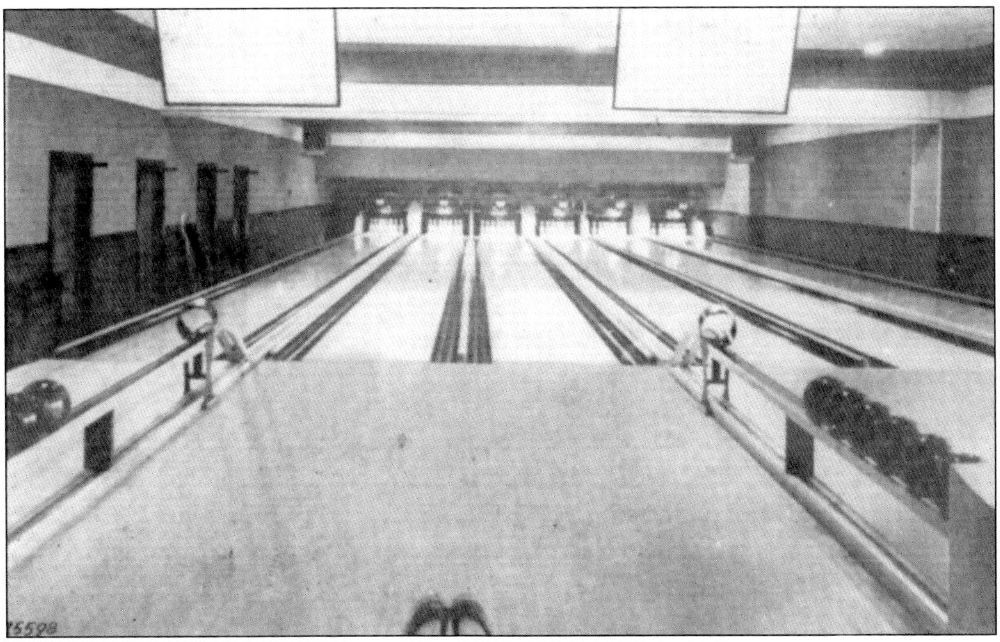

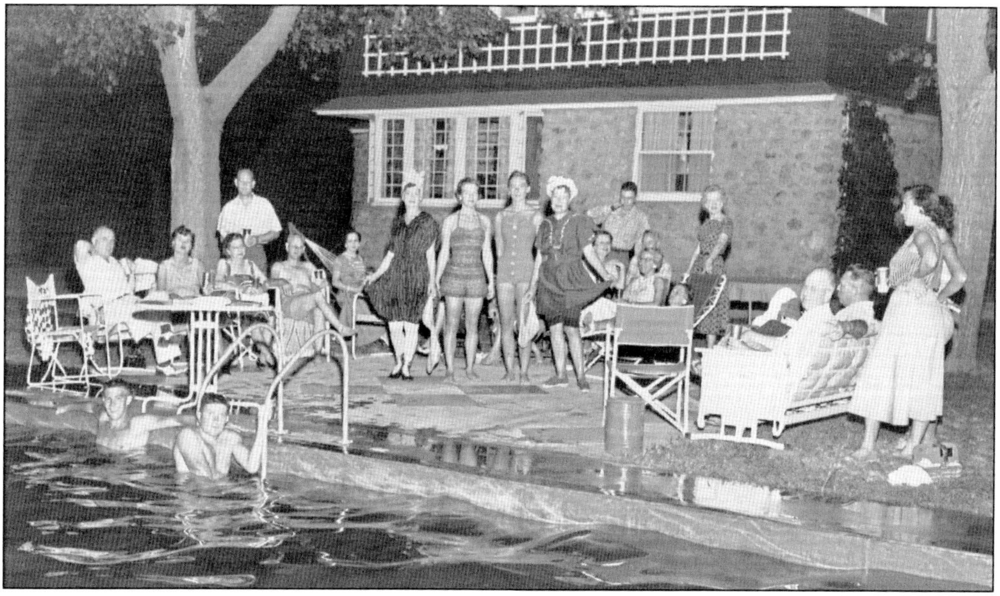

Michel Home, 1562 West Fairview Avenue. Carthage friends gather in the 1960s for a pool party. In the center are Marian Powers Winchester, Jane Putnam, Van Hartman Ellis, and Margaret Michel. Mrs. Winchester and Mrs. Michel are modeling antique bathing suits, which are now part of the museum collection. The Michel house was built in 1910 as a country home for Judge Joseph Perkins, father of Marlin Perkins.

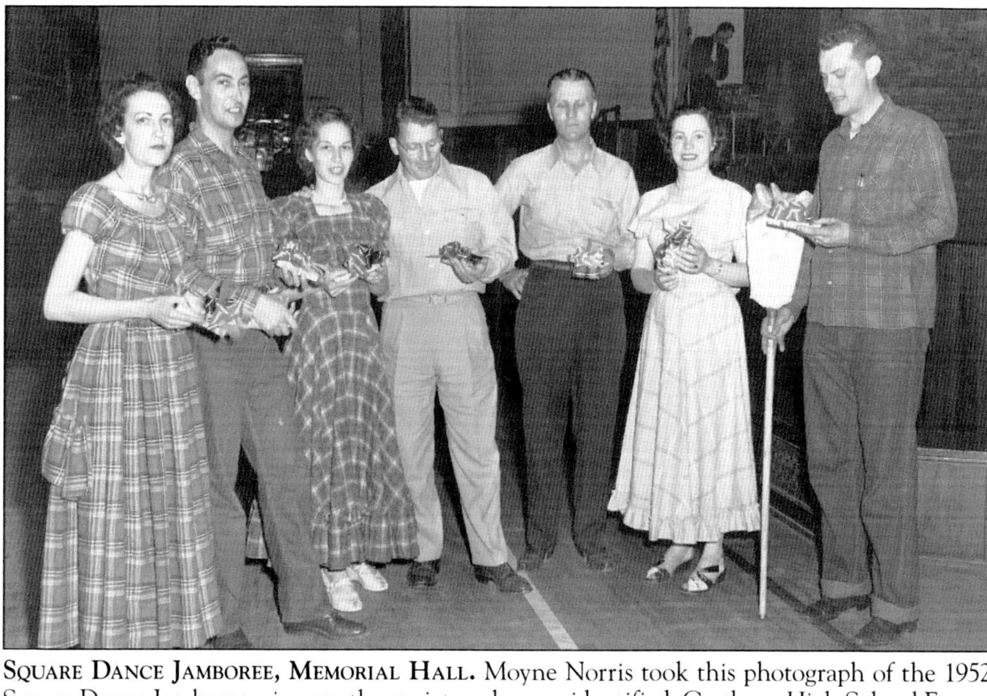

Square Dance Jamboree, Memorial Hall. Moyne Norris took this photograph of the 1952 Square Dance Jamboree winners; those pictured are unidentified. Carthage High School Future Farmers of America and Carthage firefighters coordinated decorations. It was sponsored by the Soroptimists and called by Ernie Boucher of Monett, Missouri. Ray Stanley of Carthage also gave an old-fashioned square dancing demonstration.

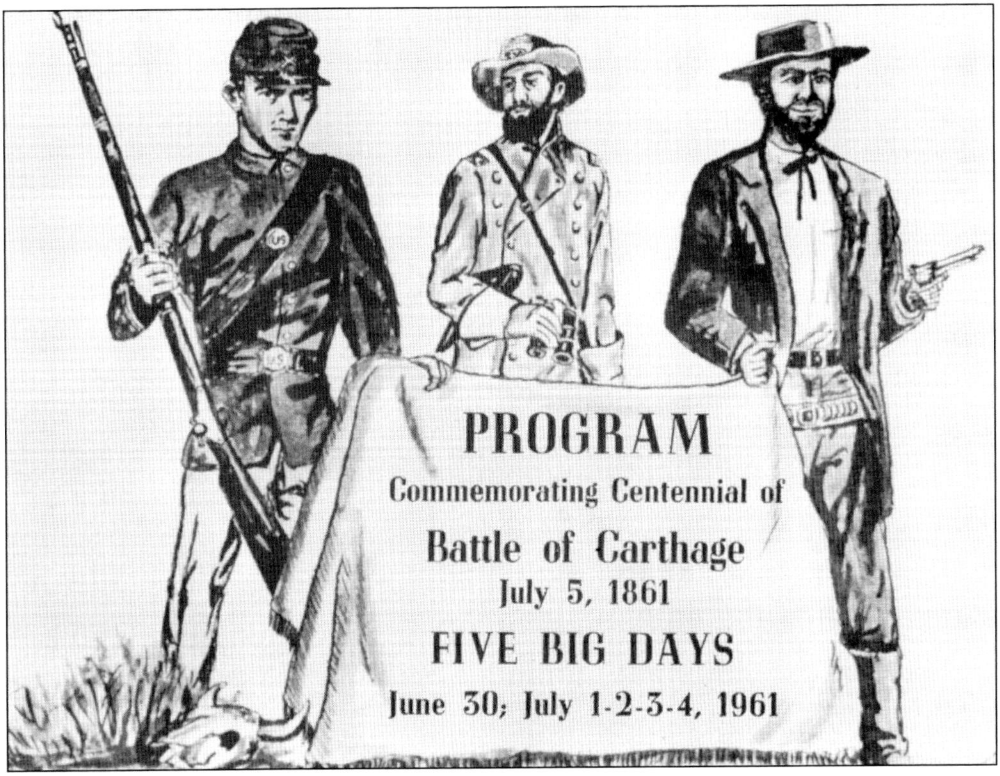

BATTLE OF CARTHAGE CENTENNIAL. Honoring the July 5, 1861, Battle of Carthage, a variety of events over the course of June 30 and July 1–4, 1961, were held. These included a square dance and historic fashion show on the square, guns and weapons displays, a pilgrimage to Civil War historic sites, an old fiddlers' contest, and the traditional Fourth of July fireworks in Municipal Park.

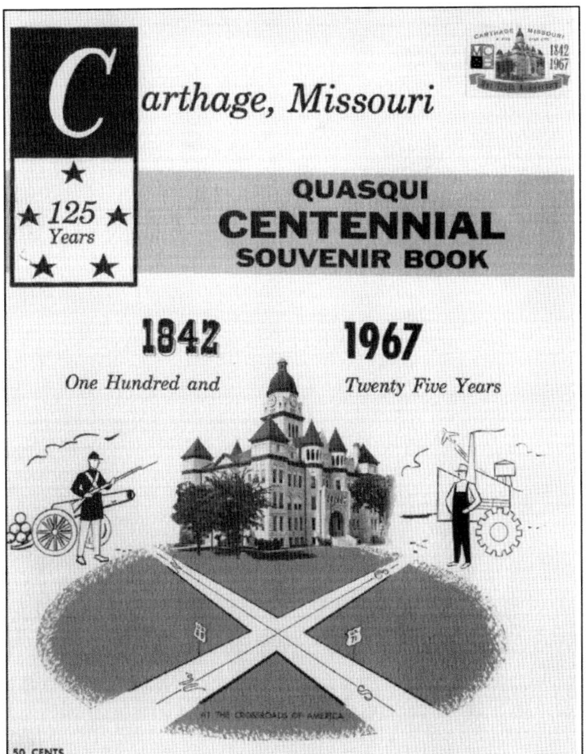

CARTHAGE QUASQUICENTENNIAL CELEBRATION. Six years later, during October 14–21, 1967, Missouri governor Warren Hearnes and Carthage celebrated the town's 125th birthday with another series of events including a horse show, Native American dances, Belle Starr Day, a ball with the Jimmy Dorsey Orchestra, rededication of Memorial Hall, two parades, two football games, and other historical activities and displays downtown.

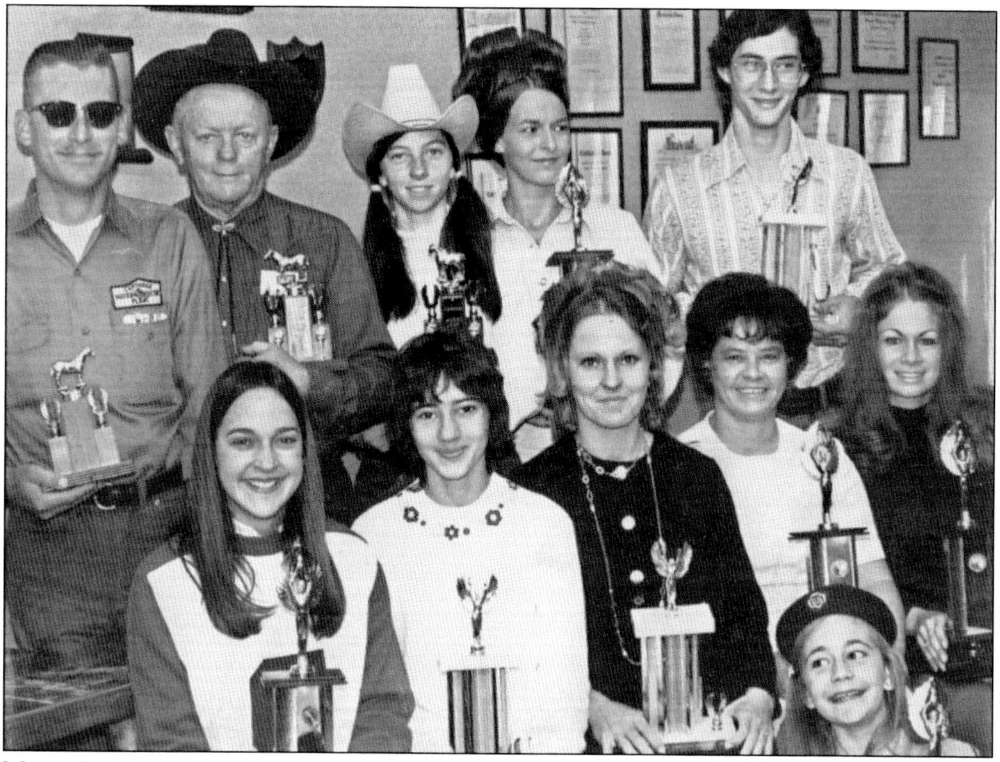

MAPLE LEAF FESTIVAL. Due to the success of the 125th anniversary celebration, the chamber of commerce decided to create a new community event known today as the Maple Leaf Festival. Pictured above are 1971 festival parade winners, and a 1989 festival parade automobile with members of the Rhoda Fairchild Chapter of the National Society of Daughters of the American Revolution is pictured below. The following are just a few of the Maple Leaf Parade marshals over the years: Governor Hearnes (1968), Congressman Gene Taylor (1973, 1974, and 1978), Marlin Perkins (1984), and the Foggy River Boys (1993).

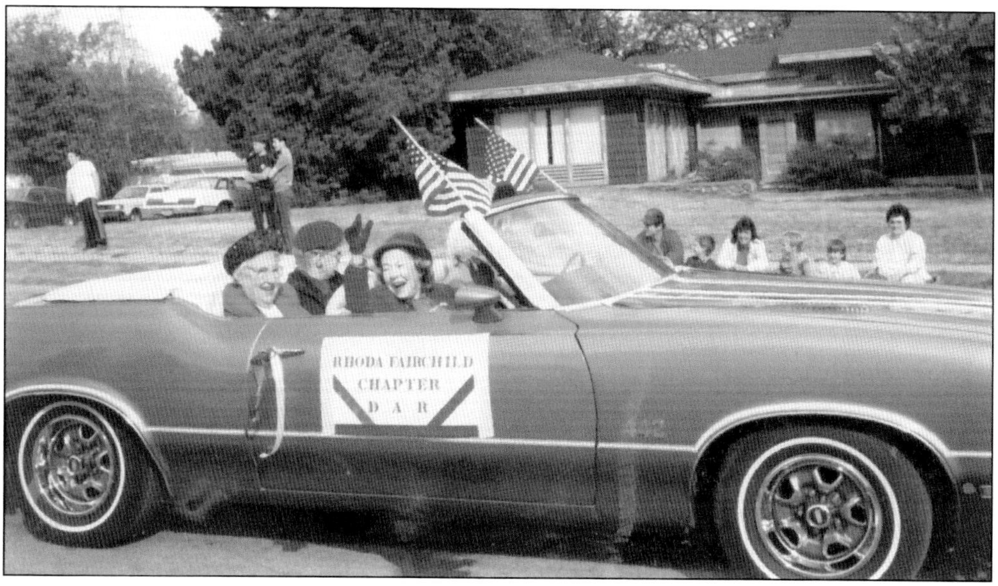

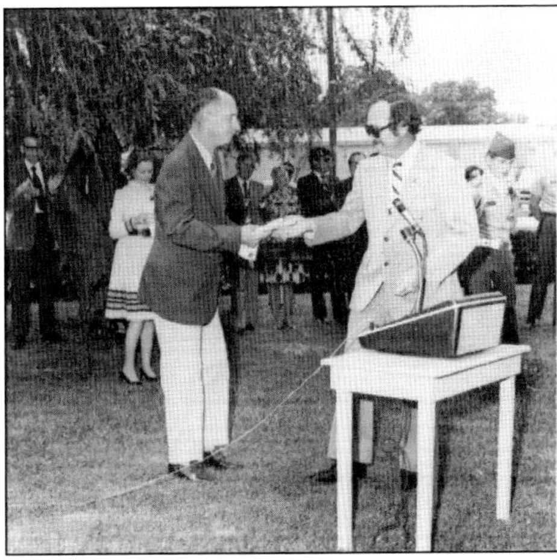

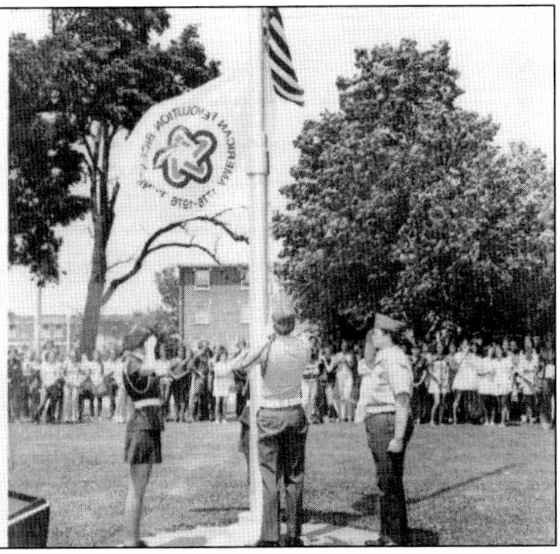

CARTHAGE BICENTENNIAL CELEBRATION. Carthage became an official Bicentennial City in 1974 with this ROTC flag-raising event at Carthage High School. The Spirit of '76 Committee was in charge and planned three years of events. Mayor Byron Hallam and Ken White with the Missouri Bicentennial Administration presided over the activities pictured here.

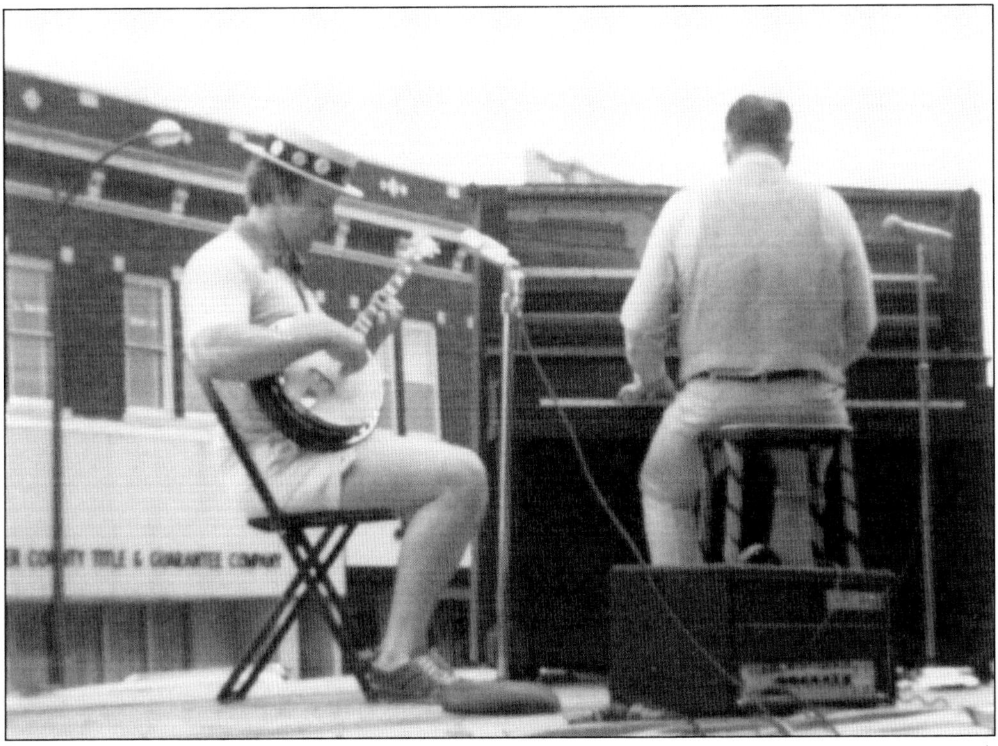

CARTHAGE RAGTIME FESTIVAL. As part of the many activities the Spirit of '76 Committee arranged, the first ragtime music festival in 1976 was held to celebrate Carthage's ragtime heritage as represented by composer James Scott (1885–1938). Here, Ray Rose (at the piano) and Tom Farig (playing the banjo) perform in an outdoor concert on the courthouse square.

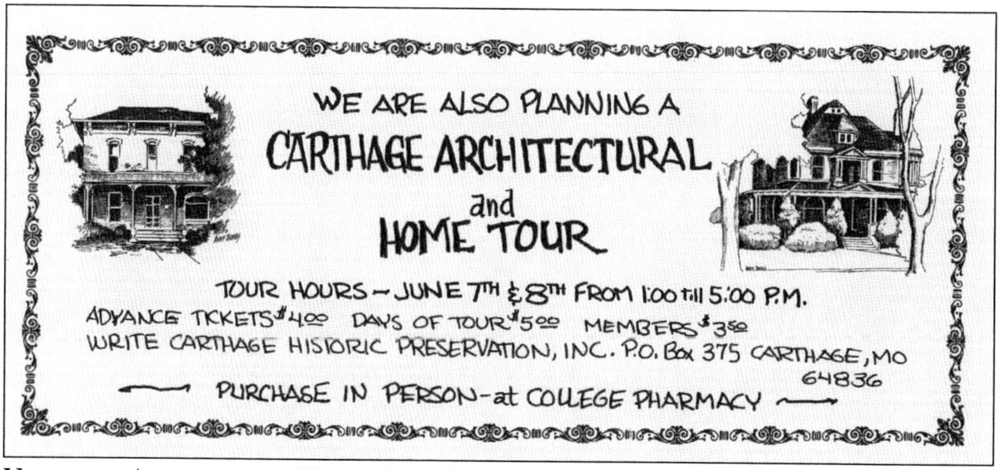

Victorian Architecture Home Tour. Carthage Historic Preservation (CHP) was founded in 1979 and began promoting the preservation of Carthage's architectural heritage. Among the homes featured on the 1980 tour was the 1876 Goucher Home (left) at 1309 South Main Street and the 1888 Davey Home (right) at 1130 Grand Avenue. Today, CHP maintains the historic Phelps House at 1146 Grand Avenue.

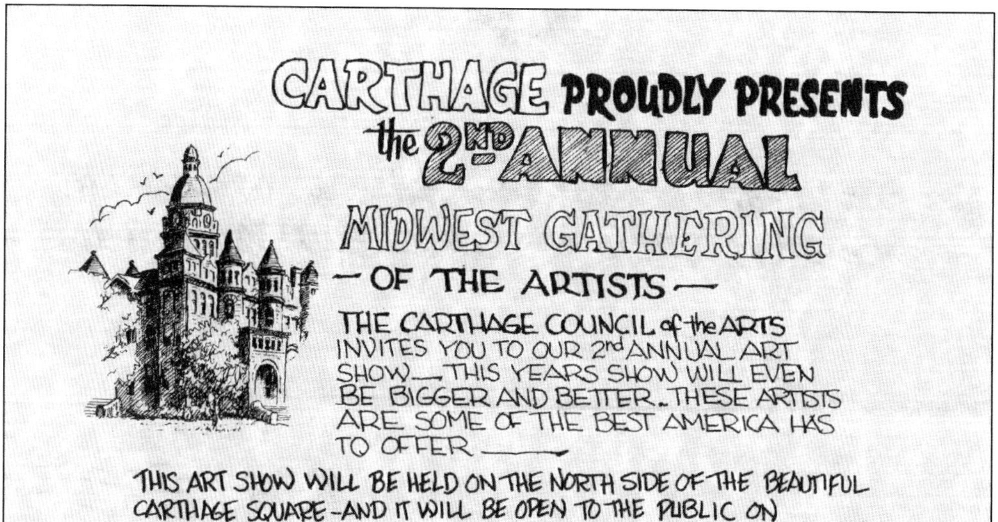

Midwest Gathering of Artists. Established in 1979 and continuing today, the Midwest Gathering of the Artists show was created by Bob Tommey, Lowell Davis, and Danny Hensley. In the second event held on the north side of the square in 1980, Tommey, Davis, and Jerry Ellis participated with 18 other artists who traveled to Carthage.

Seven

In and Around Carthage

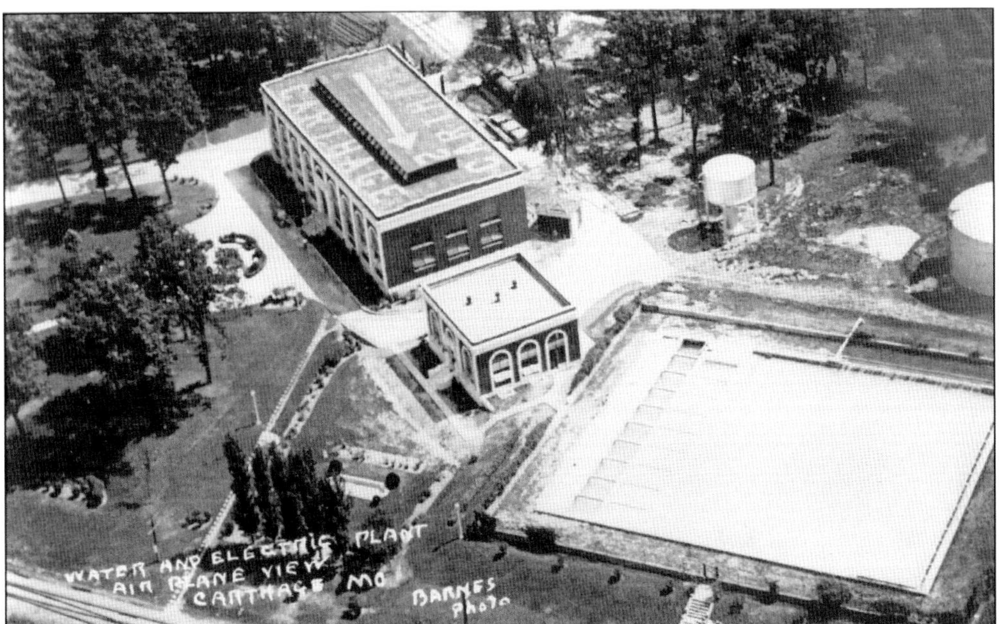

Carthage Water and Electric Plant (CW&EP), 300 South River Avenue. Carthage's municipally owned utility has been operating from this site since 1927. This c. 1941 aerial view shows the plant's main building and reservoir. Between those features is the water softening facility. In 1947, CW&EP provided water service through 86 miles of underground water mains.

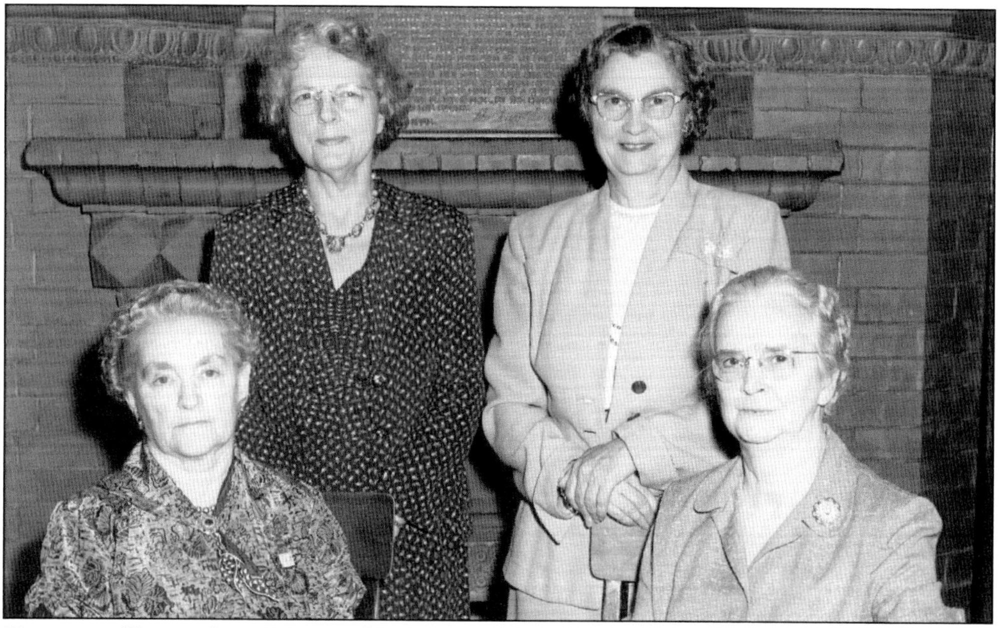

CARTHAGE PUBLIC LIBRARY, 612 SOUTH GARRISON AVENUE. From left to right are librarian Jessie Stemmons and assistants Helen Jones, Ethel Keeper, and Frances Cushman on the library's 50th anniversary of opening to the public; Carl Taylor took this photograph. The June 1955 celebration was presided over by library board president Laurence Flanigan and secretary Edith Allen. (Courtesy of Carthage Public Library.)

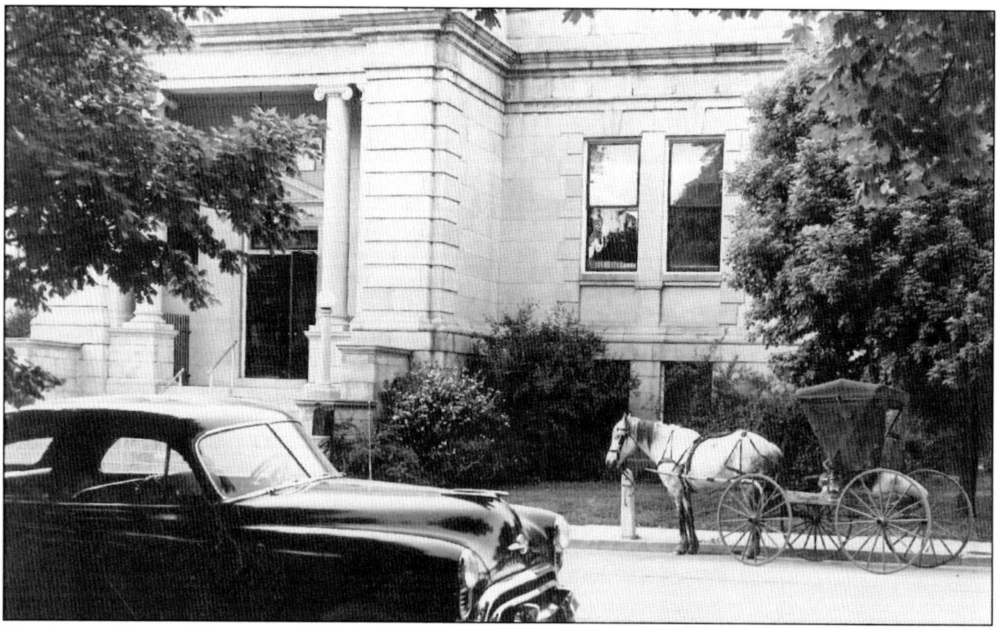

CARTHAGE PUBLIC LIBRARY. Moyne Norris caught this library scene on film in 1951. Librarian Stemmons's car is in front of the library along with the Lowry twins' horse and buggy tied to a hitching post, which was installed in 1904 by Wetherell and Company contractors. In 1953, the post was struck by a car and converted to a birdbath east of the building. (Courtesy of Carthage Public Library.)

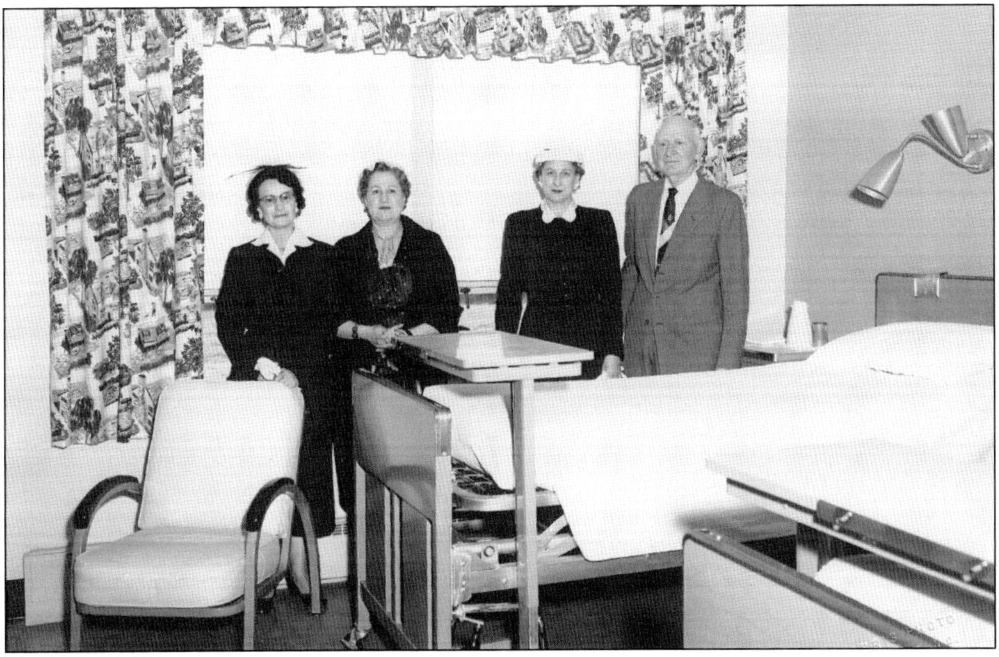

McCune-Brooks Hospital, 627 West Centennial Avenue. Soroptimist members Ruby Ott (middle) and Edith Pemberton (right) are with hospital administrator George Masters in the new hospital room that the service organization furnished with a $550 gift to the hospital at the time of the north wing expansion project in 1957.

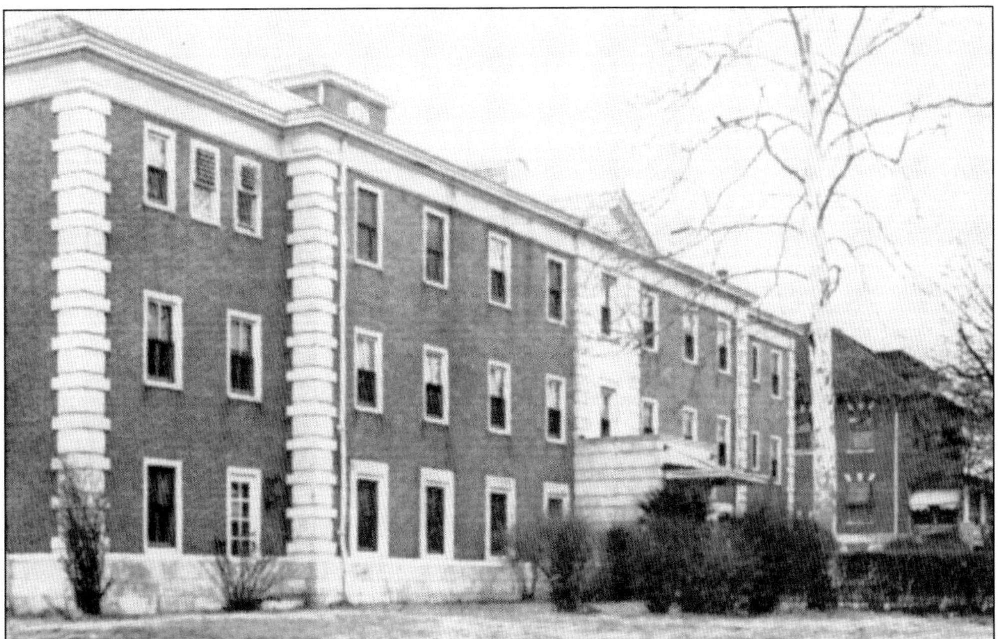

McCune-Brooks Hospital. This image is from a 1950s hospital brochure that advertised private rooms at $9–$12 per night and operating room charges for major surgery of $15. The first Carthage Hospital, erected in 1906–1907 to the right of the main building, was torn down in 1972 for a hospital expansion project to the 1929 main building.

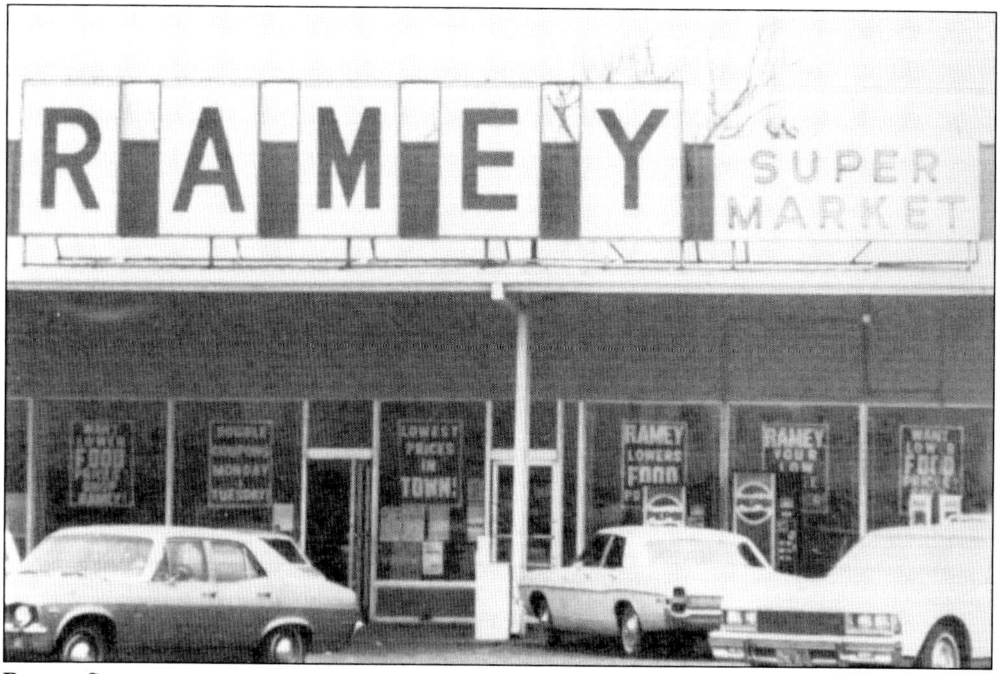

RAMEY SUPERMARKET, 1223 WEST CENTRAL AVENUE. As businesses looked for locations to expand, West Central Avenue became a target in the late 1950s. By the late 1960s, Carthage's first Walmart Discount City and Food Store was built at 1211 and 1213 West Central. Eventually, the building complex expanded to the west. By 1977, Ramey's offered groceries at 1223 while Walmart had expanded its general merchandise to the east.

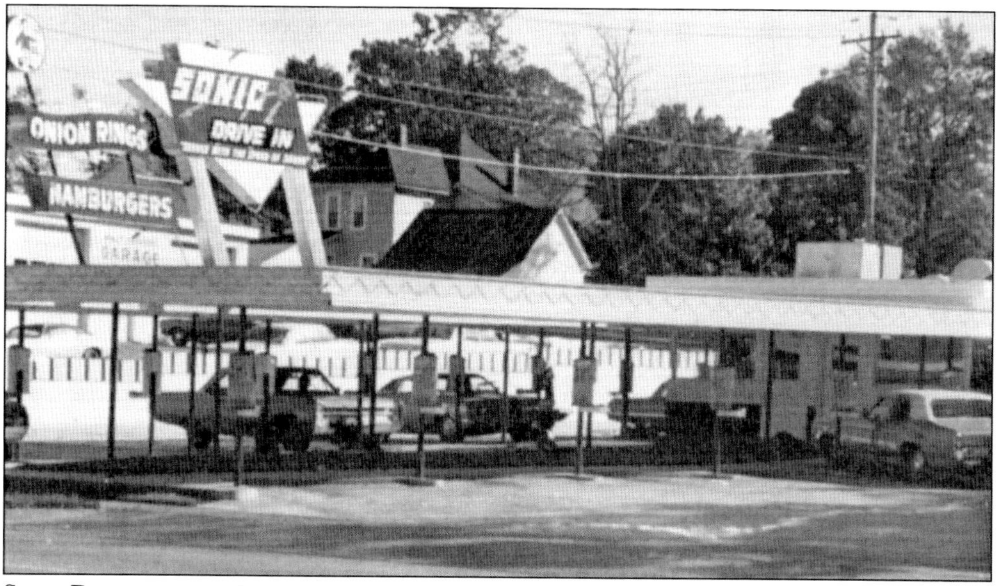

SONIC DRIVE-IN, 1000 WEST CENTRAL AVENUE. The commercialization of West Central Avenue continued in the 1960s and the 1970s as US Highway 66 was diverted from Oak Street. Opened in 1972, Sonic continued the long line of fast food drive-ins in Carthage. Others on Central Avenue were Tastee Freeze (1962), formerly at 1007 West Central, and McDonald's (1975) at 1111 West Central. Sonic relocated to 1106 West Central in 2003.

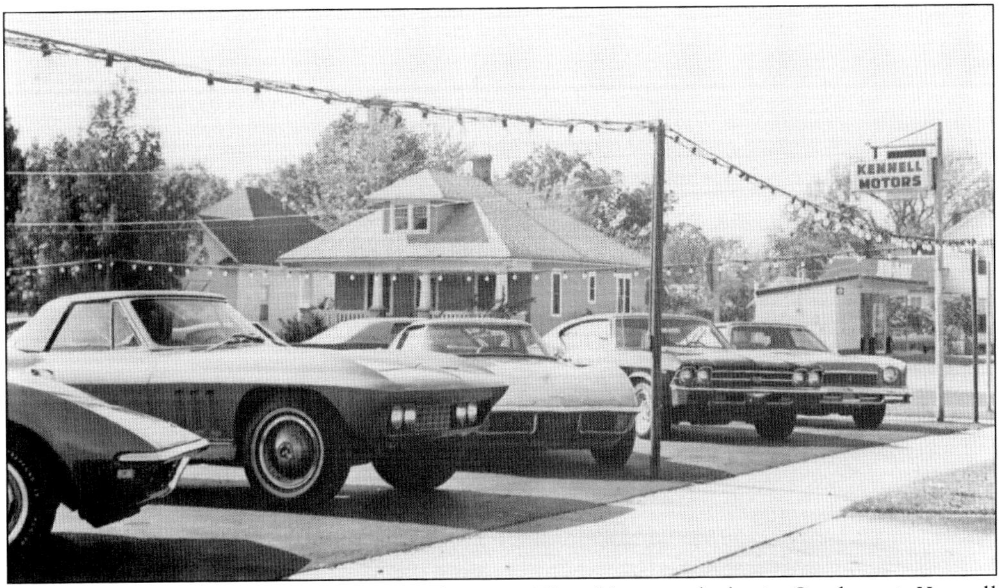

Kennell Motors, 426 West Central Avenue. The oldest car dealer in Carthage is Kennell Motors, which has been located in various locations since its establishment in 1938. It moved to West Central Avenue in the 1960s, first at 1027 and then settling at its current location. The company continues to operate under the ownership of Cliff and Kel Kennell.

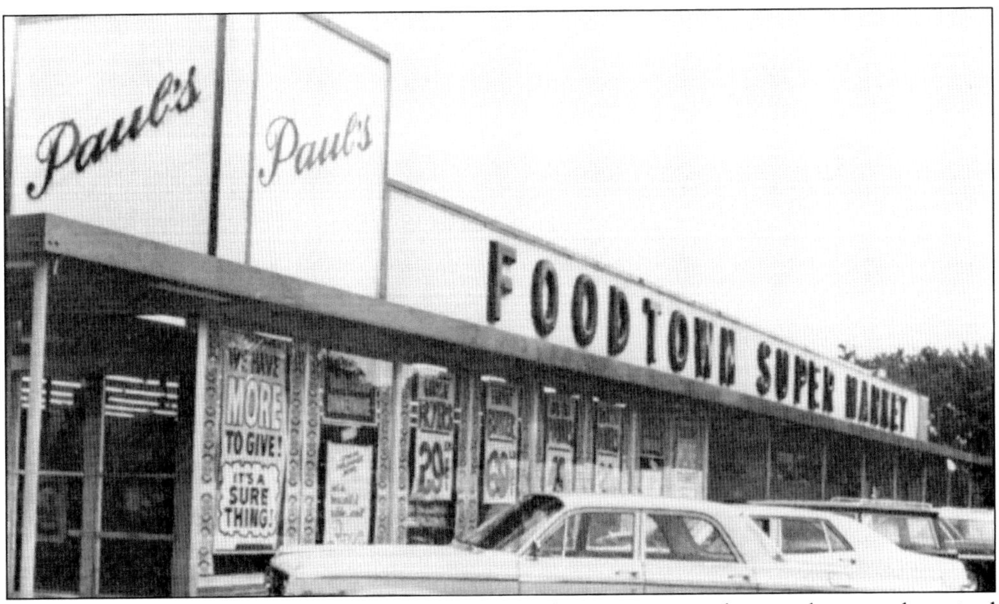

Paul's Foodtown, 1937 South Garrison Avenue. As grocery stores became larger and required their own parking areas, they moved from the courthouse square. This trend also started the demise of neighborhood groceries. Foodtown was constructed in 1959 and managed by Paul Feagan. Another example of expansion in the mid-1950s was Rhinehart's Grocery with its IGA Foodliner at 308 East Central Avenue.

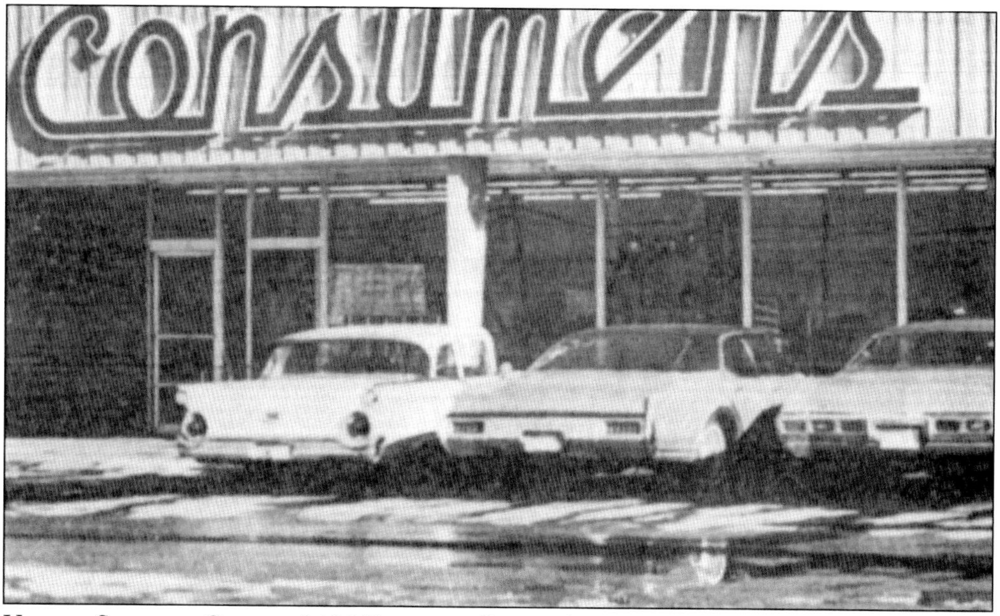

VILLAGE SHOPPING CENTER, 2400 BLOCK OF GRAND AVENUE. As Carthage grew to the south, a new commercial center was built at the southern end of Grand Avenue in 1970–1971. Among the first stores were Consumers Supermarket, Dollar United, Dutch Maid Laundry, and Glo Dry Cleaning. A year later, the Plaza One Office building was added.

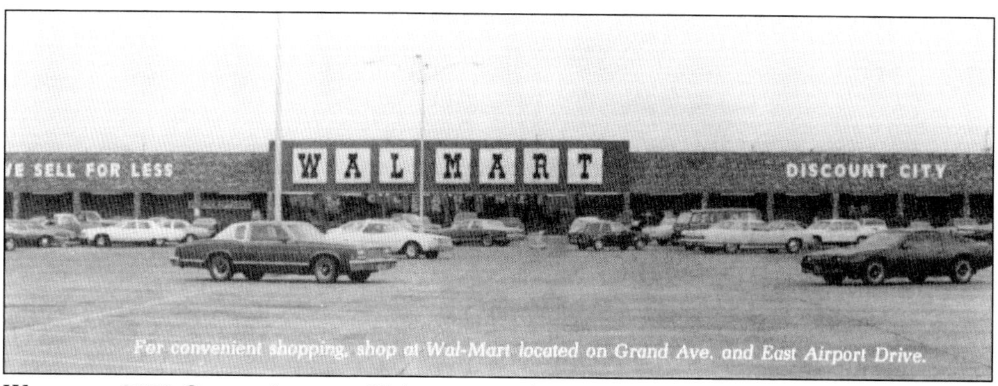

WALMART, 2330 GRAND AVENUE. Walmart moved to its second location in 1979. Constructed nearby were the apartment complexes Highland Meadows (1977) and Dearfield Meadows (1979) on Airport Drive and Andy's Restaurant at 2342 Grand Avenue (1982), which is now a Wendy's Restaurant. Walmart moved to its current location at 2705 Grand in 1999.

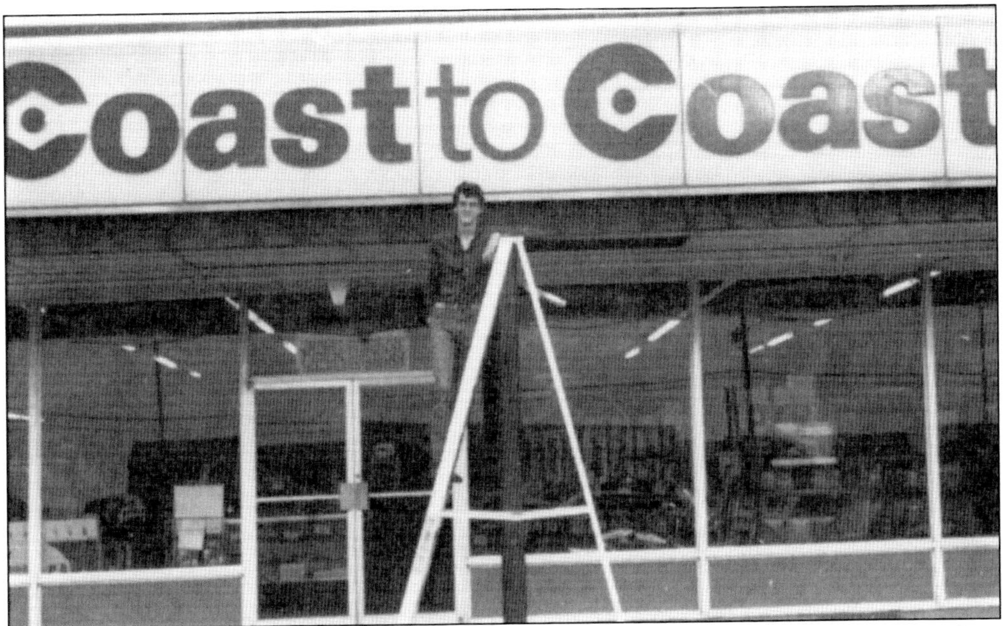

VILLAGE SHOPPING CENTER, 2400 BLOCK OF GRAND AVENUE. In 1972, an addition was made to the Village Shopping Center to provide more stores, including Fabrific Fabric Center, P.N. Hirsch Department Store, and Coast-to-Coast. Built farther to the south of the center in the 1970s was Sirloin House (2506 Grand Avenue), which is now Mazoos, and the Federal Land Bank (2540 Grand Avenue), which is now Suddenlink.

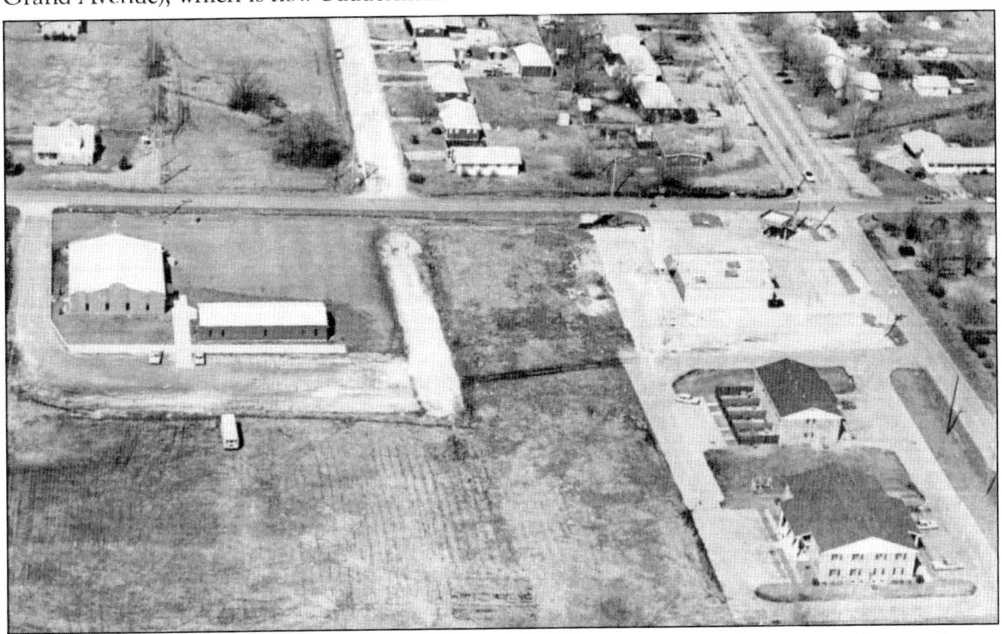

RIVER STREET AND FAIRVIEW AVENUE. Carthage's growth to the southeast is evident in this c. 1977 aerial photograph. Calvary Cumberland Presbyterian Church (now Full Faith Church) at 736 East Fairview Avenue, Ravenwoods Apartments at 2027 and 2037 South River Avenue, 7-Eleven convenience store (now The Corner) at 824 East Fairview Avenue, and several homes are visible.

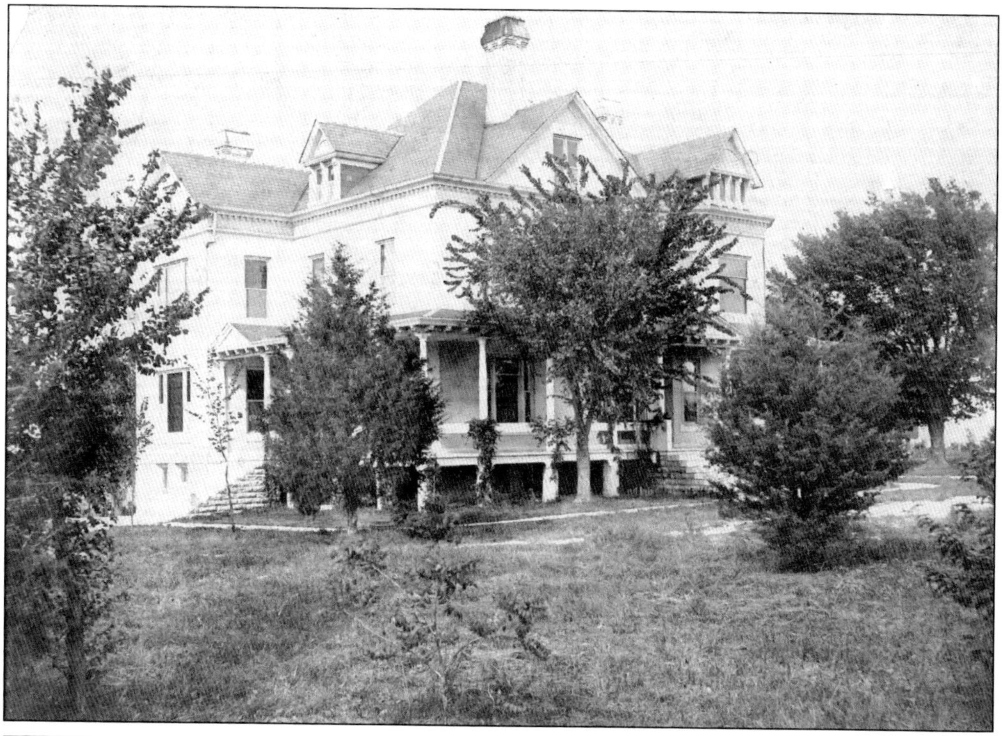

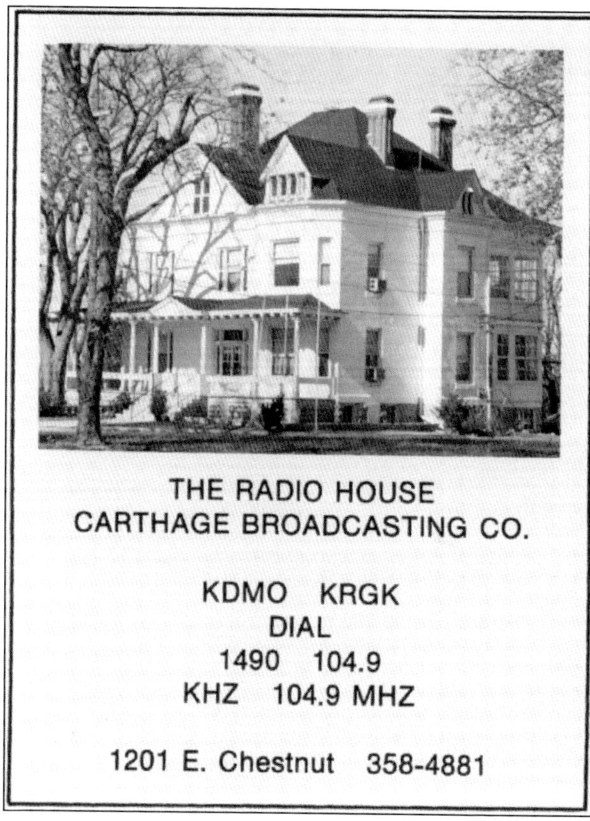

DR. CARTER HOME, EAST CHESTNUT STREET. Constructed by one of Carthage's earliest post–Civil War physicians, Carter's home was located on a bluff overlooking James Springs (later called Carter Springs), a site used by both sides at different times during the 1861 Battle of Carthage. This private home was extensively restored to its Victorian appearance in the late 1980s and 1990s.

RADIO HOUSE, EAST CHESTNUT STREET. In 1947, Lloyd McKenney and John Daly established local radio in Carthage. In 1962, George and Ruth Kolpin purchased the radio operations located in the historic Carter home. Eventually, offices were moved to 223 East Third Street, and in 1990 Ruth's son Ron Peterson purchased the business.

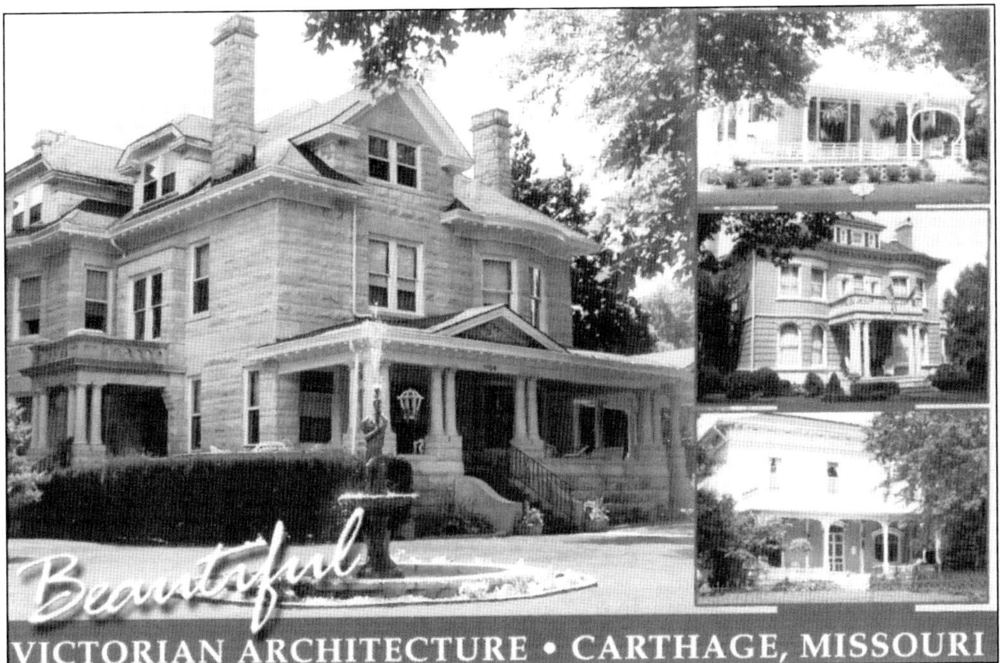

VICTORIAN ARCHITECTURE IN CARTHAGE. As advertised in the early 1970s, "the charm of Carthage, Missouri . . . the combination of contrasts between the old and the new" was a feature to be promoted with her "abundance of well-maintained, turn-of-the-century mansions." (Courtesy of Carthage Convention & Visitors Bureau.)

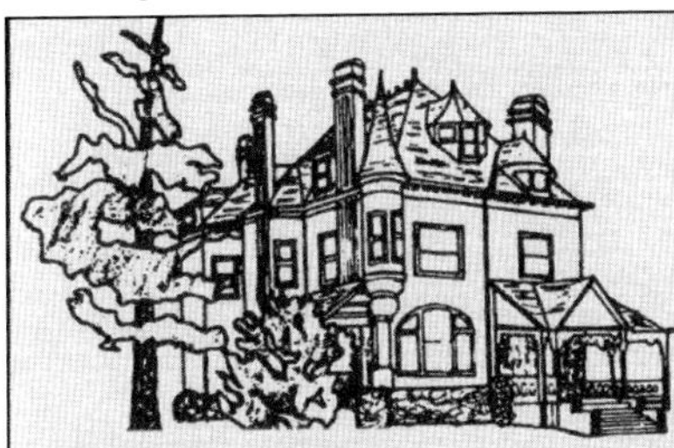

HILL HOUSE

Dean and Ella Mae Scoville
Bed and Breakfast • Antique and Gift Shop
Magnificent Victorian Mansion Circa 1887
• 10 Fireplaces • 6 Chimneys • 5 Porches
• Slate Roof • Copper Gutters • Stained Glass Windows
• Marble Sidewalks • Original Chandeliers
TOURS I:00 PM - 5:00 PM Daily

1157 S. MAIN **TEL. (417) 358-6145**

The Leggett House

"...A Bed and Breakfast on Historic Drive."

- The Victorian Carthage stone house completed in 1901 as a family residence for industrial pioneer J. P. Leggett, provides a glimpse of gracious living at the turn of the century.
- Enjoy a continental breakfast in the formal dining room or out of doors if you like.
- Tours Available
- 10 Minutes To Precious Moments

1106 GRAND 417-358-0683

LEGGETT HOUSE AND HILL HOUSE. Appreciation of Carthage's historic architecture spurred development of two bed-and-breakfast establishments. The Hill house, built in 1886, was operated by Dean and Ella Scoville and was a tour home and antique shop in the mid-1980s. The Leggett house, erected in 1901, was restored by Nolan and Nancy Henry in 1989. Both homes have returned to private residences, but two other bed-and-breakfasts, Grand Avenue and The White Rose, operate today.

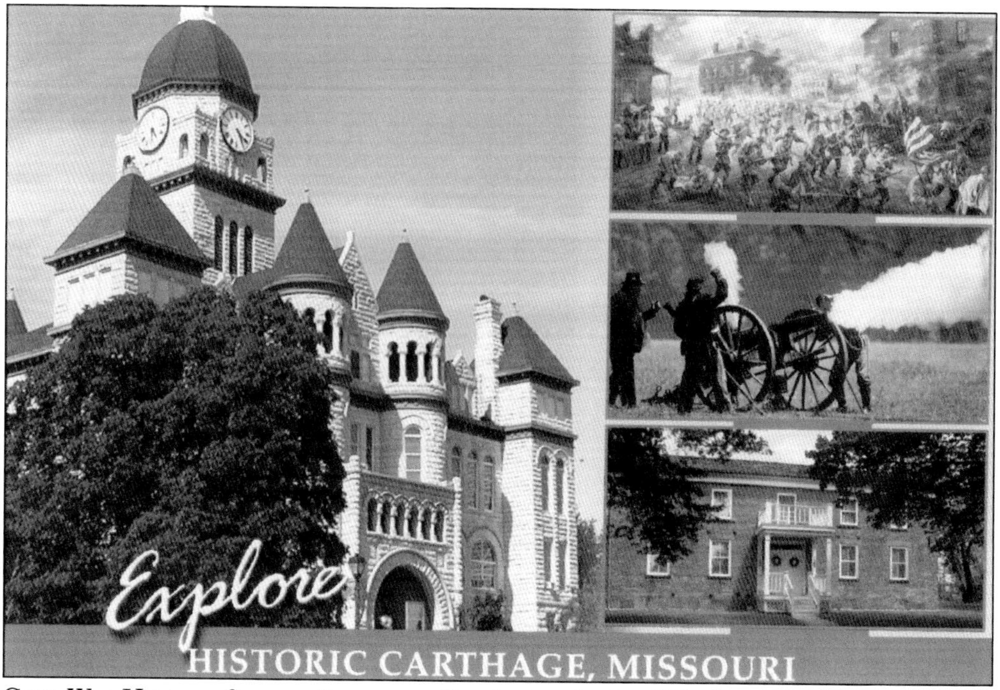

Civil War Historic Sites in Carthage. Developing the Civil War heritage of this community has been gaining importance since the 1961 Civil War Centennial. Through the efforts of state senator Richard Webster and local historian and journalist Marvin VanGilder, the Battle of Carthage State Historic Site was created in 1988. The Carthage Civil War Museum, seen on the top right side of the postcard above as well as in the photograph below, was opened in 1992. The Kendrick House, pictured at the bottom of the postcard, is found north of Carthage and is recognized as the only area home standing after the Civil War. It was restored in the late 1980s by Victorian Carthage. A Civil War reenactment was held in 1990, and scholarly publications on the Civil War began to appear for the first time since the 1920s. (Above image courtesy of Carthage Convention & Visitors Bureau.)

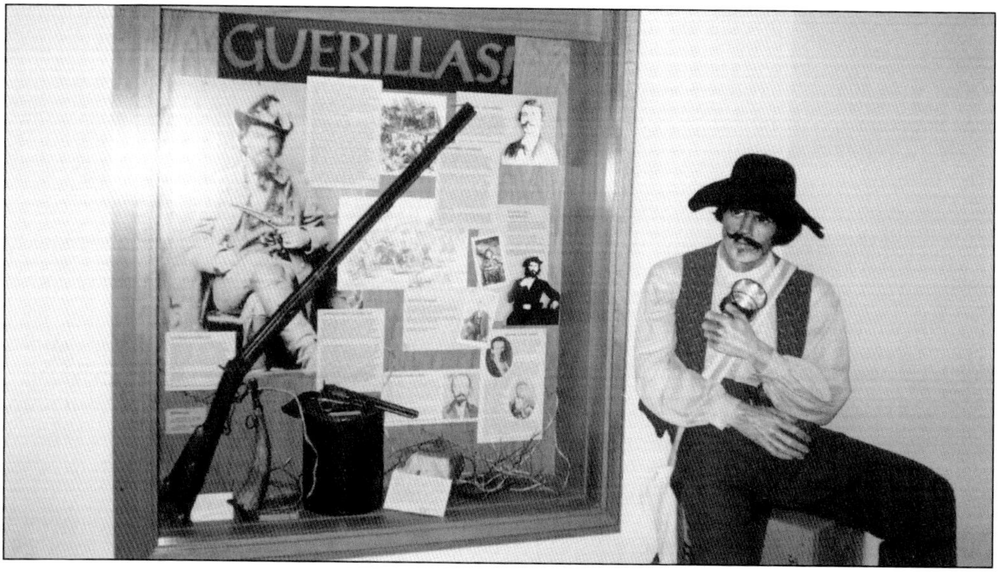

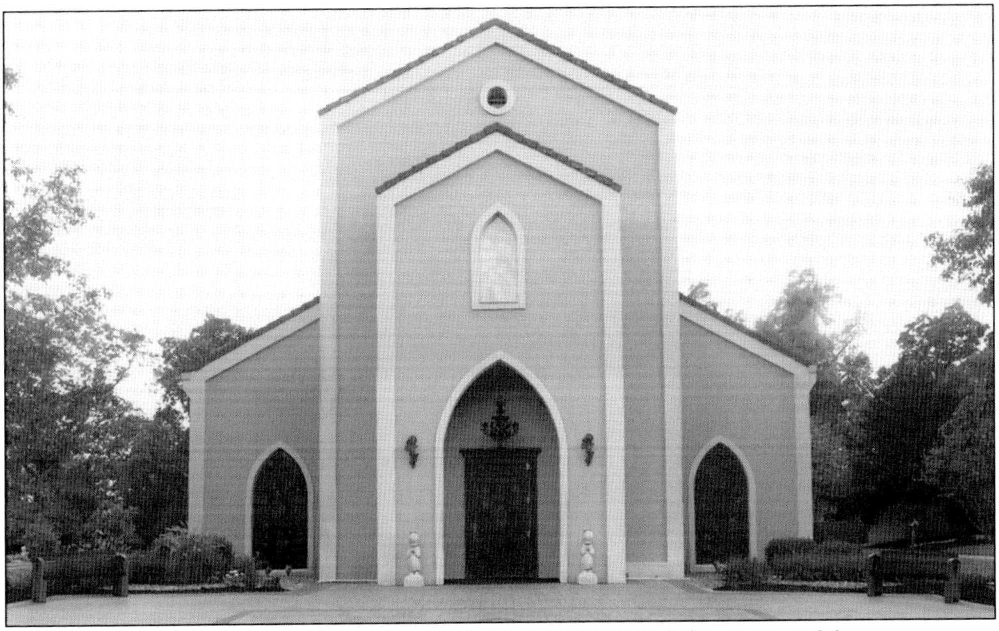

PRECIOUS MOMENTS CHAPEL, SOUTHWEST OF CARTHAGE. Built by Precious Moments creator Sam Butcher (below), the Precious Moments Chapel (above) opened in 1989 after three years of planning and painting. Artist Sam Butcher painted a re-creation of Michelangelo's Sistine Chapel on the ceiling of the chapel using the Precious Moments characters while elsewhere Biblical scenes are depicted through murals, stained-glass windows, and other artwork. Once opened, the chapel became a destination for tourists visiting the Missouri Ozarks. In 1988, Butcher served as grand marshal of the Maple Leaf Parade and was named Citizen of the Year in 1995. He continued to develop attractions at the chapel complex through the 1990s. (Both images courtesy of Precious Moments Supporting Foundation.)

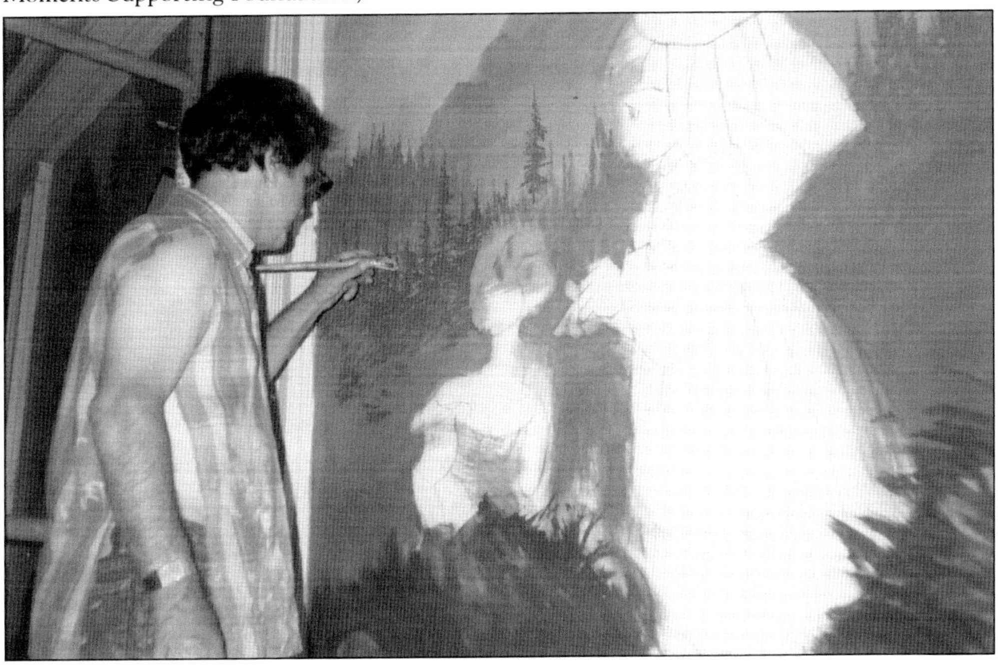

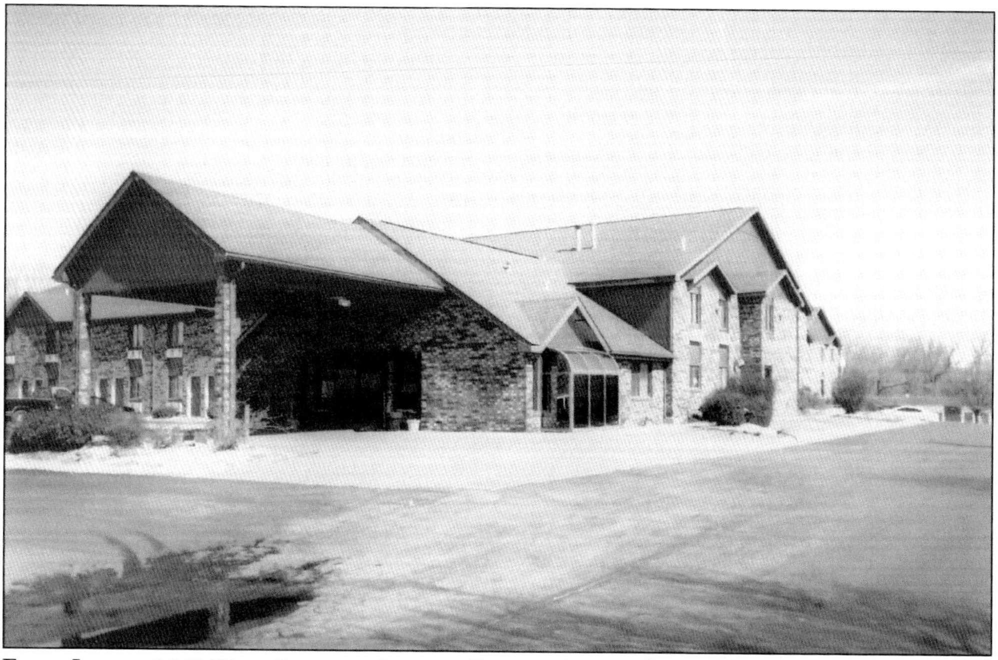

EconoLodge, 1441 West Central Avenue. Serving the traveling public through the hospitality industry has become important again to Carthage. This motel opened in 1987. The Stratford House Motel at 2244 Grand Avenue (now Carthage Inn) was completed earlier in 1982. Precious Moments Best Western Hotel and the Super 8 Motel would come in the next decade.

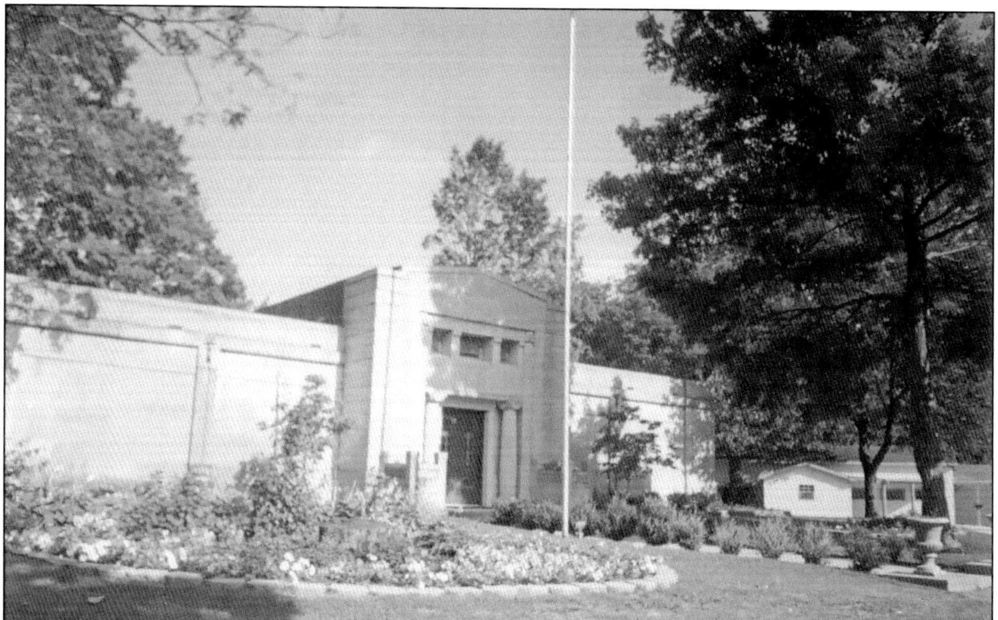

Park Cemetery Mausoleum, 801 South Baker Boulevard. Established in 1879 by Timothy Regan, Park Cemetery has gained a reputation as a site for monuments, including the one for the Grand Army of the Republic. It is also noted for its maple trees and their display of fall colors. The mausoleum was built in an Egyptian Revival style of architecture using Carthage limestone.

JESSE THACKER MEMORIAL IN PARK CEMETERY. One of the most outstanding memorials in the cemetery is Jesse Thacker's. Thacker (1818–1887) was a hardware man and capitalist in the banking, real estate, and mining enterprises of this region. At the time of the memorial's construction, it was the most expensive monument placed in the cemetery. It features a life-size sculpture of Thacker made from Italian marble and a Scottish granite base.

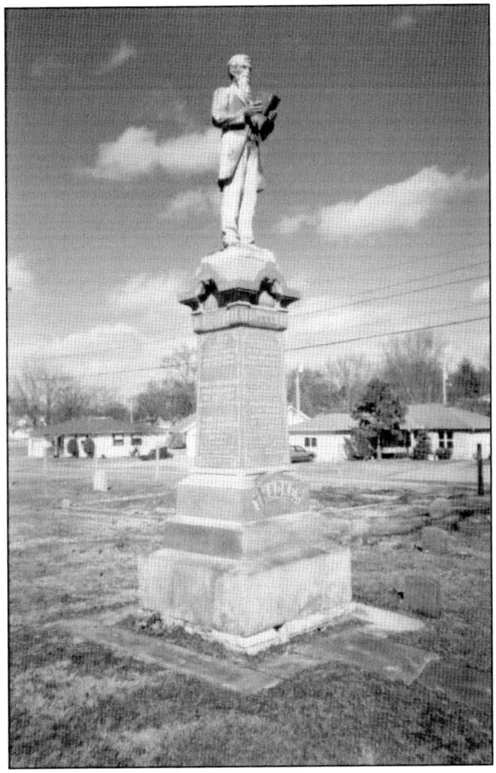

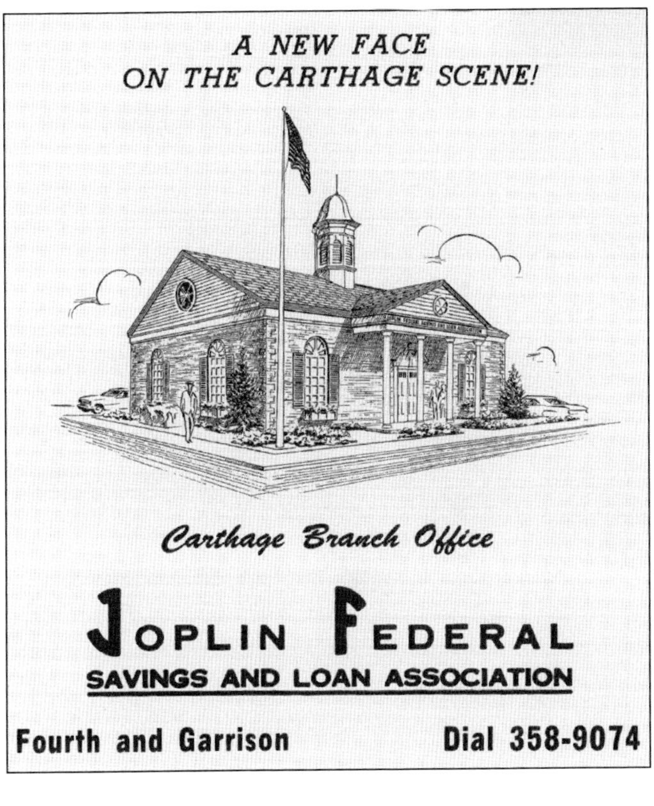

JOPLIN FEDERAL SAVINGS AND LOAN ASSOCIATION, 404 SOUTH GARRISON AVENUE. Opened in 1976, this structure has housed several financial institutions, the last being Great Southern Bank. As of 2003, it has been home to the Carthage Chamber of Commerce and the Carthage Convention & Visitors Bureau. That same year, the chamber donated many scrapbooks to the Powers Museum, documenting the organization from the 1940s to the 1980s.

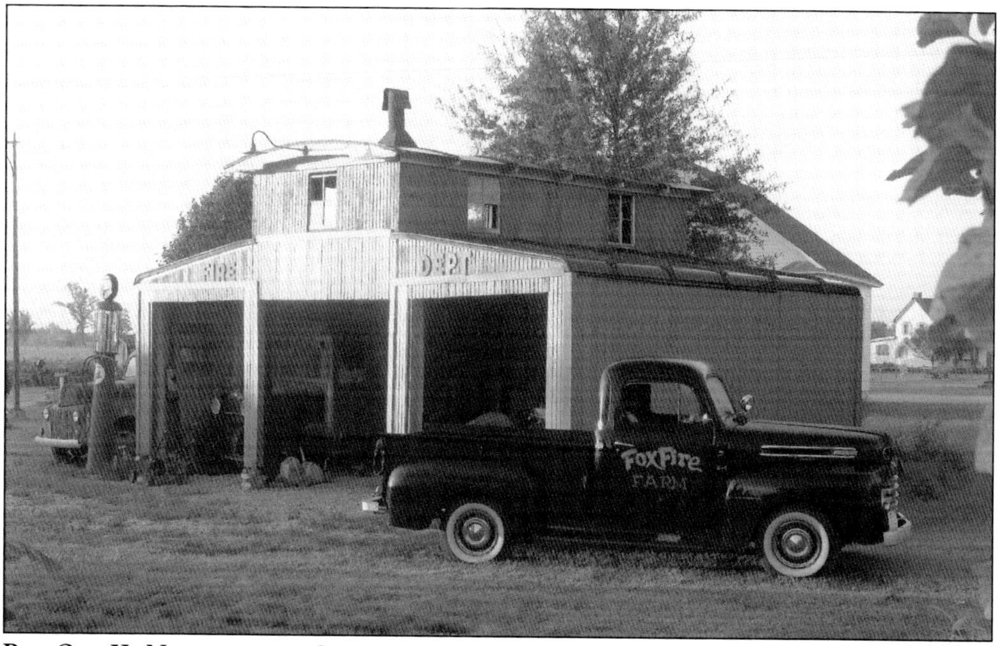

RED OAK II, NORTHEAST OF CARTHAGE. Artist Lowell Davis started moving old buildings to his farm in 1987. Although the historic village was sold by Davis, visitors can still walk the grounds, which over three dozen buildings call home, including this firestation. (Photograph by Patty Johnson.)

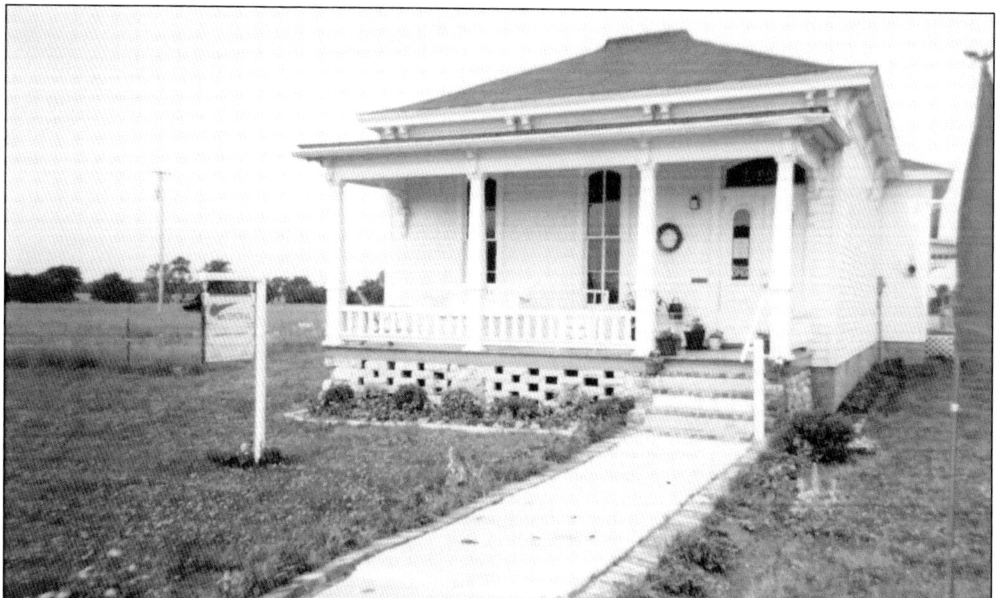

GERANIUM HOUSE AT RED OAK II. The arts have been supported from 1940 to 1990 by many organizations including CAST & Company, which was later renamed artCentral. The group, founded by Sandy Higgins in 1987, began holding events in the IGA Building on East Central Avenue but moved to Geranium House in the late 1990s. Beginning in 1999, this organization became headquartered in the former Hyde home at 1110 East Thirteenth Street. (Courtesy of artCentral.)

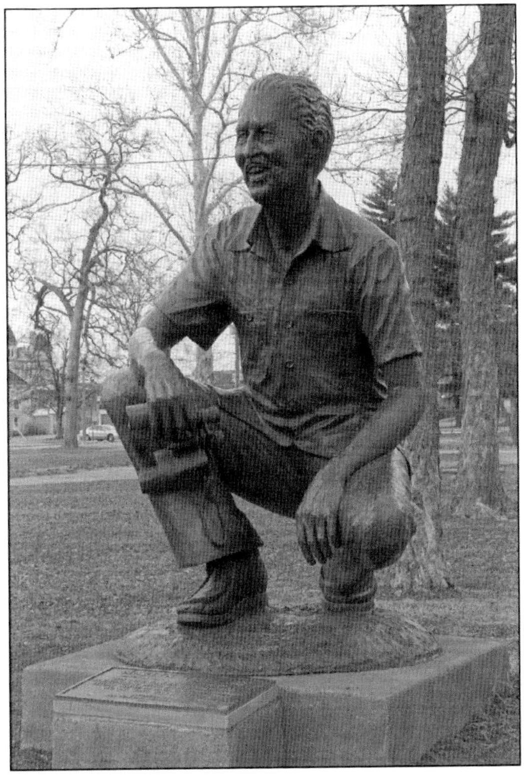

Marlin Perkins Statue in Central Park. After the death of Marlin Perkins in 1986, artists Bill Snow and Bob Tommey created this statue to honor the Carthage-born zoologist. Funded by private donations, it was dedicated in 1988 by Carol Perkins and people associated with the *Mutual of Omaha's Wild Kingdom* television show, which Perkins hosted from 1963 to 1985. In 2013, the Perkins family donated to the Powers Museum several papers and books of Marlin Perkins and his father, Judge Joseph Perkins. (Photograph by Koral Martin.)

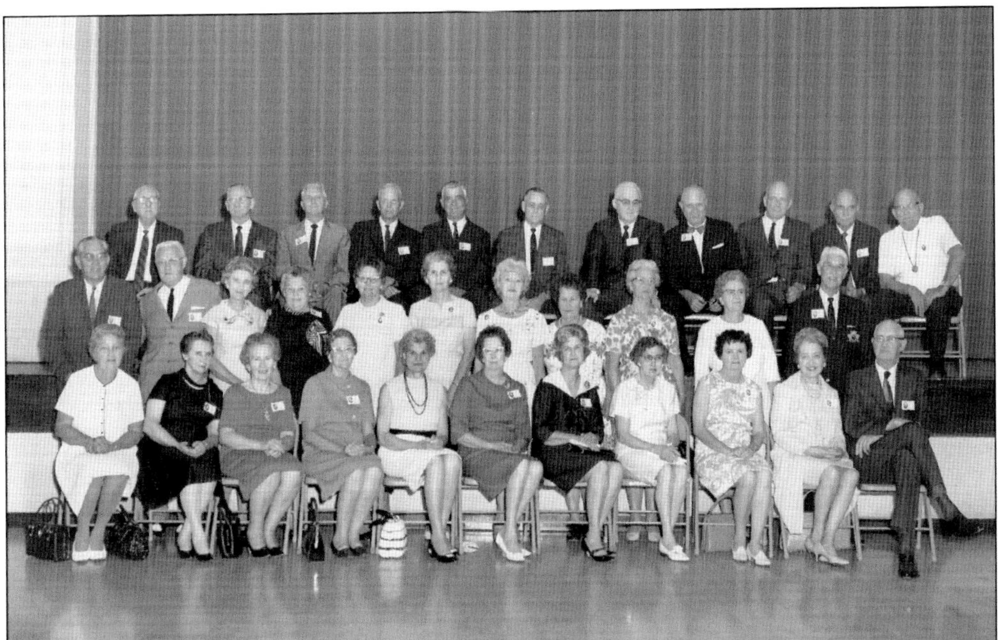

Carthage High School Class of 1923 Reunion. Born in 1905, Perkins lived at 905 South Main Street and graduated from high school in 1923. In 1968, he returned for a class reunion and posed with his classmates, pictured at the far right on the second row. In 1960, he was honored by the 4-H and FFA with "Marlin Perkins Day." In 1984, he was Maple Leaf Parade marshal.

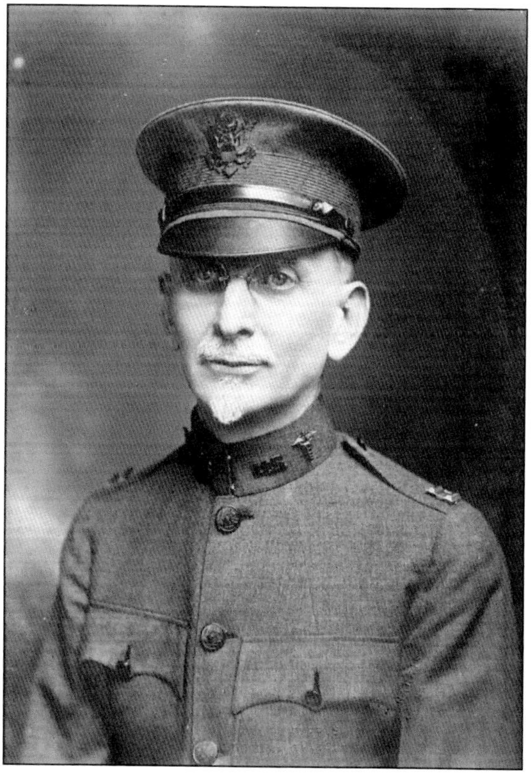

Dr. Everett Powers. Born in Labaddie, Missouri, in 1869, to Dr. John Alexander Powers and Maria Crowder Powers, Everett attend Eclectic Medical College in Cincinnati, Ohio, and received his first medical degree from there but went on to get additional degrees, including one from Jefferson Medical College in Philadelphia, Pennsylvania. He moved to Carthage in 1902 and set up a specialized practice for the eye, nose, throat, and ear. He died in 1954.

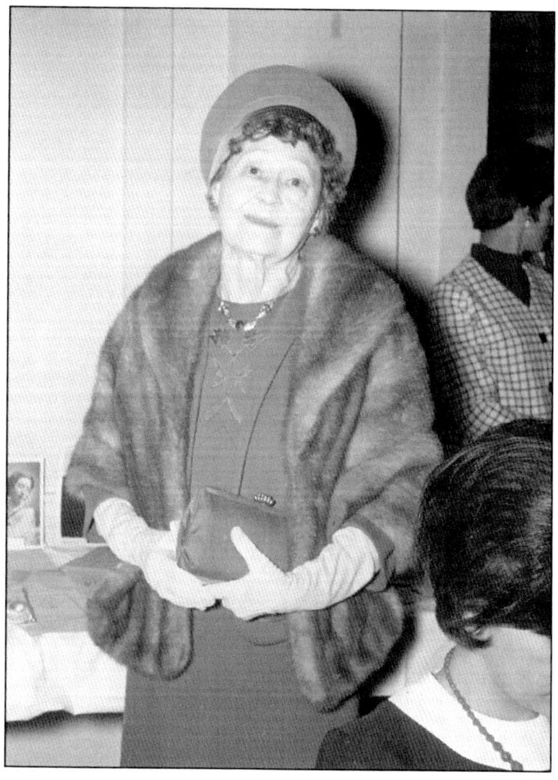

Marian Wright Powers. Born in 1880 in Connersville, Indiana, Marian Powers came to Carthage in 1889. Her father was one of the owners of the Troup Mine, near Prosperity, and the Carthage Stone Company. She graduated from Carthage Collegiate Institute and studied music in America and France, pursuing a career as a coloratura soprano in this region. Powers said she "had married and buried half of Jasper County," singing at weddings and funerals. She died in 1969.

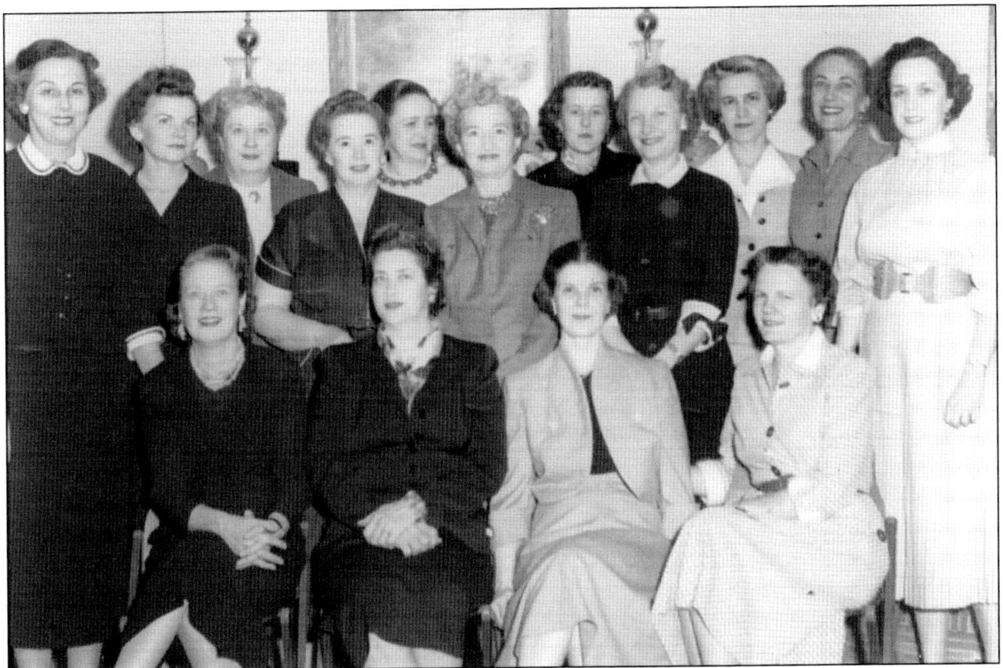

Sorosis Club. Like her mother, Marian L. Powers Winchester was an active club woman during her life (1905–1981). She is seen in the middle of the back row in this 1949 image. Club memberships for her mother, Marian W. Powers, included PEO, Daughters of the American Revolution (DAR), and Junior Shakespeare Society. Both women had been involved with the American Red Cross, and in the late 1930s through World War II, Marian Louisa Powers was the local chapter's executive secretary of the American Red Cross.

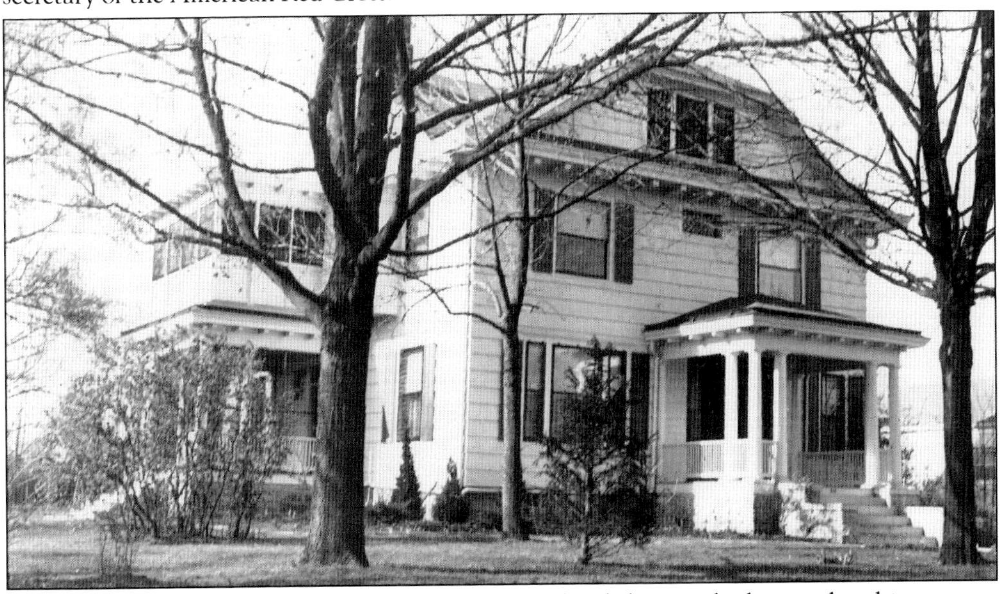

Powers Home, 314 Euclid Boulevard. The Powers family home, which moved to this property in 1917, is seen in 1940 after being remodeled with white shingle siding and green shutters to match the green roof. Each family member lived out their lives in this home, including daughter Marian and son-in-law W.L. "Bill" Winchester (1907–1962).

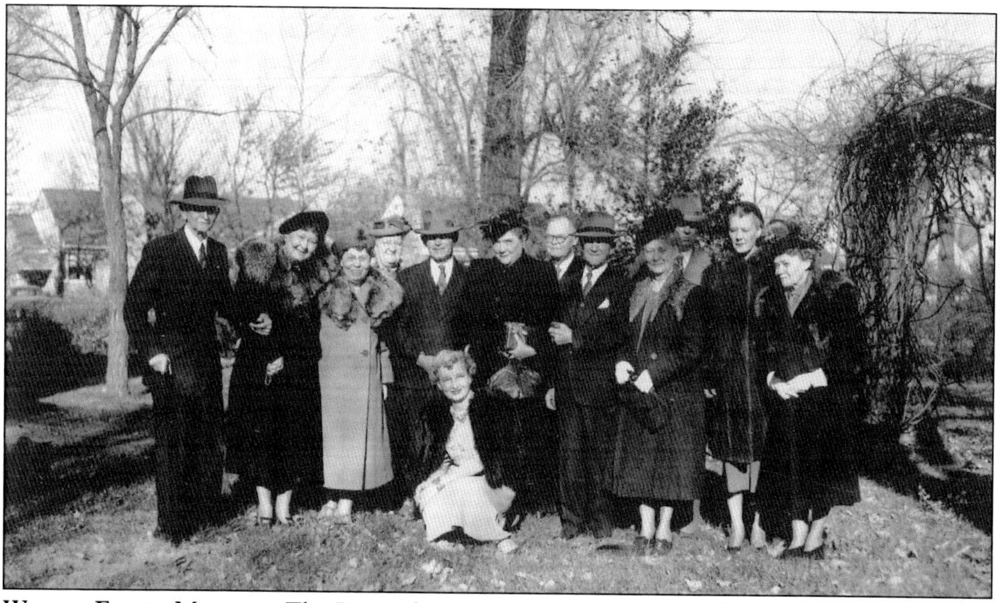

Wright Family Members. The Powers home was the scene of many family reunions, including this one on Thanksgiving 1949. Pictured from left to right are Dr. and Mrs. Powers, Etha Wright, Emma and Robert Wright, Gail and Curtis Wright Jr., George and Matilda Wright Hench, Firman and Nira Hench Carswell, Nira Wright, and Marian Powers Winchester in front.

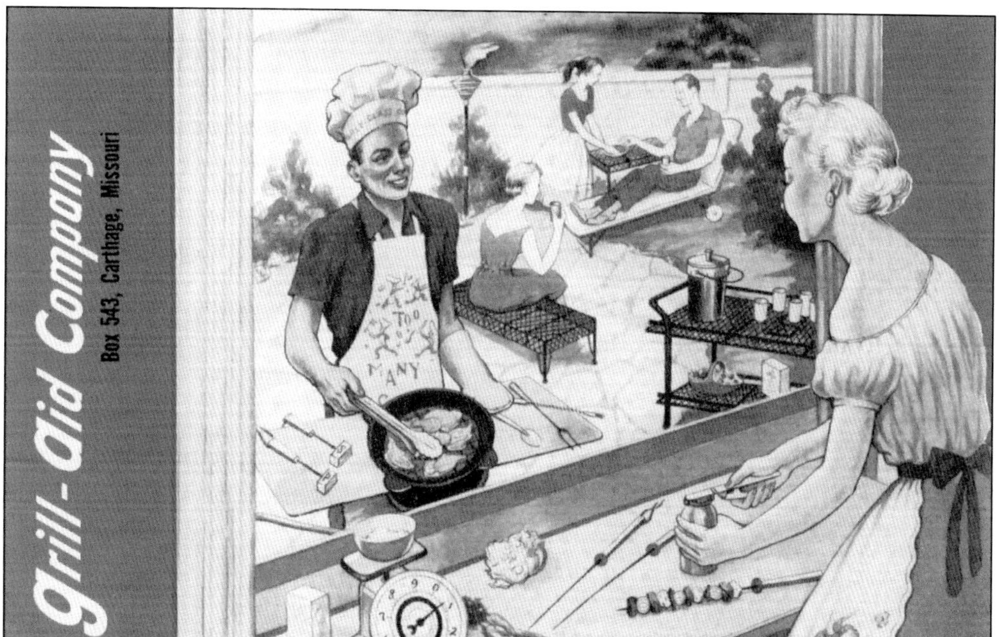

Grill Aid of Carthage. Bill Winchester started a mail order business in 1955 called Grill Aid, selling iron patio furniture and barbecue accessories. By 1957, this business expanded into Winchester's of Carthage, selling all types of novelties and household items shipped from its base at 420 Grant Street. The business was sold in 1963 after Bill's death.

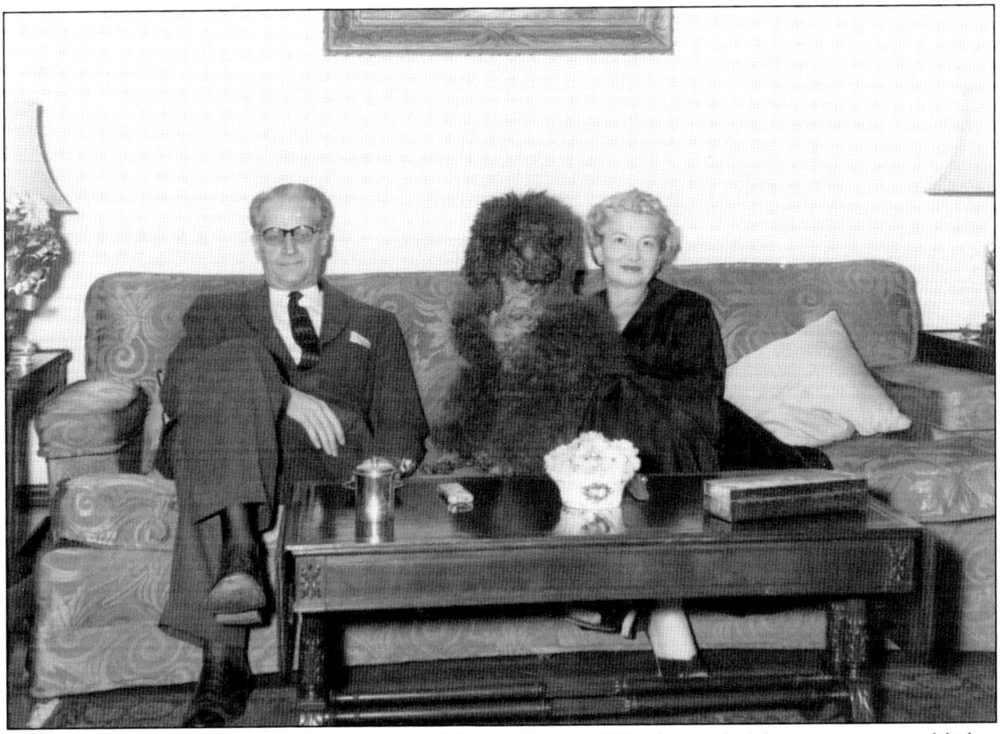

W.L. AND MARIAN POWERS WINCHESTER. Marian Powers Winchester left her estate to establish a museum for her beloved town and requested the museum's name honor her parents. The museum opened in mid-June 1988. Powers Museum board members who presided over the opening were Mary Beimdiek, president; Mary Lou Glauber, vice president; Sharon Heisten, secretary; Jim Farley and Robert Oexman, board members; along with advisory committee members June Luke, Dale Rife, John O. Phelps, and Elizabeth Wright.

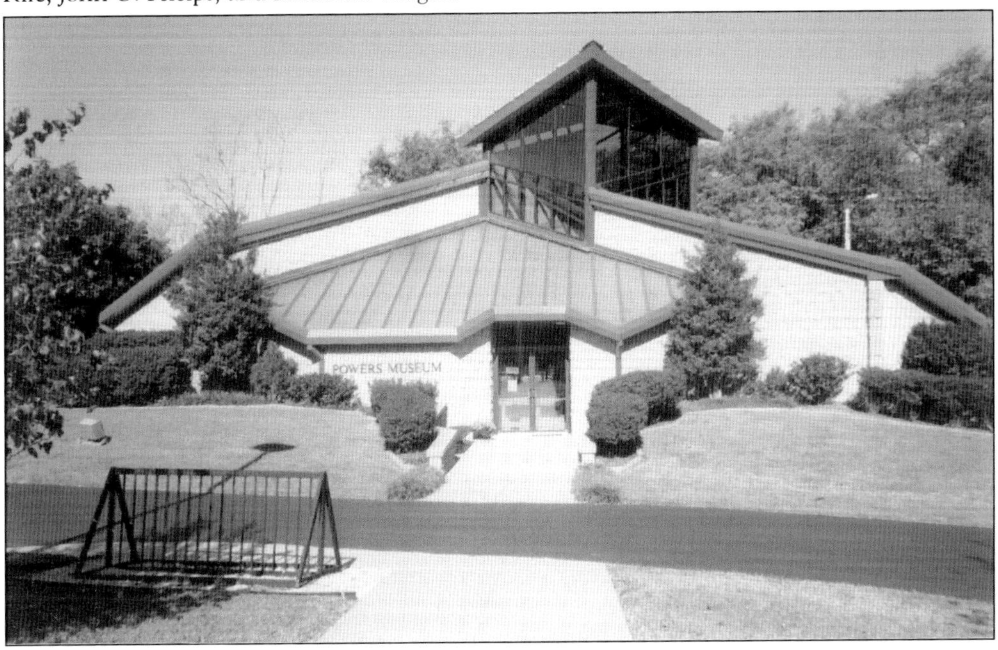

Bibliography

A Pictorial History of Carthage, Missouri. Carthage, MO: The Carthage Press & D-Books Publishing, Inc., 2008.

Ferguson, Richard. *Bank of Carthage: 100 Years of Banking and Community Service*. Carthage, MO: Bank of Carthage, 1968.

Hall, John G. *Majoring in the Minors: A Glimpse of Baseball in a Small Town*. Stillwater, OK: Oklahoma Bylines, Inc., 1996.

Hansford, Michele Newton. *Carthage, Missouri*. Mount Pleasant, SC: Arcadia Publishing, 2000.

Rodegen, Jeffery L. *The Legend of Leggett & Platt*. Fort Lauderdale, FL: Write Stuff Enterprises, Inc., 2008.

Sonderman, Joe. *Missouri Route 66 in the Ozarks*. Mount Pleasant, SC: Arcadia Publishing, 2009.

Vandergriff, Sue. *Then and Now: An Architectural History of the Carthage, Missouri Square & Nearby Structures*. Cassville, MO: Litho Printers & Bindery, 2003.

VanGilder, Marvin L. "Civil War Centennial Edition of Carthage Press, June 28, 1961." Carthage, MO: *Carthage Evening Press*, 1961.

———. *Legacy of Love*. Carthage, MO: Clayton E. Smith and Scottie Conkling Smith, 2005.

———. *Jasper County: The First Two Hundred Years*. Carthage, MO: Jasper County Commission, 1995.

All titles can be consulted at the Powers Museum during public hours except *Legacy of Love*, which is available only at the Jasper County Record Center, 125 Lincoln Street.

About the Organization

The estate of Marian L. Powers Winchester created the Powers Museum. It had long been the desire of Marian L. Powers Winchester, as well as her mother, that Carthage have its own museum. With her generous gift to the City of Carthage, Winchester made that dream possible. Per her wishes, the museum's name honors her parents, Dr. Everett Powers and Marian Wright Powers.

Processing the estate took several years, and it was not until 1987 that land was purchased and construction of a facility began. Once opened in June 1988, the museum has focused on promoting the local history of Carthage through exhibitions, public programming, and cooperative community events with other organizations. National commemorations such as the Lewis and Clark Bicentennial and the Civil War Bicentennial have been explored, too.

Digital projects have been embraced by the museum including a special project on the Missouri State Archive's Missouri Digital Heritage website called "Riches from the Earth" (http://www.sos.mo.gov/archives/mdh_splash/default.asp?coll=riches). Beginning July 2013, hundreds of collection artifacts and archival pieces will be online at http://powersmuseum.pastperfect-online.com so that more of the museum's resources can be shared with visitors and researchers than can be accommodated each year in the museum's rotating exhibition gallery. By 2015, the museum hopes to have placed several thousand items online. Publishing projects, such as this title, also share the museum's resources to a wider audience.

Your book purchase will enhance the expanding educational and exhibit mission of the Powers Museum. If you wish further information on volunteer opportunities or additional avenues to financially support the organization, please contact the museum.

Powers Museum
(located at 1617 West Oak Street on the Route 66 Scenic Byway)
PO Box 593
Carthage, Missouri 64836-0593
417-237-0456
www.powersmuseum.com

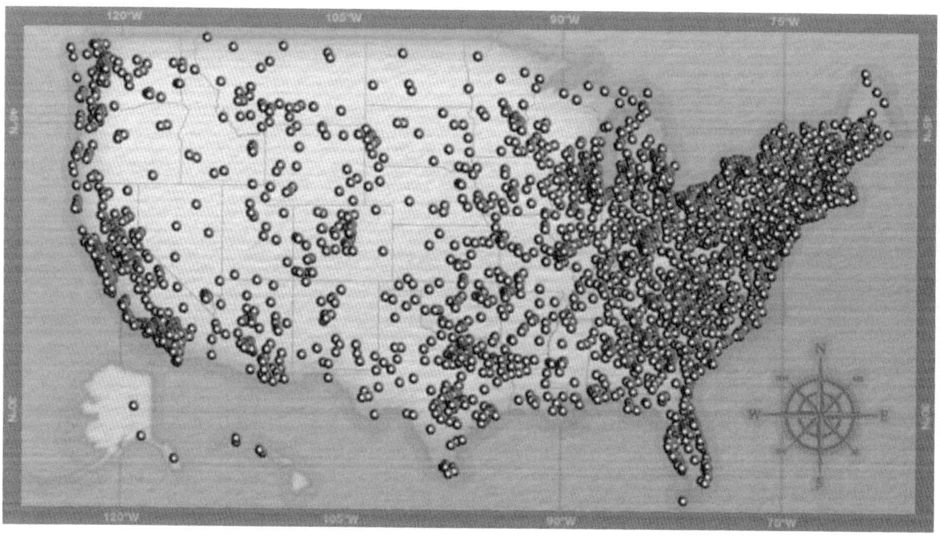